David Smith.

3-95

BIBLICAL CRITICISM

BIBLICAL CRITICISM

by

WICK BROOMALL, A.M., TH.M.
Professor of Hebrew and Systematic Theology
Erskine Theological Seminary
Due West, South Carolina
Author of *The Holy Spirit*

OLIPHANTS LTD.
LONDON   EDINBURGH

OLIPHANTS LTD.
1-5 PORTPOOL LANE,
HOLBORN, LONDON, E.C.1

AUSTRALIA
317 COLLINS STREET,
MELBOURNE.

NEW ZEALAND
23 MONTGOMERY ROAD,
ROTHESAY BAY,
AUCKLAND.

CANADA
EVANGELICAL PUBLISHERS,
241 YONGE STREET,
TORONTO.

U.S.A.
ZONDERVAN PUBLISHING HOUSE,
1415 LAKE DRIVE, S.E.
GRAND RAPIDS 6, MICHIGAN

First Published 1957

PRINTED IN GREAT BRITAIN BY
LOWE AND BRYDONE (PRINTERS) LIMITED, LONDON, N.W.10

To
the memory of
my FATHER *and my* MOTHER
and
my teacher
DR. ROBERT DICK WILSON

PREFACE

This book is the outgrowth of a course which the author taught for a number of years in the Columbia Bible College, Columbia, S. C. It was felt at the time he was teaching this course that there was need for a solid presentation of the conservative side of Biblical criticism. The most cursory acquaintance with literature being published today on the Bible will reveal the sad fact that the vast majority of such works are written by scholars who have accepted the modern approach to the Bible. Conservatives have been criticized for being unproductive in critical scholarship. And such is really the case. The present volume is an attempt to supply a need on the conservative side.

This work does not attempt to be so scholarly as to be beyond the reach of most ministers and Bible students. References to other works could have been considerably multiplied on almost any page. Lengthy footnotes could have been added at will. But it was the author's desire to keep the book as popular as the subject would allow. There will be those, of course, who will complain that the material is too technical for their comprehension. To all such we would suggest the thought that, if conservatives are to meet attacks on the Bible from critical circles, they must deal with these attacks on approximately the same level of scholarship.

The present volume is naturally a defense of what is now known as the conservative (which is often generally equated with the traditional or historic) view of the Bible. The author is thoroughly persuaded that this position is defensible — in fact, that it is the only view that will stand up under the scrutiny of historical research and investigation.

It is not likely, therefore, that the statements and conclusions put forth in this book will be acceptable to those who belong to what is called the liberal or modern school of Biblical criticism. It is our hope, however, that that school will find nothing herein that is an untrue presentation of their viewpoint. Neither conservatives nor liberals like to have their viewpoints misrepresented. We have tried to be fair in the description of every aspect of the modern approach to the Bible. We believe that authorities could be cited for every major view put forth in the name of modern liberalism. If we have erred in any detail in the characterization of the modern view, we trust that error will be called to our attention.

No one will realize more than the author how inadequate his treatment of the subject really is. This book was written in the midst of a busy life and under trying circumstances. If it serves a useful purpose in giving a foundation for the Bible-believing Christian to stand upon, as he faces the attacks of unbelieving critics, the long hours of labor will have been more than justified.

The Bible references are cited from the American Standard Version of 1901.

Parts of the manuscript of this book were read by Prof. George A. Anderson, dean of Presbyterian College, Clinton, S. C., and by Dr. Tunis Romein of Erskine College, Due West, S. C. For their helpful suggestions the author is indebted. Mr. O. Z. White, student in the Erskine Theological Seminary, helped type part of the manuscript.

With the hope and prayer that this book will confirm the faith of many in the truthfulness of the Bible in these days of spiritual declension, the author sends it forth, under God, on its mission.

WICK BROOMALL

Due West, South Carolina

CONTENTS

CHAPTER ONE

THE INSPIRATION OF THE BIBLE

I. IMPORTANCE OF THE SUBJECT

There is hardly any subject in the realm of theology which is more crucial than that which relates to the nature of the Bible. On this subject volumes have been written and are still being written. Some hold that the inspiration of the Bible is a relic of uncritical times when dogmatism ruled in Biblical studies; others hold that this doctrine is of the very essence of Christianity — without which real Christianity could hardly exist. Between these views there are many variations of opinions of liberal or conservative slant. In order that we may have a clear view of the importance of the inspiration of the Bible, let us note at the beginning of our study why this is of such paramount importance.

A. *Inspiration Fundamental to Other Truths*

Back of all the great facts and doctrines of the Bible stands, like a mighty fortress, the supernatural inspiration of the written documents in which these facts and doctrines are recorded. If these documents are of purely human origin, and thus subject to all the limitations of man-made productions, then it logically follows that the authority of the facts and doctrines recorded in the Scriptures will be no higher than that which men accord to writings of non-inspired sources. If, on the other hand, the Biblical records were produced by men directed and controlled by the Holy Spirit, then we have every reason to believe that the facts and doctrines recorded in the Bible are free of those imperfections and blemishes that characterize all purely human productions. If this latter assumption be the true one, as we believe it actually is, then it naturally follows that we will give to the Bible, in its record of events and doctrines, that

11

authority over our minds and wills that we cannot give to even the best of uninspired men.

It follows, furthermore, that here is such a logical consistency between Biblical inspiration and the facts and doctrines of the Bible that, if the former is denied or questioned, the facts and doctrines will eventually lose their authority over us. This is the road over which many have traveled in their so-called flight from Fundamentalism to Modernism. Men who originally held the Bible in the highest place of honor and esteem as the ultimate authority in all matters of faith and conduct have, by the denial or questioning of the inspiration of the sacred writers, come to a place where the authority of the Bible is rejected where it runs counter to the modern mind or the dictates of science.

B. *Inspiration Basic to Christianity*

It is undoubtedly true that Christianity could have existed as a world religion — similar to Islam — even if those who produced its historical and theological documents had had no direct inspiration from the true God. The bare facts of the new faith could have been reliably reported for posterity even if there had been no inspired apostles to report such facts. The Church Fathers, for example, give us the main facts and doctrines of the Christian faith, but the historic Church has never given to such men the rank of inspired apostles. These Church Fathers, living in the early centuries following the apostolic age, firmly held to the inspiration of the Biblical documents but did not believe in their own inspiration.

But the decisive factor that differentiates Christianity as the only true and authoritative faith is found in the divine inspiration of its records. The Early Church Fathers knew instinctively that, in the writings of the inspired prophets and apostles, they were listening to the voice of God. It was this voice, vibrating and pulsating with divine life, that made the canonical Scriptures infinitely more than a bare recital of facts or precepts such as we find in the Koran, the bible of Islam. Basically it is the fact that Christianity has back of it an inspired Bible that puts it in a category all by itself among the so-called religions of mankind. Had this not been true, the Christian faith might have survived, but it would never have had a message vibrant with life and authoritative in doctrine. Deny the inspiration of the Bible and you rob Christianity of its claim as the final and authoritative voice of God to mankind.

C. *Inspiration a Test of Orthodoxy*

The great divide between historic, conservative Christianity and what is known as Liberalism is found in the concept of Biblical inspiration. Those who call themselves conservatives believe in the inspiration of the Bible, although they may differ on some minor points of doctrine, such as, whether the Lord's coming is according to the premillennial, dispensational, postmillennial or amillennial scheme of things to come. Those who belong to the liberal camp of Biblical scholarship are united in their conviction that the Bible, if inspired at all, is surely not inerrant and infallible. The conservative defines inspiration in terms of inerrancy; the liberal treats the Bible, as we shall see later, as a book that contains many mistakes in history and science and even in moral truths.

Thus, as a matter of fact, the acceptance or rejection of Biblical inspiration is becoming increasingly a test, if it is not already such, of a scholar's theological viewpoint. Let us know what his position is regarding this vital issue and one can practically predetermine what his views will be about all the other great truths in the Christian system.

D. *Consequences of Denying Inspiration*

Our fourth and final reason for the importance of the subject of the inspiration of the Bible is found in the consequences that inevitably follow when this doctrine is denied or minimized. There is such a logical connection between the Bible's inspiration and other doctrines of our Christian faith that the former has a direct bearing upon the latter. Rejecting the inspiration of the Biblical writers means an ultimate rejection of what these same writers say in every aspect of their teaching. Let us illustrate with an example. Was Christ born of the Virgin Mary? This is essentially a question of facts. But where do we have the facts upon which to make a decision? Without controversy, these facts are found only in the New Testament documents. The unprejudiced historian will tell us that, on the basis of the obvious meaning of the Gospels, Christ was undoubtedly born of the Virgin Mary. The theologian, however, who has already rejected the inspiration of Matthew and Luke, will hardly acquiesce in such a simple conclusion. If he has been bold enough to deny the inspiration of the Biblical writers, and all that is involved in that term, it is hardly likely that he will accept Matthew's or Luke's statements about Christ's conception and birth at their par value. Not accepting their inspiration, he will treat their writings from a purely human standpoint and find mistakes and discrepancies in the narratives, fill the account with legendary or mythological elements, and otherwise so twist and pervert the simple and unadulterated story as to empty it of all spiritual significance in the sequence of events that began at the incarnation and reached a climax in Christ's resurrection and ascension. The denial of Biblical inspiration, though accounted by some a minor thing in the Christian system, is a deadly virus that eventually corrupts our whole body of theology and pollutes and contaminates the water of eternal life found in the Scriptures.

II. DEFINITION OF INSPIRATION

It is important at the outset of our investigation that we define accurately what is meant by Biblical inspiration. On this subject there has been a great deal of confusion. Some have maintained that the Bible never gives an exact definition as to what it means by inspiration. That this view is not true will be shown shortly. Suffice it here to maintain that the elements or factors that enter into a definition are surely found in the Biblical writings. There is, for example, no scientific definition of the Trinity in the Scriptures, but no competent scholar would deny that the Bible contains teaching on this subject that naturally leads to a definition.

A. A Creedal Definition

Many definitions of inspiration are given in works on this subject. Some of these we shall cite a little later. At the present time we wish to present a classic definition as found in the historic *Westminster Confession of Faith* (1646). This famous document, perhaps the most complete and definitive of the post-Reformation Protestant creeds, defines exactly the scope and nature of inspiration in its first chapter. We may accept as true that this Confession represents what Protestants universally believed regarding the Bible about three centuries ago and up until the rise of modern higher criticism in the nineteenth century. Summarizing the Confession, we give the following propositions as therein contained.

1. Only the sixty-six canonical books belong to Scripture; all other books, including the Apocrypha, lack "divine inspiration" and are, therefore, "no part of the canon of the Scripture." As such, these uncanonical books possess "no authority in the Church of God," and are to be used only as "other human writings" might be consulted.

2. Only the sixty-six canonical books constitute "the word of God written." These books were "immediately inspired by God."

3. Only the Bible, as originally existing in the autographs, is inspired by God. In "all controversies of religion the church is finally to appeal unto" this Bible. Translations are to be made from the original to the common languages "that the word of God dwelling plentifully" in such versions, people may worship God "in an acceptable manner."

4. Only in the Scriptures do we find those truths necessary for our salvation. The Bible contains the "whole counsel of God, concerning all things necessary for His own glory, man's salvation, faith and life."

5. Only the Spirit can give absolute authentication of His Word. Concerning the Bible "our full persuasion and assurance of the infallible truth, and divine authority thereof, is from the inward work of the Holy Spirit, bearing witness by and with the word in our hearts."

6. Only the Spirit can illuminate the passages of Scripture to our minds. We must "acknowledge the inward illumination of the Spirit of God to be necessary for the saving understanding of such things as are revealed in the word."

7. Only the Word of God can adequately interpret the

Word. "The infallible rule of interpretation of Scripture is the Scripture itself." The difficult places can be "known by other places that speak more clearly."

8. Only the Scriptures constitute the Supreme Judge. The settlement of all controversies of religion can be obtained only through "the Holy Spirit speaking in the Scriptures."

This brief resumé of the teaching of the *Westminster Confession of Faith* on the nature of the Bible shows clearly and unambiguously what was the faith of the Reformation churches on inspiration. To the Reformers and their followers, the Bible was inspired by the Holy Spirit and was the infallible Word of God, above which there was no higher court of appeal on earth.

B. *Definitions of Theologians*

We cite here several definitions taken from some of the principal writers on the subject of inspiration. This list is representative and by no means exhaustive.

1. L. Gaussen: Inspiration is ". . . that inexplicable power which the Divine Spirit put forth of old on the authors of holy Scripture, in order to their guidance even in the employment of the words they used, and to preserve them alike from all error and from all omission" (*Theopneustia*: *The Plenary Inspiration of the Holy Scriptures* [n.d.], p. 34).

2. B. B. Warfield: "The Church, then, has held from the beginning that the Bible is the Word of God in such a sense that its words, though written by men and bearing indelibly impressed upon them the marks of their human origin, were written, nevertheless, under such an influence of the Holy Ghost as to be also the words of God, the adequate expression of His mind and will. It has always recognized that this conception of co-authorship implies that the Spirit's superintendence extends to the choice of the words by the human authors (verbal inspiration), and preserves its product from everything inconsistent with a divine authorship — thus securing, among other things, that entire truthfulness which is everywhere presupposed in and asserted for Scripture by the Biblical writers (inerrancy). Whatever minor variations may now and again have entered into the mode of state-

ment, this has always been the core of the Church doctrine of inspiration" (*Revelation and Inspiration* [1927], p. 173).

3. Robert Watts: "By Verbal Inspiration is meant such an agency of the Holy Spirit as rendered the sacred writers absolutely infallible in the communication of the Divine will to men, determining not only the substance (which were all one with Revelation), but the form also of the message they were commissioned to deliver, and extending, not simply to the ideas (which were Revelation again), but reaching to the words in which the Revelation was conveyed" (*The Rule of Faith* [1885], pp. 97f.).

4. F. Turretin: "The sacred writers were so moved and inspired by the Holy Ghost, both in respect to thought (*res ipsas*) and language, that they were kept from all error, and their writings are truly authentic and divine" (quoted in William G. T. Shedd's *Dogmatic Theology* [1891], Vol. 1, p. 72).

5. Webster's Dictionary: "The supernatural influence of the Spirit of God on the human mind, by which prophets, apostles, and sacred writers were qualified to set forth Divine truth without any mixture of error" (quoted by John Urquhart, *The Inspiration and Accuracy of the Holy Scriptures* [n.d.], p. 15, as a fair description of the Church of England around 1863).

6. Loraine Boettner: "The inspiration for which we contend is, of course, that of the original Hebrew and Greek words as written by the prophets and apostles. We believe that if these are understood in their intended sense — plain statements of fact, figures of speech, idioms and poetry as such — the Bible is without error from Genesis to Revelation" (*The Inspiration of the Scriptures* [2nd ed.; 1940], p. 17).

C. Biblical Definition

It is sometimes quite dogmatically asserted that the Bible neither has a specific definition of its inspiration nor does it provide the materials out of which a legitimate concept of inspiration can be constructed. Neither of these assertions actually presents the Biblical viewpoint regarding its inspiration. Granting that there is no scientific definition that would

B

be acceptable to the modern theologian, there is, nevertheless, as we shall soon see, sufficient evidence found in the
sacred documents out of which a realistic definition can be
erected. This fact, not so obvious on the surface, will become increasingly clear as we examine some of the basic
statements in the Scriptures regarding their inspiration.

1. Interpretation of basic passages. There are a number
of texts of Scripture that deal with the problem of inspiration. It is not necessary for us to deal with all such passages
in order to ascertain what the Bible really means by inspiration. We select a few of the major passages which might
be considered as classical expressions of Biblical inspiration.

a) II Timothy 3:15f. This Pauline text is, beyond question, the Mount Everest of passages dealing with our project.
No one can honestly by-pass it if he is to formulate a doctrine of inspiration. We shall consider it under the following heads:

(1) The exegesis of the passage. The AV and RSV ren-
derings are much to be preferred to the faulty ASV rendering ("Every scripture inspired of God is also profitable,"
etc.). The Greek verbal adjective *theopneustos* (used here
undoubtedly in the passive sense as "God-breathed") is co-
ordinate with the other predicate describing "all scripture"
and is co-ordinate with the other predicate adjective translated "profitable." The two predicate adjectives ("God-
breathed" or "inspired by God" and "profitable") are joined
together by the co-ordinate conjunction *kai* ("and"). Simple
exegesis demands that we affirm that Paul is dogmatically
asserting that "all scripture" is theopneustic; that is, "God-
breathed" or "inspired by God."

(2) The meaning of the passage. There are three things
that Paul affirms in this text regarding Scripture. (*a*) The nature of Scripture — it is theopneustic. (*b*) The consequences
of its theopneustic character — it is "profitable for teaching,
for reproof; for correction, for instruction which is in righteousness" (ASV). (*c*) The spiritual purpose of its inspiration — "that the man of God may be complete, furnished
completely unto every good work" (ASV).

(3) Some questions regarding the passage. Several such

questions must here be considered, among which the following are important. (a) Does "all scripture" here refer only to the Old Testament? On any interpretation of Paul's words "all scripture" must surely include the Old Testament, since "scripture" in the New Testament writings almost everywhere designates the Old Testament documents. However, there is no fact here or elsewhere that requires us to exclude the New Testament writings (even though some were as yet unwritten when Paul wrote) from the category of "all scripture." If Peter (II Pet. 3:16) could classify Paul's letters as "scripture" (placing them on the same level with the Old Testament), surely there is no a priori reason why Paul could not designate his own writings and the writings of the other apostles as "scripture." (b) Is Paul here giving a definition of the nature of inspiration when he affirms that Scripture is theopneustic? Our answer must be affirmative, for it is the common practice of Biblical writers to give short, concise definition of sacred truths. Sin, for example, is defined tersely in I John 3:4; 5:17; Romans 14:23, and elsewhere. In a similar subject-predicate form God's nature is defined in John 4:24; I John 1:5; 4:8. In a negative-positive relationship the kingdom of God is defined in Romans 14:17. The true Jew (that is, Christian) is defined in Romans 2:28f; 10:6ff. So it well conforms to the practice of Scripture when we see in II Timothy 3:16 a definitive statement regarding its inspiration. (c) Does theopneustos include such ideas as infallibility, inerrancy and authority? Although Paul does not elaborate on the psychological processes of inspiration, we are surely to conclude from the theopneustic character of "all scripture" that God has not breathed into His Word anything that borders on error of any kind. If like begets like in the natural realm, the same principle must operate in the spiritual realm. If God is the Source and Author of all truth in nature and in revelation, it is inconceivable that He would breathe into one of His messengers that which was lacking in veracity and truthfulness. Satan is the author of the lie (John 8:44); but God cannot lie (Tit. 1:2). It follows that the God-breathed Scriptures cannot lie, that is, they cannot err in any realm, whether it be in history, science or spiritual truths. If this be so, as it most assuredly is, inspiration includes inerrancy, infallibility and authority.

b) II Peter 1:21. Without going into critical matters here, we accept this passage as a genuine utterance of the prince of the apostles. It supports and corroborates, with beautiful harmony, the conclusions we have just arrived at from Paul's classic statement. We shall deal with it here as briefly as its importance will allow.

(1) The exegesis of the passage. The literal translation of this text reads as follows: "For not by man's will was brought a prophecy at any time, but by the Holy Spirit being carried spake from God men." We have followed here the Greek order. Several things call for careful attention. For one thing, we must take note of the passive voice in the main verb ("was brought") and in the present participle ("being carried" or "being borne along"). The passive is further indicated by the personal agency of the Spirit ("by the Holy Spirit"). There could hardly be a more definite statement regarding the passivity of man in the process of divine inspiration as men "spake from God" (the "from" indicating the source whence their "speaking" — that is, their words — came). There can be no ambiguity in the meaning of Peter's words in this passage.

(2) The meaning of the passage. As just indicated, the meaning is crystal clear. To elaborate just a little we note: (a) The origin of prophecy is considered negatively as not being due to man's will (cf. Gal. 1:1; John 1:13 for similar negations). Nor is a prophecy subject to individual interpretation (II Pet. 1:20). (b) The origin of prophecy is described positively. Men spake (cf. Heb. 1:1) from God as their Source. These same men spake as or while they were being carried along (as a twig, for example, is borne by the stream) by the Holy Spirit.

(3) Remarks. The secret of this passage is found in the adverb *pote*, which, with the negative *ou*, must here be translated as "ever." The basic idea, therefore, is that no prophecy ever (whether in the Old or the New Testaments) originated out of the mere will of a man. On this we must

again request the student to compare the negative assertion made in John 1:13.

Peter here is in complete harmony with Paul's statement in II Timothy 3:16. Both writers assert in the most unequivocal language that the Bible is of divine origin. In fact, so unconcerned are they about modern notions of man's part in the Bible's composition, that they practically put man in a very secondary place as God's mouthpiece.

c) II Corinthians 13:3. This text, though rather unobtrusive, is pregnant with mighty implications. It is one of the casual utterances arising out of a historical situation. It is of sufficient importance to demand a careful interpretation and explanation.

(1) Exegesis of the passage. Literally the passage reads as follows: "because if I should come unto thee again not will I spare, since you are seeking a proof of the in-me-speaking Christ." The following facts are significant: (a) The main verb is present and indicates continuous action ("you are seeking" or "you keep on seeking"). (b) The object of their continuous search is some "proof" of Paul's apostleship and authority (as the two letters to the Corinthian church make manifestly plain). (c) The participle is also present and adjectival, restrictively modifying Christ ("the in-me-speaking Christ" or, more idiomatically in English, "the Christ who is speaking in me"). (d) We should also note the significant preposition "in" used here. Paul did not use *dia* (indicating agency and usually translated by "through") but rather he used *en* (meaning "in"). This, of course, cannot be construed to mean that Paul taught that he was an incarnation of Christ; but it can and does mean that, in his office as an inspired apostle, he considered himself as the mouthpiece of the Lord Jesus Christ.

(2) Meaning. This verse must be understood in the light of the context; and, in this particular case, the context includes all of Paul's correspondence with the turbulent church of Corinth. His right to teach and act with apostolic authority was undoubtedly questioned by some in Corinth. In the closing chapter of his second letter he faces this challenge head-on. He recognized clearly that he could deal with the

rebellious and obnoxious with the authority which the Lord
had given him for building up, rather than tearing down
(II Cor. 13:10). But this would be the idea of a deranged
mind unless his authority, recognizable by him and by his
readers, was based on the indubitable fact that the Lord
whom they worshiped was actually speaking authoritatively
in His servant Paul.

We must also call attention to another important fact. In
verse 5 of the chapter under consideration, Paul challenges
his readers to try to prove the reality of their faith as to
whether Christ is really in them. If that be not so, they
are reprobates. On the other hand, if they are really Christians, so the implication seems to be quite obvious, they
will readily recognize that Christ is speaking in Paul. Christ
lives "in" all who are real believers; but Christ speaks "in"
Paul because he is Christ's inspired mouthpiece. To reject
Paul is to reject Christ.

d) John 10:35. This passage, arising out of a controversy
with Jewish leaders, expresses the unbreakable authority of
the Word of God. The following remarks but faintly indicate
the major importance of this text.

(1) Exegesis of the passage. The "if" here is a first-class
condition (assuming the supposition to be true). We can
translate the passage somewhat like this: "If He characterized
those to be gods to whom the word of God came (literally,
became) — and the Scripture cannot be broken — do you say
of Him whom the Father sanctified and sent into the world,
'Thou dost blaspheme!' because I said, 'I am God's Son'?"
The scripture referred to here is undoubtedly Psalm 82:6.
Compare Exodus 22:28.

(2) Meaning. Several things are undoubtedly implied here
regarding the Bible. (a) There is the recognition that the
passage referred to (Ps. 82:6) is the Word of God. By implication the whole Old Testament is included in this term.
(b) There is the argument from the lesser to the greater.
The Jews must recognize that in their Scriptures even unworthy judges are called "gods" (elohim). If that be so of
mere men, how much more must it be so of the One who
has intrinsic right to that title because of His nature ("sanc-

tified") and His commission ("sent into the world")? Christ, like the Jews, believed in the unbreakable character of even one verse of Scripture (Ps. 82:6). Logically it follows that if one verse is unbreakable in authority (and thus could be appealed to by Christ to nullify the charge of blasphemy), then all Scripture bears that same absolute and unbreakable authority.

2. Elements in the Biblical definition. Using the passages which we have exegetically considered above (II Tim. 3:15f; II Pet. 1:21; II Cor. 13:3; John 10:35), we are able to construct a very satisfying dogmatic definition as to what Biblical inspiration really is. It will be understood, of course, that the passages under consideration are simply typical of others that bear the same consistent testimony to the unique inspiration of Biblical documents. The following synthesis will indicate briefly the nature of sacred inspiration.

a) The Bible is inspired. Undoubtedly this is the basic meaning of Paul's description in II Timothy 3:16. The assertion is made there that "all Scripture" is theopneustic, that is, "God-breathed" or "inspired by God." This is, without question, the highest statement that could possibly be made of the divine origin of the Bible. No theologian can question, if he accepts the Bible at all, that it teaches the doctrine of inspiration in the most unambiguous language.

b) The Bible is plenarily inspired. By this we mean that the Bible is wholly and in every part inspired. When Paul said that "all Scripture" is "God-breathed" he included in that designation all of Scripture. Christ Himself believed that neither an iota nor a dot could pass from the law until all was fulfilled (Matt. 5:18, RSV). The Bible knows nothing of the idea of degrees of inspiration as if some parts of the Bible were more inspired than other parts. God "spake" in the Old Testament just as much as in the New Testament (Heb. 1:1; II Pet. 1:21).

c) The Bible is verbally inspired. Many of the liberal school equate verbal inspiration with dictation and try to make the conservative position ludicrous. But, whatever may be the unjust caricature of the conservative view, the Bible most deliberately teaches the verbal inspiration of its documents. Christ (John 10:35) and Paul (Gal. 3:16) and others make appeal to divine inspiration in the very choice of words used in the original documents. The modern idea that only the thought (but not the words) was inspired is utterly foreign to the Scriptures and absolutely obnoxious to any true view of inspiration. It is significant that Paul asserted in II Timothy 3:16 that "all Scripture" (that is, the written words) is theopneustic — "God-breathed." Christ's thrice-repeated "It is written" (Matt. 4:6, 7, 10) is an eloquent reminder of our Lord's high view of verbal inspiration.

d) The Bible is true. God's law is truth (Ps. 119:142); the sum of His Word is truth (Ps. 119:160). Christ affirmed that God's Word is truth (John 17:17). When we posit "truth" as an attribute of the Word of God, we are not permitted to mix that truth with error as is the practice among liberals. It is absolutely repugnant to the whole tenor of the sacred writers to suppose for one moment that they would attribute to God's Word that which is erroneous or faulty. To them it was truth — truth in every category, whether it be in the realm of historical fact or in the sphere of physical phenomena or in the kingdom of spiritual and eternal truth.

e) The Bible is authoritative. It is the "Supreme Authority" beyond which the sacred writers know no higher appeal. "To the law and to the testimony! if they speak not according to this word, surely there is no morning for them" (Isa. 8:20, ASV). Even Christ, the Son of God, could cite no higher authority against Satan than the written Word of God (Matt. 4:6, 7, 10). To the Biblical writers the modern notion that man's mind should sit in judgment on God's Word deciding what shall be accepted and what rejected — such an idea was utterly detestable to them! The Bible is a critic of man (Heb. 4:12). Man dare not usurp that authority over the Bible!

III. PROOF FOR BIBLICAL INSPIRATION

There are two extreme positions with reference to the need of any proof for the Bible's inspiration. At the extreme left stands the haughty scoffer who ridicules the idea that the Bible could be proved to be of divine origin. On the extreme right stands the Bible-believing Christian who in his simple childlike faith accepts the Bible as the very Word of God without asking for, or desiring, any logical proof for the Bible's inspiration, apart from the fact that it speaks truth to his heart. Most Christians, however, while accepting with their hearts that the Bible is God's Word, desire to have the reasons for their faith stated after a logical fashion. We give proofs for most of our beliefs (such as, for example, the deity and resurrection of Christ) and it is no less spiritual to seek proofs for the Bible's inspiration. At least it would seem that we are on Scriptural ground when we give a reason for the hope that lies in us (cf. I Pet. 3:15). That is what we propose to do just now.

A. *The Bible's Testimony to Its Own Inspiration*

We begin our investigation with the testimony of the Bible itself. We simply want to find out whether, after all, the Biblical writers were conscious of any special inspiration which guided and controlled them in their writings. We readily recognize the fact that there are some in the modern world who deny us the right to begin with the Bible, or to appeal to the Bible at all in this matter. Their specious plea is that it is unfair to use the Bible's testimony in its own behalf. More particularly it is argued, with a flair of imperiousness, that this is a sort of reasoning in a circle which amounts to nothing and convinces none, except those who already believe the Bible to be the Word of God. But this argument is nothing but pretense. In human law, for example, every man is allowed the right to defend himself in a court and his testimony must be accepted as valid unless and until the contrary is proved. Even so it is in science. Does not every scientist appeal to the elemental laws of his own science in proving a principle that belongs to his particular science? Does not the physicist use the already existing laws of physics to prove a physical law? Does not a botanist use the laws of botany? And the chemist must use the laws of chemistry. The same could be said about the astronomer and all other scientists. It is

simply ridiculous to deny the Biblical scholar the same right
that others enjoy in their fields. If we have no right to
appeal to the Bible's statements regarding its inspiration,
then, logically, the physician has no right to appeal to the
human body to prove the circulatory system or any other
thing about the human body. We accept it as an undeniable
right, therefore, to use the Bible's own testimony to its
inspiration.

1. The inspiration of the Old Testament. Our investigation, of course, must begin with the Old Testament. It is
hardly likely that the truth of the Bible's plenary inspiration can be successfully maintained unless we include the
Old Testament, for the whole trend of modern critical studies
has been to jeopardize and call in question the inspiration
of that portion of Scripture. It is highly imperative, since
the Old Testament is an integral and essential part of "all
Scripture," that we maintain its divine origin and inspiration.
To prove the fact of Old Testament inspiration we must first
find out what is said therein about this subject; after that,
we shall see what Christ and the New Testament writers
say about its inspiration. All in all, we shall find a wonderful harmony of unified statements about this theme.

a) The testimony of the Old Testament to its inspiration.
Our approach here must be somewhat different from the
New Testament approach. In the latter portion of Scripture we have such specific statements as II Timothy 3:16
and II Peter 1:21, which we have already considered. We
have no such passages in the Old Testament. Our approach
must, therefore, be more indirect. In the end, however, we
shall have just as high a degree of certainty about the Old
Testament's inspiration as if Isaiah had written II Timothy
3:16 or Jeremiah had penned II Peter 1:21. This conclusion
will result, we believe, from the following facts.

(1) Divine attestations of a prophet's mission. Just as
Christ appealed to certain signs or factors in His divine
mission (see John 5:30-47), so an Old Testament prophet
could, if necessary, cite one or more proofs of his mission
as a prophet of God. These attestations are the following:
(a) Miraculous signs. Such supernatural signs were used

to authenticate Moses' mission as Israel's leader out of Egypt (Exodus 4:1-9). In Elijah's combat with Ahab and Baalism, we find several cases of the working of miracles to prove the truth of Elijah's ministry (I Kings 17:1ff; I Kings 18: 21-40). Signs and wonders by themselves, apart from other considerations, could never constitute an absolute proof of a prophet's divine commission (see Deut. 13:1-3). (b) Fulfillment of prediction. Frequently Isaiah cites the fact that only God can know the future (41:22; 42:9; 44:7; 45:21; 46:10). The gods of the pagans cannot do this; therefore, they are false gods. But those who are true prophets know the future in so far as God wills to reveal it unto them — and their prophecies come to pass (I Kings 17:1; 18:1). It is a sure sign that a prophet is false if his prediction fails of accomplishment (Deut. 18:20-22). (c) Harmony of revealed teaching. If a prophet should arise, teaching the people of Israel to worship other gods instead of Jehovah, that would be a sure indication that that prophet was simply "a dreamer of dreams" and not a true prophet (Deut. 13: 1-3). The whole principle is summarized in the words of Isaiah: "To the law and to the testimony! if they speak not according to this word, surely there is no morning for them" (8:20, ASV). A subsequent revelation must always harmonize with the essential truths already revealed to God's chosen people; otherwise, it is spurious and fraudulent. (d) A divine call. God called His servants, the prophets, sometimes outwardly by visible appointment and anointing (I Kings 19:16, 19), but always internally with a consciousness on the prophet's part that he had been called, even before his birth (Jer. 1:5; cf. Gal. 1:15) and in the midst of fluctuating human frailties (Jer. 20:7-13; cf. Luke 7:18-23), to declare the will of God ("Thus saith the Lord") to his generation. This consciousness of divine mission is expressed vigorously by Micah in the following words: "But as for me, I am full of power by the Spirit of Jehovah, and of judgment, and of might, to declare unto Jacob his transgression, and to Israel his sin" (3:8).

(2) Representations of the Holy Spirit's activity among the prophets in the Old Testament dispensation. The fol-

lowing acts or relationships are indicated: (a) God puts His Spirit upon men (Num. 11:25, 29; Ex. 28:3; 31:3). (b) God pours out His Spirit upon men (Joel 2:28; Ezek. 39:29; Isa. 32:15; 44:3). (c) God's Spirit falls upon men (Ezek. 11:5). (d) The Spirit is said to rest or come upon men (Num. 11:26; 24:2; I Sam. 10:6; II Chron. 15:1). (e) The Spirit of God enters into men (Ezek. 2:2; 3:24). (f) The Spirit clothes Himself with men (I Chron. 12:18; II Chron. 24:20; Judg. 6:34; see ASV margin on these passages). (g) The Spirit fills men (Mic. 3:8).

It will be noticed that in the references given above prophets are mainly, if not exclusively, in mind. And let us remember that in the Old Testament times the term prophet included much more than prediction. Historians and others who had the office or the gift of prophecy were included in the terminology. With this fact before us, let us summarize briefly the relevant facts bearing on the inspiration of the prophets.

(3) Facts supporting the inspiration of the Old Testament prophet. Not any one of these facts by itself would conclusively prove that the prophet was sent on a divine mission to Israel; but, taken together, they constitute an unbreakable chain of evidence corroborating the inspiration of the Old Testament prophet. We list here a few of the facts: (a) The prophet was conscious that he was sent by God to declare God's will to Israel (Mic. 3:8). (b) He was also conscious of the fact that God had in a special way communicated His revelation to him (Amos 3:7 — "Surely the Lord Jehovah will do nothing, except he reveal his secret unto his servants the prophets"; cf. I Pet. 1:12). (c) The prophets considered all prophets who prophesied without a divine commission as false (cf. Jer. 23:13-40). (d) Furthermore, they considered the evidence so clear that almost any one could perceive the difference between true and false prophets (I Kings 22:24-28; II Chron. 18:23). (e) The prophets looked upon themselves as belonging to a line of prophets who spake the same message to Israel (Neh. 9:30 — "Yet many years didst thou bear with them, and testifiedst against them by thy Spirit through thy prophets: yet would they

not give ear: therefore gavest thou them into the hand of the peoples of the land"; cf. also Zech. 7:12). (*f*) The prophets always considered writings of prior prophets of God as historical, genuine and authentic; there is not the slightest insinuation that their writings were erroneous, or that they contained myths and legends. Almost any page in the Old Testament would confirm this statement (e.g. Haggai 2:5; Zech. 1:6). (*g*) The prophets considered themselves so much the mouthpiece of God that, if their words were rejected, it was the same as if God Himself were rejected (Amos 7:10-17).

The right evaluation of the facts mentioned above can lead to but one conclusion — the inspiration of the Old Testament Scriptures. This conclusion is the only natural one that is possible in the light of the evidence. A different estimate of the facts must be due to a preconceived theory of naturalism that necessarily excludes the supernatural. And our conclusion here is confirmed by the highest authority known to the believing child of God; namely, the Lord Jesus Christ Himself.

b) The testimony of Christ to the inspiration of the Old Testament. Before we can deal adequately with Christ's testimony, we must first consider the debated matter pertaining to His authority in such questions.

(1) The challenge of Christ's authority. Down through the centuries Christ's words with reference to the Old Testament Scriptures have been taken at their face value in the Christian church; but, since the advent of higher criticism in the last century, His right or authority to speak on such matters has been challenged by a large number of critical scholars, many of whom profess to be followers of Jesus Christ. We must, therefore, first establish upon solid ground, Christ's right to speak authoritatively on such matters, before we take up His positive testimony to the Old Testament Scriptures.

(*a*) Facts supporting Christ's authority. Surely it must be considered a rather daring thing for a man who professes to acknowledge Jesus Christ as his Lord to question His right to speak authoritatively on the subject of the Old

Testament. And such it really is, especially in view of the fact that there are so many evidences supporting Christ's right. Let us look at a few of them: First, we have His nature — He is God's Only begotten Son. As such He has a unique knowledge of God the Father (Matt. 11:27). Next, we note the fact that He claimed to come into this world on a divine commission from the Father (John 8:42; 13:3; 16:28, 30; 17:8). In the third place, it is to be noted that this claim was corroborated by miracles and other works (John 5:30-47). Fourthly, in His ministry He always spoke the truth; in fact, He came into the world to bear witness to the truth (John 1:14; 8:14, 45; 18:37). Fifthly, there was no sin nor error in Him or in His teaching. No man could convict Him of sin (John 8:46); and we may also say, no man could or can convict Him of error. Sixthly, Christ, by His predictions and their fulfillment, showed that He had supernatural knowledge. If He could foresee the future accurately, He could much more know the past. We have every reason, therefore, to conclude that when Christ referred to the Old Testament, even in the slightest allusions, His words must carry the highest degree of authority with us. But in spite of this unimpeachable line of evidence, there are some in the modern critical world who undermine Christ's authority in such matters by some very subtle theories to which we must now address ourselves.

(*b*) Theories attempting to discount Christ's authority. There are three negative theories that we must deal with briefly at this point in order to clear the ground for Christ's positive testimony to the Old Testament Scriptures.

First, the theory of kenosis. According to this theory, based presumably on Philippians 2:5ff, Christ divested Himself of His attribute of omniscience in His act of incarnation. Thus it is uncritically used to give support to the questionable assumption that Christ's statements, with reference to the Old Testament, must be taken as the words of an ordinary man. Because He was limited, His knowledge was also limited and, therefore, so the theory runs, we need not take His statements as absolutely binding on us. To this theory there are some weighty objections that annihilate it entirely. Among these objections we cite the following. In the first place, the theory, if true, proves too much; for, if Christ were limited in one category, He was limited in all. We could not be sure that any one of His statements or teachings is true. If He erred about the Old Testament, He could also err about everything that He taught men to believe concerning Him and concerning their salvation. Thus the theory actually leads us into agnosticism. In the second place, this theory is built upon a wrong exegetical foundation. The "emptying" is explained by the "taking the form of a servant" that immediately follows. This interpretation is quite natural to the context. Nothing here is said by Paul of Christ's divesting Himself of His divine attributes — that idea is read into it by the critical mind. In the third place, there is no evidence in the Gospels that Christ considered Himself as talking about spiritual or historical things as a fallible man would speak. He exercised His omniscience repeatedly whenever the occasion made it necessary.

Second, the theory of accommodation. The idea here is that Christ actually knew that certain matters about the Old Testament were not true, but, because He did not want to rub the Jewish prejudices the wrong way, He accommodated His references to the Old Testament to their popular ideas. This theory sounds very plausible on the surface, but, in reality, is as subtle as the devil himself. To uncover its nefariousness, let us note the following facts. First, it implicates Christ in moral evil; it makes him out-Jesuitize the Jesuits in the trade of questionable distinctions. If the Jews were wrong in their views about Old Testament matters, they should have been corrected by Christ. If, for example, the Jews thought that the story about Jonah was really historical, and yet Christ knew that it was only an allegory (as the modern, critical view tells us), then it was morally wrong for Christ to appeal to Jonah's experience as a parallel to His approaching death and resurrection (cf. Matt. 12:38ff). Secondly, this theory actually undermines the authority of our blessed Lord as a teacher of truth. If He allowed certain erroneous views to pass by unchallenged, can we be

too sure that He did not compromise the truth in other
realms? If, for example, modern criticism has discovered
certain places where Christ's statements do not harmonize
with the facts as uncovered in our day, then does it not
follow, as a matter of logic, that Christ's statements and
teaching will be eventually undermined throughout? An unsafe teacher in one department of truth is also an unsafe
teacher in another department. If Christ cannot be accepted
as an absolute guide in historical and literary matters about
the Old Testament, need we still accept Him as such a
guide in spiritual matters about that portion or any other
portion of Scripture? Thirdly, if we scrutinize the Gospels
carefully, we will find that there is no evidence supporting
this theory. Christ was not the "popular" preacher that this
theory would visualize. He rebuked evil without fear of
the consequences. Read the twenty-second chapter of Matthew for His scathing denunciation of the hypocrisy of the
scribes and Pharisees. Can we suppose that Christ would
leave unchallenged the faulty and erroneous conceptions
of the Old Testament that the Jew presumably entertained
— according to the modern, critical view? Not so!

Third, the theory of disinterestedness. According to this
view, Christ could not concern Himself about petty matters
concerning the authorship of Old Testament books or the
actuality of historical events therein recorded. His mission
was greater than the settlement of questions as to whether
the historic Isaiah or some unknown prophet of the fifth
century before Christ wrote the fifty-third chapter of the
book bearing his name. Did David write the one hundred
tenth Psalm? As far as Christ was concerned, according
to the theory under examination, it did not matter one way
or another. Against this theory the following things may
be said by way of refutation. First, this theory is the child
of desperation. Something has to be done to get rid of
the evidence that Christ had a very high view of the Old
Testament — that He supported, so to speak, the historic
church view of the inspiration and historicity of that portion
of Scripture. So it is affirmed, contrary to all the evidence,
that Christ simply was not interested in technical questions

of date and authorship and the like with reference to Old Testament books and events. This position will simply not stand up under examination. Second, the so-called "technical questions," which it is asserted Christ was not concerned about because of their insignificance as compared with the great doctrines and truths which He promulgated, are not as insignificant as one might suppose. It often happens in life that little things make a world of difference. Is it a little matter that Christ cited a prophecy as unfulfilled as yet and referred the prophecy to Daniel (Matt. 24:15)? Christ considered the statement as a real prediction of a historic person by the name of Daniel, but the almost universal, critical view today is that the statement cited was neither a real prediction (as Christ thought it was) nor was it authored by the historic Daniel (as also Christ thought it was). It might seem a small matter to some, but, really, the difference between Christ's view here and the modern, critical view is the difference between supernaturalism and naturalism.

Thus we have now considered three theories which have been offered by the modern, critical world in an effort to undermine the authority of our Lord in matters pertaining to the Old Testament Scriptures. We have seen that each theory is beset with serious difficulties which make it utterly unacceptable to all who still hold high views of our Lord's person and works. Any one of the theories, if consistently held, cannot but weaken the whole structure of the Bible and Christianity. We, therefore, regard each one of them as objects of repugnance.

(2) Christ's positive testimony to the inspiration and authority of the Old Testament. This is a large and vastly important subject and our treatment will be necessarily inadequate. At the same time, though brief, the salient facts will be mentioned upon which a valid conclusion can be erected. We shall deal with Christ's treatment and estimate of the Old Testament under His objective testimony and His subjective testimony. This division is for the purpose of more clearly presenting the material.

(a) Christ's objective testimony to the Old Testament.

C

Under this heading we place His testimony to the historical, predictive, and Messianic character of the Old Testament Scriptures. Let us now consider each in turn briefly.

First, Christ's testimony to the historical character of the Old Testament. Christ cited a number of events from Old Testament times and always considered them as real events. The creation of man (Matt. 19:4) was just as real as the institution of marriage (Matt. 19:4); and the flood in Noah's time was just as historical as the destruction of Sodom (Matt. 24:27, 39; Luke 17:28f). The typical significance of the brazen serpent in no wise affected its historicity (John 3: 14). According to grammatical law, Christ considered the events concerning Jonah, though typical in significance, to be just as firmly grounded in objective reality as His approaching death and resurrection — the "as" statement is just as real as the "so" statement. There is not the slightest suggestion in all that Christ said that He considered any part of the Old Testament as even bordering on the realm of myth or legend. It was real history written with a purpose and pregnant with spiritual and typical significance.

Second, Christ's testimony to the predictive character of the Old Testament. We shall not attempt here to list those passages in which Christ cited the Old Testament as predictive. One, already referred to, must suffice — namely, Matthew 24:15, where Daniel is cited as predicting an event which Christ considered as still unfulfilled. We but allude to the fact that Christ's view of the predictive character of the Old Testament is entirely contrary to the dominant school of Old Testament criticism today.

Third, Christ's testimony to the Messianic nature of the Old Testament. This obviously is the core of His teaching about the Old Testament. "And beginning from Moses and all the prophets, he interpreted to them in all the scriptures the things concerning himself" (Luke 24:27). "And he said unto them, These are my words which I spake unto you, while I was yet with you, that all things must needs be fulfilled, which are written in the law of Moses, and the prophets, and the psalms, concerning me" (Luke 24:14). Could words be more transparent than these? Again we but allude to the fact that Christ here stands on absolutely different ground from modern critics who pose as His interpreters. To Christ the Old Testament is replete with Messianic meaning; to the modern critic there is but little, if any, prediction that can be called Messianic. Are we not told in current, liberal books that Isaiah 53 does not refer to Christ and that we are not to read into Daniel's prophecies (especially chapter 9) any Messianic significance? But these modern views would have been utterly repugnant to our blessed Lord.

Thus it is as certain as truth is truth that Christ believed that the Old Testament is historical, predictive and Messianic. To all who hold that the Gospels give us a valid description of Christ's words and ministry there can be no other conclusion regarding His testimony to the Old Testament Scriptures.

(b) Christ's subjective testimony to the Old Testament. By "subjective" here we mean the internal reasons in Christ and in the Holy Scriptures why He considered the Old Testament objectively historical, predictive, and Messianic. These reasons are found in the fact that Christ looked upon the Old Testament as inspired, infallible, and authoritative. On each of these aspects a few remarks are necessary.

First, Christ's testimony to the inspiration of the Old Testament. In Matthew 4:4 Christ cites Deuteronomy 8:3 ("Man shall not live by bread alone, but by every word that proceedeth out of the mouth of God") in His reply to Satan's temptation. Here Christ gives His approval to the belief that the Old Testament comes "out of the mouth of God" (cf. Heb. 1:1). In Matthew 5:18 He asserts in the strongest terms the verbal inspiration of the Law ("Till heaven and earth pass away, one jot or one tittle shall in no wise pass away from the law, till all things be accomplished"). In citing Psalm 110:1 Christ affirms that David spoke that verse "in the Spirit" (Matt. 22:43; cf. II Sam. 23:2; Rev. 1:10). In John 10:35 (already considered above), Christ emphasizes the verbal authority of the Old Testament. Christ rebukes the Jews for making void the Word of God (the Old Testament) by their traditions (Mark 7:

13). Christ attributes the commandments directly to God (Matt. 15:4 — "For God said," etc.). We need not cite further instances to prove that Christ received the Old Testament as a revelation of the true God and as inspired in its words.

Second, Christ's testimony to the infallibility of the Old Testament. Infallibility and inspiration go hand in hand; if a book is inspired it must be infallible; if it is infallible it is because it was inspired. We need not, therefore, belabor this point. In addition to the passages cited under the previous heading, we here call attention to the negative fact that Christ nowhere insinuates that the Old Testament is erroneous in any detail. Its history is absolutely true (e.g., Matt. 24:37f; Mark 2:24-28; John 3:14). There is not the slightest suggestion that it is in need of correction. Even His famous "but I say unto you" as found in the Sermon on the Mount (Matt. 5:22, etc.) is not to be interpreted as a correction of the former revelation but is to be understood as a correction of Jewish misunderstanding of the Old Testament teaching. It is, therefore, most certain that Christ esteemed the Old Testament as infallible in its teaching and in its historical statements.

Third, Christ's testimony to the authority of the Old Testament. Here we find that Christ held the Old Testament as a final authority in dealing with matters of faith and conduct. He appealed to it frequently with His characteristic "It is written" — as if to say, God has spoken in His Word and that settles it (Matt. 4:4, 7, 10). He even cited examples out of the Old Testament as authoritative for His own conduct (Mark 2:25ff). Its statements about legal matters were considered authoritative (John 8:17). And its predictions concerning Him were looked upon as true and of supreme authority in deciding His Messianic claims (Luke 24:25-27, 44ff; John 5:45f). The voice of Moses and the prophets was considered as authoritative in matters of the soul's destiny (Luke 16:29-31). Christ believed that if a principle or truth were taught in the Old Testament, there was no need to appeal to a higher authority.

Thus, to summarize, Christ's objective testimony to the

Old Testament consists in His belief that it is historical, predictive and Messianic. His subjective testimony consists in His conviction that it is inspired, infallible and authoritative. These six statements are a unit that cannot be broken. Logically, we must accept one and all, or none. Because the Old Testament is inspired by God, it is, therefore, infallible; and because it is infallible, it is authoritative. And because it is inspired, infallible and authoritative, it is also historical predictive and Messianic. One cannot stop in this logical process until he has accepted or rejected all the elements that go into it. We have, therefore, the most profound of all reasons to believe the Old Testament as coming from God on the basis of Christ's direct claim that it is of God.

c) The testimony of the New Testament writers to the inspiration of the Old Testament. The evidence afforded by an investigation of the apostolic writings is just as conclusive in regard to the Old Testament theopneustic character as the testimony of Christ which we have just examined. On this point there is absolute unanimity of belief. The followers of Christ present a united front in their belief regarding the supernatural origin of the Old Testament Scriptures. That this is not a forced statement will be shown in the following examination of details.

(1) The apostolic writers quote the Old Testament as authored by God or the Spirit. In some places even the human writer is ignored entirely as the quotation is referred immediately to God (Acts 2:17; cf. 4:25; Heb. 4:7; 8:8) or to the Holy Spirit (Heb. 3:7). Just as Christ attributed the same quotation to Moses (Mark 7:10) and to God (Matt. 15:4), so the New Testament writers attribute a quotation to the human author (e.g., Rom. 10:18-20) or to the Divine Author (e.g., Heb. 8:8; 10:15f) or to both the human and Divine together (Acts 28:25).

(2) The apostolic writers held the Old Testament to be inspired by God. Already we have dealt at length with the classic statements in II Timothy 3:16 and II Peter 1:21. In addition to these passages, which surely apply to the Old Testament, we note that in Hebrews 1:1 God is described as the One who "spoke" in both the Old and New Testa-

ments. Furthermore, "the Spirit of Christ" was in the prophets of old (I Pet. 1:11) just as much as in Paul when he spoke (II Cor. 13:3).

(3) The New Testament authors looked upon the Old Testament as verbally inspired. Constantly we hear the Old Testament referred to as "the sacred writings" (II Tim. 3:15), "the oracles of God" (Acts 7:38; Rom. 3:2), "the scripture" (I Tim. 5:18), "scripture" (I Pet. 2:6), "the word of God" (Rom. 9:6). It is "every scripture" (that is, the words that make up the document) that is inspired by God (II Tim. 3:16). Paul even bases an argument on the difference between the singular and plural of an Old Testament word (Gal. 3:16; cf. Matt. 22:42f; John 10:35, 36).

(4) The apostolic authors recognized real history in the Old Testament documents. Not even Paul's use of allegory in Galatians 4:21-31 can be construed to mean that he did not consider the details of the account historical. This very account is called a part of "the scripture" (Gal. 4:30, citing Gen. 21:10, 12). Old Testament history, however, was written not as a bare recital of historic details, but, according to the apostles, it was written with a didactic purpose. It was an objective portrayal of events as they actually occurred (without any doctoring or coloring of the facts), but the events so related were selected with a subjective purpose in mind. They were written for examples (I Cor. 10:6, 11) and to instruct us (II Tim. 3:16).

(5) The New Testament writers assign the Old Testament books to their traditional authors. Thus they run contrary to the views of modern critics. Passages are attributed to Isaiah, for example, whether they come from the earlier part (cf. Acts 28:25-27; Rom. 9:29) or the latter part (Rom. 10:20) of the book. The New Testament writers were utterly ignorant of the critical notion of two or more Isaiahs. Moses is, in their view, the writer of the Law or the Pentateuch (Rom. 10:19). David writes the Psalms (Acts 2:25; 4:25; Rom. 4:6; 11:9). Joel writes his prophecy (Acts 2:16-21), and Hosea authors his book (Rom. 9:25-27). Thus it can be truthfully said that the New Testament writers recognized the same human authors of the Old Testament as appears

in the Old Testament books themselves and as held universally by the ancient Jews and the Christian Church down to the advent of destructive criticism in the nineteenth century.

(6) The New Testament authors held to the prophetic character of the Old Testament. They believed that the prophets of the Old Testament really foresaw and preannounced events in New Testament times. The Holy Spirit, for example, caused David to pen the fact of Judas' transgression about a millennium before the event (Acts 1:16). Joel described centuries in advance the events of Pentecost (Acts 2:16ff). Isaiah foresaw Israel's rejection and hardness of heart (Acts 28:25 — "Well spake the Holy Spirit through Isaiah the prophet," etc.). The call of the Gentiles was predicted by Hosea (Rom. 9:25f). The introduction of the new covenant was in Jeremiah's predictions (Heb. 8:8ff). These references should be sufficient to prove that the New Testament writers saw in the Old Testament things concerning "these days" in which we live (Acts 3:24).

(7) The apostolic writers held that the great theme of the Old Testament concerned the coming of the Messiah. To them it was essentially Messianic. They affirm that "all the prophets" (Acts 3:18) spoke of Messiah's advent, suffering, death and resurrection. Paul affirms that his gospel is in perfect harmony with "what the prophets and Moses did say should come; how that the Christ must suffer, and how that he first by the resurrection of the dead should proclaim light both to the people and to the Gentiles" (Acts 26:22f). Cf. I Peter 1:11.

(8) The New Testament writers considered that the Old Testament had evidential value in proving Christianity to be true. The resurrection of Christ, for example, proved the Old Testament to be true (Acts 2:24-32; 13:33). Christ came to confirm the promises made to the Old Testament saints (Rom. 15:8ff; Heb. 11:39f). The inclusion of the Gentiles in the Christian Church is corroborated by the prophets (Acts 15:15-18). Israel's rejection of the Messiah is proved on the basis of Old Testament prophecy (Acts 13:40f; Rom. 9:32; 10:16-21; 11:1-32; I Pet. 2:6-8).

(9) The New Testament writers teach that, though the Old Testament writers were inspired, the prophets of the old dispensation did not always understand the real significance of their prophecies. They lacked illumination at times regarding the nature of their prediction (I Pet. 1:10ff). This was not a moral fault on their part, as it was in the case of the Jews at Christ's first advent who wilfully misunderstood their Old Testament prophets and were thereby punished with spiritual blindness (cf. John 9:39-41; 12:37-40). And their lack of illumination was perfectly consistent with their inspiration.

We have now covered the subject of the inspiration of the Old Testament, proving that that portion of Scripture is God's revelation and is inspired because it bears witness itself to its inspiration, because our Lord bears witness to its inspiration, and because the New Testament writers testify to its inspiration. This threefold chain is not easily broken and should be conclusive to all who sincerely want to know the truth. We turn now to the inspiration of the New Testament.

2. The inspiration of the New Testament. It will be perfectly evident to most Christians that, if any part of that which we call the Bible is theopneustic, it surely must be the New Testament part. If, therefore, we can prove, as we have just finished doing, the theopneustic character of the Old Testament, it seems quite obvious that that description ought to be applied more readily and with less debate to the New Testament Scriptures. And such is actually the case. However, we are not to suppose that the inspiration of the New Testament is so widely entertained that there are no opponents of it in the modern world. Men who formerly spent their time and talents in undermining the Old Testament find that their case cannot be won, unless they exercise equal ingenuity in seeking to undermine and discount the inspiration and authority of Christ and His apostles in the New Testament. We simply cannot, therefore, pass by the evidence for the inspiration of the New Testament documents. There are five points that we must take up in turn, namely: Christ's own inspiration;

Christ's promise of inspiration to His apostles; the claim that the New Testament writers make themselves for their inspiration; the testimony of the post-apostolic church concerning the inspiration of the New Testament; and the negative witness of the apocryphal writings.

a) Christ's own inspiration. Since we have previously dealt with this subject when we considered Christ's testimony to the inspiration of the Old Testament, it will be unnecessary here to elaborate further on this point. Suffice it to say, that if Christ Himself is not inspired, then it is surely true that neither those who preceded Him nor those who followed Him are inspired. That would mean that neither the prophets nor the apostles were theopneustic. Though Christ was inspired, His inspiration differed from the inspiration of all others in the following ways: (1) Christ was inspired at all times; prophets and apostles were inspired only as the Spirit came upon them for the purpose of recording Scripture. (2) Christ was inspired and illuminated at the same time; the prophets and apostles were inspired but not sinless. (3) In Christ inspiration preceded (I Pet. 1:11) and followed (II Cor. 13:3) His incarnation; in prophets and apostles inspiration began and ended in their earthly life. (4) In Christ inspiration was original (Heb. 1:1); in prophets and apostles it was derived (II Pet. 1:21 — "from God"). (5) Christ considered Himself to be the center of inspired writings (Luke 24:44 — "concerning me"; cf. II Cor. 1:19f; Rev. 19:10); no prophet or apostle looked upon himself as such (I Pet. 1:12). (6) Christ commissioned a group of men to write about Him (John 16:12-14); no prophet or apostle ever commissioned another group of inspired men to write of them. (7) In Christ (since He never wrote a part of Scripture) inspiration terminated in words spoken (John 17:8—"the words"; v. 14—"thy word"); in prophets and apostles inspiration terminated in words written (II Tim. 3:16 — "every scripture").

Christ's unique inspiration in no wise invalidates or diminishes the inspiration of prophets and apostles; rather, it assures us with the greatest degree of certainty, that both prophets and apostles, inspired by His Spirit (I Pet. 1:11), speak to us just as authoritatively as if Christ were speaking in His inspired servants (II Cor. 13:3).

b) Christ's promise of inspiration to His apostles. This promise consists of the following facts: (1) Christ recognized that His apostles were the recipients of a special revelation from the Father (Matt. 10:19, 20; 16:17; Mark 13:11). (2) Christ chose His apostles and commissioned them to go forth as deputized teachers of the new faith (Matt. 28:19; John 15:16; Acts 1:2; Gal. 1:1). (3) Christ promised the Holy Spirit to these men in order that He (a) might quicken their memories (John 14:26; cf. 2:22), (b) guide them in the truth (John 16:13), (c) bear witness to Christ (John 15:26, 27), and (d) enable them to know the future (John 16:13). All these features will be seen fulfilled in the Book of Acts and the inspired letters and writings of the apostles. (4) Christ gives to the words of His apostles the same authority as He possessed (Matt. 10:14f; Luke 10:16; John 13:20; 17:14, 18; Acts 1:2; Heb. 2:3, 4). (5) Christ promised that authenticating signs would follow His apostles (Mark 16:16-20; cf. Heb. 2:3, 4).

Thus it is as certain as anything can be that the apostles of our Lord were divinely chosen, commissioned, empowered, and authenticated as inspired recipients of the revelation that was committed to them as they penned the New Testament documents by the Holy Spirit.

However, we must consider briefly some of the major objections that scholars have made to the testimony of Christ concerning the inspiration of the New Testament writers. These objections may be conveniently summarized and answered under the following heads:

(a) It is asserted that Christ's promise (e.g., Matt. 10:19; Luke 12:12; John 14:16; 15:26; 16:7, 14) did not refer to the theopneustic nature of apostolic writings but rather concerned a general providence that enabled them to perform their ministry acceptably. The idea is that Christ promised the Spirit, not to insure infallible writings but, to guide them generally in cases of emergencies. The objections to this position are the following: 1) It is practically certain that our Lord had in mind in His statement in John 16:12-14 something more than general superintendence. His statement surely included what His disciples would write in their testimony about Him (John 15:26, 27). 2) That our Lord included the writings of the apostles in His promise seems even more certain, when we cite the fact that the risen Lord in glory communicated to the Apostle John specific directions to write a book about Him (Rev. 1:1-3, 11, 19; 22:18, 19). 3) As a final point, it is definite that the apostles understood the promise of Christ as referring to their writings, as well as their oral instructions. Note, for example, how Peter classifies Paul's writings as "scripture" (II Pet. 3:15, 16). Peter himself puts his writings and the writings of the other apostles on a level with "the words which were spoken before by the holy prophets" (II Pet. 3:1f). The commandment of the Lord is now expressed through the apostles (II Pet. 3:2). As the apostles went forth to proclaim the gospel, the Lord Himself worked with them and confirmed their word by accompanying signs (Mark 16:20; Heb. 2:3, 4).

(b) It is asserted that our Lord's promise included inspired traditions, as well as inspired documents, and even includes an inspired church in the person of the pope of Rome. This is, of course, the position of the Church of Rome and the way whereby they support their claim of an indefectible church. This is too large a subject to be dealt with here, except briefly. Suffice it to point to the following things: 1) References in apostolic writings to "traditions" (II Thess. 2:15; 3:6; I Cor. 11:2) cannot legitimately be construed to mean that the apostles approved of a secondary system of belief existing fluidly in oral traditions. The apostolic "traditions" constitute that which the apostles spoke verbally while at Thessalonica (cf. II Thess. 2:5) or Corinth (I Cor. 11:2) or elsewhere. There has never existed a body of oral tradition independent, and interpretive of, the documents now existing in the New Testament canon. 2) Christ's trenchant rebuke of the traditions of the Jews (Mark 7:1-13) is applicable to the Romanist concept of oral traditions existing, presumably, as interpretive norms of Christian belief and practices. If Christ rebuked the Pharisees for their man-made traditions that nullified the Scriptures, surely He would make the same denunciation of human traditions existing side by side with the written Scriptures in the Christian Church. 3) There is no proof that Christ's promise of inspiration to the apostles extended from them, in apostolic succession, to the present pope of Rome. There was a finality about the apostolic corpus that could not, by the very nature of their apostleship, be extended beyond their time. They understood clearly that the Faith had been delivered to them in a definitive, once-for-all form (Jude 3; Rev. 22:18, 19). 4) Finally, the irreconcilable conflict between the apostolic teaching in the New Testament and the dogmas of the Roman Catholic Church shows unmistakably that if Christ's promise of inspiration extended, as it actually did, to the former, it most assuredly did not extend to the latter. There is nothing in the New Testament to support such Roman beliefs as the immaculate conception, transubstantiation, purgatory, and the like; therefore, we conclude that Christ's promise of inspiration did not include the dogmas and beliefs of the Roman Catholic Church and, most conclusively, did not include the idea of a perpetual oracle of inspiration and infallibility in the person of the pope of Rome.

(c) It is asserted that Christ's promise of inspiration is not to be interpreted to mean that the apostolic writings are infallible and authoritative for all subsequent time. This assertion would indulge the idea that the New Testament documents, though quite reliable, are subject to revision and modification as man increases in knowledge. The idea back of this is that it is unthinkable that modern man, with all his advancement in science and discovery, should be bound to the dictates of prophets and apostles who lived in an unscientific age and whose mental environment was circumscribed by their very primitive culture. As a corollary, this view would maintain that inspiration is by no means limited to the canonical Scriptures but is rather to be found in the writings of all leaders of spiritual thought down to the present day.

Against the view presented in the previous paragraph, the following substantial arguments can be presented: 1) No subsequent writer after the apostles can possibly evidence the "signs" of his supernatural gifts, authenticating him as a mouthpiece of Deity. Not one of the "signs" of a prophet or apostle can be seen in any writer after the apostolic age. Let some man arise who actually makes a prediction that comes true or performs a miracle equal to those found in the New Testament — then we will believe his message as from God. But such a man has never arisen in the history of Christianity subsequent to the apostles. 2) Knowledge in material things does not necessarily mean knowledge in spiritual things. Granting that scientists know more about the atom than the apostles did, we do not allow that they know more about God and the spiritual life than the apostles did. Because man has developed materially does not mean that he is competent to speak authoritatively on the salvation of the soul or the destiny of the individual. A man may be a giant in knowledge of material things and yet a babe in spiritual realities. Modern man, with all of his boasted attainments, still needs to sit at the feet of prophets and apostles who received their message directly from the Maker of all things. 3) The view under consideration makes inspiration a very changeable thing. If the Scriptures are now out-of-date because of the advancement of knowledge in modern times, then will it not hold true, if there is any validity to this theory at all, that in another millennium of time, if the world endures that long, the "inspired" men of our day will likewise be out-of-date also? No generation will have an absolutely authoritative message from God because no generation can be sure that its knowledge of spiritual things will be valid in a subsequent generation. This really brings us to the place where, if the Bible is rejected as uniquely inspired and authoritative for all time, no generation has an authoritative voice that will even be accepted by its contemporaries — not to speak of later ages. 4) Nothing found in writers after the apostles can really be said to be superior in spiritual matters to that which

they wrote. All the good in later writers undoubtedly finds
its source in the Bible itself. And, in this case, it is better
to resort to the original fountain in all of its purity rather
than drink of the polluted streams that flow down through
the centuries. 5) Finally, those who have arisen in the
days since the apostles with a supposed new "revelation"
have in every case taught things that were not only contrary to the Bible but also contrary to the best interest of
man's soul. False prophets who promise men liberty from
the restrictions and restraints of the gospel have invariably
brought themselves and their devotees into a slavery to
their baser lusts (cf. II Pet. 2:10-22).

(d) It is asserted that Christ's promise of inspiration to
His apostles did not preclude the possibility of error in
their writings. Since we plan to take up more fully the
question concerning errors in the Bible, we need not de-
tain ourselves here on this subject. It is sufficient for the
present to state the following: 1) Some of the errors imputed to the apostles are of the critic's own manufacture;
a sober exegesis and an impartial interpretation will dissi-
pate practically all of the so-called mistakes of the apostles.
2) Furthermore, mistakes of a historical character (such as
some supposedly found in Luke's writings) have now been
withdrawn from the field because of the increasing vindication of the Bible by the fairly recent science of archaeology. In view of our rapidly expanding knowledge of
ancient times, due to modern excavation and discovery, one
would be rather foolhardy to affirm that there are any insoluble historical mistakes in the Bible. And as such supposedly historical mistakes reach zero in number, so the
same can be said in regard to other mistakes which some
have reportedly found in the didactic and prophetic portions of Scripture. But this must await further explication
later. 3) Finally, if Christ promised His apostles "the Spirit
of truth" (John 15:26) to guide them "into all the truth"
(John 16:13), it is inconceivable that that Spirit would
lead them into error. How could the promised Spirit be
named "the Spirit of truth" if He, as a matter of fact, actually led the apostles into error? Did not the apostles

themselves recognize that there were "the Spirit of truth" and "the spirit of error" operating in the world (I John 4: 1-6)? But they professed to be following the truth (I John 2:19). If error entered into their writings, could they not say that "the Spirit of Truth" promised to them by Christ had turned out to be "the spirit of error?"

Having now considered some of the objections made by critics against Christ's promise of the Spirit to guide His apostles in their writings, and having also seen that these objections are insufficient to overthrow the doctrine of apostolic inspiration as a gift from Christ, we turn now to our third proof for the inspiration of the New Testament.

c) The claim that the New Testament writers make for their own inspiration. It is a reasonable thing to expect, in view of the Lord's promise to them, that the apostles actually possessed the gift of inspiration. This is the fact that we wish at the present time to make abundantly and indubitably clear in the details that follow.

(1) Specific and didactic statements regarding their inspiration. Since we have cited these passages previously and have commented on them also, we need not here do more than mention them again. Obviously such passages as II Timothy 3:16; II Corinthians 13:3 and II Peter 1:21; 3:2 prove a high doctrine of inspiration. The "every scripture" in II Timothy 3:16 must, we believe, include the New Testament documents as well as the Old Testament. Paul commended the Thessalonica Christians because they received the message which he preached "not as the word of men, but, as it is in truth, the word of God, which also worketh in you that believe" (I Thess. 2:13). This terse statement in Paul's first letter to any of his churches indicates emphatically and unambiguously the standpoint from which he wrote. In none of Paul's subsequent letters to the end of his life is there any deviation from this absolute position.

(2) Statements in which apostles recognize the inspiration of other apostles. There are, indeed, very few cross-references in the New Testament writings where one apostle refers to, or cites, another apostle's letters. There was un-

doubtedly a reason for this situation. Since they all received their authority from the risen Lord, they did not need to confirm this authority by reference to another apostle's testimony concerning them. Paul affirms that he received his gospel directly from Jesus Christ (Gal. 1:1, 12). There is one striking passage, however, in which Peter refers to Paul's letters and puts them on the same level with "the other scriptures" (II Pet. 3:15, 16). Though names are not mentioned, such passages as John 21:25; Jude 3 ("the faith"); and Revelation 22:18, 19 ("this book") would seem to have a larger reference than to the book in which the reference is found. Be that as it may, there can be little doubt that each apostle, if the occasion demanded it, would have gladly testified in behalf of his fellow-apostle's inspiration.

(3) The authentication of their inspiration by certain signs or marks. Just as in the Old Testament (which we have already considered), so in the New Testament, we find certain signs which gave evidence to any reasonable person that the recipient of the signs was duly authenticated as an inspired messenger of the faith. In the New Testament these signs are exactly the same (though not particularized as such) as in the Old Testament. They are the following: (a) The performance of miracles. This is an authentication that is written large in the apostolic history. God, as promised, bore witness to the genuineness of their mission by confirming the apostles' testimony "by signs and wonders, and by manifold powers, and by gifts of the Holy Spirit" (Heb. 2:4; cf. Mark 16:20). (b) Prediction. No one but God can foretell the future. The apostles are conscious that they are instruments of "the Spirit of truth" who was to declare unto them "the things that are to come" (John 16:13). So they could attribute their predictions to the Holy Spirit (I Tim. 4:1). They could even call attention to the fulfillment of prophecy that was already taking place in their day (II Thess. 2:5-7; II Tim. 4:17f; II Pet. 1:12; 3:1ff; I John 2:18). (c) The harmony of their teaching with previous revelation. This can be looked at in a twofold fashion. In the first place, the apostles considered them-

selves in perfect concord with the prior Old Testament revelation. Paul affirmed dogmatically that he taught "nothing but what the prophets and Moses did say should come" (Acts 26:22f). The letter to the Hebrews states that the Old Testament revelation is authored by the same God who is revealed in Jesus Christ (Heb. 1:1) and that the two dispensations make one whole plan of redemption (11:39f). Peter informs us that all the prophets from Samuel onward have spoken of "these days" (Acts 3:24; cf. I Pet. 1:10-12). In the second place, the New Testament writers consider their teaching as in perfect conformity with the teaching of Jesus Christ their Lord. Since this concerns the unity of God's revelation, we shall have occasion in a subsequent chapter to discuss it more fully. We thus pass it by for the present. (d) The divine call to apostleship. In view of the fact that Christ especially chose and commissioned His immediate apostles and endowed them with supernatural gifts for the performance of their ministry, it is likely that we shall find in their writings reverberations of their divine call. Paul regarded His call as peculiarly unique (Gal. 1:1, 11, 15-17; II Cor. 12:1ff). The Gospel of God had been committed to his trust (I Cor. 15:1ff; Gal. 2:7; I Thess. 2:4; I Tim. 1:11). In one sense it could be said that the household of God was built "upon the foundation of the apostles and prophets, Christ Jesus himself being the chief cornerstone" (Eph. 2:20). The apostles as a class had been divinely put first in the Early Church (I Cor. 12:28; Eph. 4:11). They were conscious that their position in the community of believers was exceptional and distinctive. This consciousness on their part was a natural consequence of their supernatural call to a unique ministry.

(4) Statements of the apostles which indicate that they spoke with divine authority. This fact is so intermingled with their teaching that it is difficult to distinguish in just so many words. But the apostles, being divinely commissioned and empowered by the Holy Spirit to teach and to write down for posterity the essentials of the New Testament faith, did, as the occasion demanded, express unequivocally that authority with which the risen Lord had

D

clothed them. Paul could, for example, come to a church "with a rod" (I Cor. 4:2), dealing with it "sharply, according to the authority which the Lord gave me for building up, and not for casting down" (II Cor. 13:10). Either the apostles actually possessed the authority which they professed or, on the other hand, they were men possessed of a fanatical spirit of delusion. That the first alternative is the only one consistent with the facts will be the opinion and consequently conviction of all those who are competent to judge all the factors involved. And this conviction rises to assurance when we postulate the fact that these men who were called apostles were also agents of "the Spirit of truth." They wrote as God-inspired men with all the authority which only God can delegate to men. Without inspiration their words carry no authority; with inspiration their every utterance is pregnant with divine authority — an authority which is still resident in the Word of God down to the end of time. The apostles radiate this authority in their writings just as the face of Moses glowed because of his being in the divine presence. Those who have become "partakers of the divine nature" (II Pet. 1:4) will instinctively recognize and honor this authority of the apostolic writings.

(5) Statements of the apostles in which they indicate that they were free of error. Paul affirms that his exhortation was "not of error" (I Thess. 2:3). This same apostle had a great deal to say about those who turn from the truth to fables (I Tim. 1:4; 4:7; II Tim. 4:4; Titus 1:14). Peter professes that he did not "follow cunningly devised fables" (II Pet. 1:16). John firmly believed that his teaching was "of the truth" (I John 3:19), of which no lie was possible (I John 2:21). There is not the slightest suggestion in any apostolic writing that the writer thereof thought for one moment that his teaching veered away from the absolute truth by even a hair's breadth.

(6) The remarkable unity of the New Testament writers is another strong proof of their inspiration. Since we shall deal with this subject more fully in a subsequent chapter,

it will not be necessary to cite details that confirm this phenomenon. Suffice it for the present to call attention to the fact that there is a threefold unity evident among the New Testament writers. First, there is unity between them and the recorded teachings of the Lord Jesus Christ. Second, there is unity between one writer (such as Paul) and another writer (such as Peter) in their doctrines and statements of facts. Finally, there is unity of teaching in each individual writer. Paul, who writes the Thessalonian letters, does not contradict Paul, who writes the Pastoral letters. Likewise, Peter's sermons in Acts are in harmony with Peter's two letters. The same is true of all the New Testament writers. With this brief summary we need not pursue this subject more at the present time.

d) The fourth proof we advance for the inspiration of the New Testament writers is found in the fact that the Early Church writers, who lived in the centuries immediately succeeding the apostles, bear witness to the fact that the apostles were uniquely inspired in their writings. The evidence for this statement is so adequately given in W. Sanday's *Inspiration* (Bampton Lectures for 1893) and Westcott's *An Introduction to the Study of the Gospels* (Appendix B) that we need but invite the reader to turn to these well-documented sources of information. Since that may not be possible, we give here a very brief summary of the evidence found in the post-apostolic period for the first few centuries.

(1) The Scriptures are cited as of divine origin. Such attributes as "divine" or "holy" are ascribed to the Scriptures by such church fathers as Theophilus of Antioch, Clement of Alexandria, Origen, Cyprian and others.

(2) The New Testament documents composing the sacred canon were put on the same level of inspiration and authority as the books composing the Old Testament canon. God is the author of both portions of Scripture; and the two parts make one whole. The authoritative voice of God is in both.

(3) The Sacred Scriptures are regarded as inspired by

the Holy Spirit. Tertullian describes the apostles as having their minds "flooded" by the Holy Spirit. The word *theopneustos* (II Tim. 3:16) is applied to the New Testament by such writers as Clement, Origen, Eusebius and others. Clement considers obeying the Scriptures as the same as obeying the Lord. The statement that Christ speaks in the apostles (II Cor. 13:3) is regarded as indicating the process of inspiration.

(4) The Scriptures are looked upon as verbally inspired. The regulation, for example, that a bishop should have only one wife (Titus 1:6) is cited as an illustration of the "foresight" of the Holy Spirit in guarding the church from later heresies. The record from creation to the time of Abraham was given to Moses by the Holy Spirit. The Holy Spirit is regarded as the real author of the accounts of our Lord's life and teaching as given in the four Gospels.

(5) This high doctrine of inspiration among the early Church Fathers reaches its climax in their view that the Scriptures are perfect and infallible. Methodius, bishop of Olympus, asserts that there can be no contradiction in Holy Writ. Origen denies that the writers of Scripture can have a lapse of memory. Novatian regards the Scriptures as infallible.

(6) As a natural consequence of the foregoing positions, it is obvious that the Church Fathers will appeal to the Scriptures as the absolute rule of faith for Christians. And this is the case: all parties, orthodox and heterodox, an Athanasius and an Arius, cite the Scriptures in confirmation of their position and in refutation of their opponents. To ascertain the true meaning of Scripture was to find an end to all controversy.

It will be evident from the foregoing that it was the almost universal belief among the early church writers that the Scriptures of the New Testament occupied a place of unique authority and finality. These church writers, therefore, bear an indirect testimony to the inspiration of the sacred writers of the New Testament. This testimony is even more conclusive when it is remembered that the church writers did not claim to possess the gift of inspiration themselves. They looked upon themselves simply as fallible interpreters of the infallible Scriptures of the Old and New Testaments.

e) The final proof for the inspiration of the New Testament is found in the significant contrast between the writings of the inspired apostles and those who tried to imitate them and whose writings are now classified as Apocryphal Gospels, Acts, Epistles, and Apocalypses. It is a well-known fact that, in the centuries following the apostolic age, documents arose which purported to be of apostolic origin. These spurious documents give us a strong (even if it be negative in nature) argument for the uniqueness and inspiration of the writings found in the New Testament canon. That this statement is true will be readily perceived when we consider the following particulars.

(1) The New Testament documents are true history; the apocryphal literature contains much that is unashamedly fictitious and legendary. Even the New Testament writers themselves recognize the natural tendency among men to embellish spiritual truth with fables and myths (cf. Luke 1:1-4; I Tim. 4:7; 6:3, 4). The apocryphal literature that arose as early as the second century illustrates, in all of its disregard for objective fact, the myth-working tendency of the unbridled human imagination. But in the New Testament we find sober history developed according to a divine pattern but without the aberrations of the uninspired mind of sinful man.

(2) The New Testament documents were written by contemporaries who lived at the time of the events recorded and were, in most cases, eye-witnesses of these events. The Gospels, for example, were penned by men who had known the living Lord in the days of His flesh (cf. John 20:30f; 21:24; I John 1:1ff). Luke was undoubtedly a companion of Paul on some of his missions (cf. Acts 16:10-17; 20:5-15; 21:1-18; 27:1; 28:16). It is an established fact, however, that the apocryphal literature did not arise until at least the second century — practically a century after the historic life of Christ and after all the eye-witnesses of His life had died. This apocryphal literature must, therefore, be prac-

tically nil as a source of objective history about the life
of Jesus. What perverted information it contains must be
due, either to a corruption and embellishment of the simple
record of the Gospels, or to the working of tradition in
favor of some of the heresies that arose in the early days
of Christianity, or the rank growth of myth and legend invented by the human imagination to fill up the gaps in
the life of our Lord about which the curious have always
desired to know more than that which is written.

(3) The New Testament literature is genuine, being
written by the authors whose names we know. There is
no established place in the New Testament where a document was passed off as the composition of another. Contrary to some liberal critics, the Pastoral letters were written
by Paul — not by some disciple of his who attempted to
write in the spirit of his teacher, Paul. The New Testament documents are not pseudonymns; they are distinctly
not "pious frauds." But when we turn to the apocryphal
literature that arose to supplement the New Testament we
find nothing but fraudulent productions. Though palmed
off in the name of Peter, James, Thomas, Paul and other
New Testament personalities, it is not certain in any case
who the real author of any particular apocryphal writing
actually was. This is all in striking contrast to the New
Testament literature.

(4) The New Testament writings are doctrinally unified;
each is an integral part of the whole structure. There is
nothing taught in one part that contradicts what is taught
in another part. All is in perfect concord and harmony.
When we turn to the apocryphal literature we find two
striking contrasts. On the one hand, there is conflict between this literature and the literature of the New Testament; on the other hand, there is conflict between one
apocryphal production and another. Arising in a time when
heresies and traditions had begun to flourish, the apocryphal
writings reflect the views of Gnosticism, Doceticism, and
Mariolatry that were making inroads on Christian truth. To
all unprejudiced investigators it appears self-evident that
there is an impassable gulf between the best of the apocry-

phal literature and the whole of the New Testament. Both cannot be from the same source; if the New Testament is divine, the apocryphal is human.

(5) The New Testament represents an objective portrayal of the events connected with the life of our Lord and of the Early Church. There is no attempt in this record to cover up certain unsavory matters (such as the defection of Peter). There is not the slightest suggestion that the apostles were trying to "idealize" their Master and thus make a God out of a mere man — as some modern critics have affirmed. But in the apocryphal literature "the idealization-tendency" has reached its wildest fancy. The New Testament writers were historians — not creators of fiction; the apocryphal writers — whoever they were — were creators (out of their fertile, though morbid, imagination), but not historians. In the New Testament fact is fundamental; in the apocryphal literature a fact is molded and shaped after the image of the writer's purpose.

(6) The New Testament literature towers above all contemporary literature as unequalled and unsurpassed; it is one of its kind — timeless and ageless. It belongs to every age and is never outdated or antiquated by the advances in man's knowledge. But these assertions could never be properly made about the literature — if such it can be called — which sprang as a rank growth out of its age, bearing all the characteristics of its environment, and died with its age, forgotten and forsaken by all but those who, with an apologetic motive, sought its survival either to de-emphasize the superiority of the New Testament or to prove the utter contrast between the New Testament and this apocryphal literature. That the Christian Church has never considered the apocryphal literature worthy of being mentioned in the same category with the New Testament is one of the truisms of critical research.

(7) Finally, by a true instinct, as just intimated, the Church has sensed in the New Testament literature the voice of God in a unique way. Calvin's doctrine of the testimony of the Spirit teaches that in the Scriptures God speaks to the Christian's heart in such a manner that all

of God's true children, indwelt by the same Spirit, can instinctively and intuitively discern their Father's voice. But this voice is not heard in the apocryphal literature. There we hear only the voice of man — and it is man as dominated by his own sinful passions and the passions of the age which surrounds him. The Jesus of the apocryphal literature is a man of hatred, malice, vindictiveness — a transcribed copy of the typical man of that age. But the Jesus that comes to us in the inspired record is the God-Man, like us yet different from us, tempted but without sin, suffering in death but rising triumphantly in victory.

CHAPTER TWO

THE INSPIRATION OF THE BIBLE
(*continued*)

In this chapter we continue our study of the inspiration of the Bible, dealing primarily with the question concerning the extent of inspiration and then the common objections to inspiration. As in the previous chapter, our purpose shall be to state facts objectively, supporting our position with evidence that can be trusted.

IV. THE EXTENT OF INSPIRATION

One of the most debated problems regarding the concept of Biblical inspiration concerns the question how much or how far the Bible is really inspired. We shall first state what we consider the true view to be on this subject and shall then deal with some other views that are definitely inadequate and erroneous.

A. *The True View*

There is, we believe, a view regarding the extent of Biblical inspiration that can be characterized as the true position. Those who hold to the modern, liberal approach to the Bible will, of course, object violently to our description. But their objection will in no wise affect our belief as to the truthfulness of the position we present and maintain. The time has come when the conservative scholar must be as aggressive in his presentation and defense of the orthodox position as the liberal is on his side.

There is a position regarding the extent of inspiration which may fairly be classified as the one held, down through the centuries, by the most devout and most learned representatives of the Christian faith. That view, because of its universal acceptation in orthodox circles, may rightly be

called the historic church view. We shall now give the
details of that view.

1. Only the Bible is inspired. The orthodox conception
of Biblical inspiration limits such inspiration to the sixty-six
canonical books of Scripture. Inspiration is a resident quality
and attribute of these books. All other books, not contained
in the sacred canon — whether such books be ancient or
modern, religious or secular, Christian or pagan — cannot
be rightly classified as inspired. Such books may be helpful
and may contain an element of truth in certain realms of
thought; but they cannot be put in the same category with
the inspired books of Scripture. The Bible alone is the Word
of God — that sacred deposit of infallible truth committed
to us by men who wrote under the direction and supervision of the Holy Spirit. Even the best in the world's literature is but a faint glow of what is found in pristine purity
in the Holy Scriptures. The Bible is indebted to no man,
race or people for its truth; but other authors — in ancient
and modern times, often without acknowledgment — have
borrowed their best ideas from this pure and inexhaustible
well of spiritual truth.

2. The Bible is fully inspired. The true view of inspiration maintains that every part of that which makes up
Scripture is inspired. This view emphatically rejects the
theory that there are degrees of inspiration — as if some
books or portions of Scripture were more inspired than
others. Inspiration is a resident quality or attribute that
permeates all parts of Scripture equally. That this assertion is true is evidenced by the following facts.

a) Quotations from the Old Testament are all considered
to be equally the Word of God and, consequently, authoritative. The New Testament knows nothing of giving greater
weight or authority to one portion of the Old Testament
over another portion. If Moses is cited often, it is not because Moses is more inspired than Jeremiah or some other
Old Testament writer, but because the Jews of Christ's day,
being professed followers of Moses, gave greater weight to
his words. The authoritative "It is written" is applied just
as much to a quotation from the Psalms (Luke 4:10) as

from Deuteronomy (Luke 4:4, 8). Joel (2:28) is called "scripture" (Rom. 10:11) in the same sense as Leviticus (19:18; Jas. 2:8). In the same verse (I Tim. 5:18), a quotation from the Old Testament (Deut. 25:4) and a quotation from Christ (Matt. 10:10) are both called "scripture." It is dogmatically certain, therefore, that the plenary or full inspiration of "all scripture" is taught deductively and conclusively in the Bible itself.

b) A second reason why we believe in the full inspiration of Sacred Writ is found in the fact that this view is the only one consistent with the facts and logically defensible. Any theory that denies the full inspiration of the Bible introduces a subjective element which makes the modern critic the ultimate and final judge as to what constitutes Scripture. And since one critic will naturally differ from another, it follows that there can be no definitive canon of sacred books which constitute the Word of God. If the Bible is not accepted in its entirety as the Word of God and court of final appeal, there can be no assurance that any part of it will be regarded as a trustworthy oracle from God. If the breaking of one commandment means that one is guilty of breaking the whole law (cf. Jas. 2:10), it logically follows that if one denies one part of the Bible to be the Word of God, he automatically undermines the entire Bible and thereby makes none of it God's Word. Logically there is no resting-place between an acceptance of the full inspiration of the Bible and a rejection of the Bible as God's infallible Word.

c) A third reason why we must accept the plenary inspiration of the Sacred Scriptures is found in the fact that Biblical inspiration is not to be equated with that which "inspires" us. There are some portions of Scripture (for example, the long list of names in I Chron., ch. 1ff) which are not edifying and would perhaps never be included in a book of Scripture-readings for devotions. But inspiration extends just as much to these genealogies as to the twenty-third Psalm. The former may not be uplifting, but they are still an essential part of Scripture. If every part of the human body has some part to play in the entire structure, and if even the lowliest parts assume an important place (cf. I Cor. 12:12-31), then it follows that even those parts of the Bible which we may consider, from a restricted viewpoint, as less important (and also less helpful) may, from a more complete understanding of God's purpose, assume a place of paramount importance. The genealogies may not edify, but without them we would be lacking proof that Jesus Christ was of the royal line of David — and without that proof or assurance the other parts of Scripture would soon lose their edifying quality. Inspiration, therefore, is by no means to be equated with that which "inspires" us. If such were the case, we would have as many canons of Scripture as we have readers of the Bible, for no two would agree as to which parts of the Bible are "inspiring." One will see in the Book of Esther nothing worthy of its being in the sacred canon; another will see therein a wonderful portrayal of the providence of God. To one the Song of Solomon is a sensual story of an oriental harem; to another it is a beautiful symbolism of Christ's love for His Church. All parts of the Sacred Scripture have a significance in God's total plan and all parts are equally inspired by God's Spirit. The devotional books cannot say to the historical books, "I have no need of thee" (I Cor. 12:21); nor can the apostles relegate the Old Testament prophets to oblivion.

3. The Bible is verbally inspired. By "verbal inspiration" we mean that the very words of Scripture are God-breathed. Liberals are constantly equating verbal inspiration with what they call mechanical inspiration or the dictation-theory. But verbal inspiration, properly understood, is by no means either one of these. Verbal inspiration regards the words of Scripture as infallibly inspired by the Spirit of God. That this is the true view will be apparent as we present the following proofs.

a) Verbal inspiration is the only view consistent with the facts of Scripture. In II Timothy 3:16 Paul affirms that "every scripture" is God-breathed. Undoubtedly "every scripture" refers to the "written words." "Every scripture is inspired by God" represents Paul's meaning here. That means that every word that makes up "scripture" is inspired by God. It is logically inconceivable to posit inspiration of "all scripture" and yet deny inspiration to each and every word that makes up "all scripture." If "all scripture" may be described as a circle, every jot and tittle in that circle is "God-breathed." If the Book of Jonah is a part of "all scripture," then that book must be "God-breathed." And since a book is made up of words, the very words of the Book of Jonah must be inspired.

This principle of inspiration is exactly what we find in the Bible itself. The highest regard for verbal accuracy is therein upheld. The difference between the singular and plural of a word (cf. Gal. 3:16) is a matter of paramount importance. Christ Himself affirmed that not even "one jot or one tittle" shall pass away until all things are accomplished. Paul categorically states that his words were the words which the Holy Spirit taught him (I Cor. 2:4). Zechariah characterizes previous messages to Israel as "the words which Jehovah of hosts had sent by his Spirit by the former prophets" (7:12). These "sacred letters" Timothy knew from a babe (II Tim. 3:15).

b) A second reason why we believe verbal inspiration is the correct view is found in the fact that this view alone safeguards the doctrinal foundation of our Christian faith. If the words of Scripture are not infallibly inspired, we cannot be sure of the meaning of Scripture, for words alone convey to us meaning. If the words are changed, the meaning must be changed also. If one regards the words lightly, he will also regard the meaning likewise. Because many do not consider the words of Scripture to be inspired and thus authoritative, they likewise do not consider the meaning of Scripture as absolutely binding upon them. In the hands of the scholar who does not hold the Bible as verbally inspired, the sacred Book becomes a piece of clay that can be molded after the fashion of the scholar's philosophical viewpoint. Texts can thereby be emended at will. Passages offensive to the scholar's premises can be called interpolations. Such things have been done by men who stand high in the scholarly world. And all this issues out of their conviction that the Bible is not verbally inspired. Such scholars, in order to cover the weakness and arbitrariness of their position, impute to the conservative the utterly repugnant theory of mechanical dictation.

To summarize, the true view of the extent of Biblical inspiration includes three essential features: first, only the Bible is inspired; second, all of the Bible is inspired; and third, the very words of the Bible are inspired. These three elements are so integrated that one cannot be logically divorced from the other. One must hold all or reject all — no eclecticism is allowable here.

B. Some False Views

Having stated clearly the true view of inspiration, we are now ready to enumerate some of the chief views on the opposite side. We shall also attempt to give a brief refutation of these views.

1. None of the Bible is inspired. This is the view of all agnostics, atheists, materialists, rationalists, and the like. There are three plausible arguments presented in defense of this position.

a) It is maintained that there is nothing supernatural in the present world-order. All things operate according to resident forces in nature itself. Inspired revelations, coming from a supernatural source, are utterly unthinkable in such a system of naturalism. Thus the philosophical premise held in common by these anti-supernaturalists excludes any concept of an inspired Bible.

b) This position further maintains that there are no sufficient evidences compelling them to believe that there is such a thing as a supernatural revelation or an inspired Bible. When they examine the internal and external proofs put forth in defense of the Bible's uniqueness, they turn away unconvinced. The exponents of this viewpoint may, at times, candidly admit that there are gems of moral insight in the Bible, but they do not allow that such gems have a supernatural origin. They are simply the products of the human mind which may be paralleled in the best of the world's literature.

c) Moreover, modern defenders of this negative position affirm that their viewpoint, once rejected as heretical and outside the Christian fold, is now baptized and made legitimate by many teachers, ministers and others, who have adopted an identical position in the modern Church. Celsus, Porphyry, Voltaire and Paine have become incarnate again in professors and preachers who teach and write books in which are found attitudes and approaches toward the Bible once rejected by the Church but now widely accepted in religious and theological circles.

It will be evident that the position presented above is absolutely contrary to the historic view of the Christian Church. The arguments against this negative position are such as the following:

(1) There is adequate and compelling evidence supporting the theistic world-view. In this view supernaturalism is an essential part. This supernaturalism permits the introduction into the history of man of a revelation from God. God not only made the world and established laws for its continuance, but He has also revealed Himself to man upon the earth. This intervention, as planned by God for man's good, is now recorded in the supernatural revelation in the Bible.

(2) Furthermore, the unbiased critic must admit that, taking all the relevant facts into consideration, there is sufficient evidence to prove to any honest doubter that the Bible gives adequate proof that man is not its ultimate author. Men have written many other books, secular and religious, but no man nor any group of men has ever written a book like the Bible, apart from supernatural revelation.

(3) The truthfulness of the Bible's inspiration does not hinge on the number or the presumed scholarship of those who, in the modern Church, take the side of ancient or modern skepticism in denying Biblical inspiration. In fact, the denial of the inspiration of the Scriptures in the modern world is a proof for inspiration, for the Bible most certainly foretells the apostasy of the Church from the historic faith toward the close of the present age (cf. II Thess. 2:1ff; I Tim. 4:1ff; II Tim. 3:1ff; 4:3, 4). Modern deniers of Bibli-

cal inspiration do, in fact, confirm the very inspiration which
they decry. Furthermore, as an additional proof for inspiration, if the Bible had been written by men apart from the
supernatural insight of the Holy Spirit, it would never have
pictured the corruption of the faith as one of the characteristics of the closing days of the present age.

2. The Bible plus something else is inspired. This is the
common view held by groups calling themselves Christians
but, at the same time, adding to the Bible other standards
of their faith that they consider equally inspired and authoritative. There are four such groups that we wish to include in this category. We shall present each one in turn,
stating and refuting the position of each.

a) The Roman Catholic position. Rome accepts the Bible
as authoritative and inspired, but practically nullifies the
Bible as a final court of appeal by accepting the authority
of certain Apocryphal books, church tradition, the decrees
of councils, the Vulgate translation of the Bible, and, since
1870 at the Vatican Council, the infallibility of the pope
of Rome. Our refutation of the Romanist view must be
brief. We call attention here to the following facts.

(1) By adding other authorities to the Bible Rome has,
in fact, repudiated the absolute authority of the Bible. That
Church, professing great reverence for the Bible, has undermined the authority of the Bible in the preference she gives
to her man-made authorities. Some of her most pernicious
errors can be supported only on the basis that either tradition or councils or the pope or some apocryphal book is equal
or superior to the authority of the Bible.

(2) Rome has on her side neither the ancient Jews, nor
Christ and His apostles, nor the consensus of the Church
Fathers in her claim that the Bible needs to be supplemented
by tradition, councils, and the dogmas of supposedly infallible popes. It is a known historic fact that the errors
of the Roman system have grown up during the Dark Ages
and that Rome, in desperation, has been compelled to accept the authority of other standards than the Bible alone
in order to sustain her perversions of Christian truth.

(3) In rejecting the absolute authority of the Bible alone,

Rome illustrates the principle that, when once the Bible is repudiated as the only inspired source of Christian truth, there is no end to the increase of errors and the corruption of the Gospel. A notorious example of this principle is seen in Mariolatry and all of its attendant evils — the immaculate conception, the perpetual virginity, and now (since 1950) the assumption of Mary. These perversions are not found in the Bible but in the other "authorities" that Rome puts on a level with the Bible — in fact, in practice, she gives greater weight to them than to the Bible itself!

b) The position of cults and isms. Under this head are to be placed all those groups which more or less accept the Bible as an infallible guide but add some revelation reportedly received by the founder of the cult involved. Many such groups have arisen in the history of the Christian Church. Mohammedanism is, of course, the most notorious example of what we have in mind. In that sinister religion the Koran has all but usurped the authority of the Bible. In modern Christendom we find such groups as Mormonism with its "inspired" prophet, Joseph Smith; Christian Science with its "inspired" Mary Baker Eddy; Seventh Day Adventism with its "inspired" prophetess, Mrs. Ellen Gould White; Jehovah's Witnesses with its "inspired" Charles Taze Russell; and similar groups. The basic idea in all these cults is found in the supposed fact that God has made a further "revelation" of His will and program to the founder of the cult involved. The following observations will show plainly the spurious nature of these pretended "revelations."

(1) The Bible teaches unambiguously that it is the final revelation to mankind (Jude 3; Rev. 22:18f). All subsequent "revelations" arising after the close of the New Testament canon must necessarily be false.

(2) Christ and His apostles repeatedly warned the Church against accepting false prophets and teachers that would arise in the course of church history (Matt. 24:11, 24; I Tim. 4:1ff; II Tim. 3:1ff; 4:3, 4; II Pet. 2:1ff; 3:3ff).

(3) In every case it can be proved that the subsequent "revelation" contains statements and inculcates principles that are incompatible with the inspired revelation in the Bible.

E

We need not enumerate details here, since our assertion is easily provable. The Bible speaks of such errors as "destructive heresies" (II Pet. 2:1). Such cults could not survive apart from the esteem and reverence they attach to their human founder and his pretended "revelation." It is unquestionable fact that such religionists attribute more authority to the "revelation" reportedly received by their founder than they do to the Bible itself.

(4) When objectively compared with the revelation given to us in God's infallible Word, the subsequent "revelations" are all found wanting in their historical trustworthiness and are all on a par with the apocryphal literature that flourished in the second and subsequent centuries of our Christian era. Whereas the Bible deals with real persons, places and things whose historical character can be corroborated by archaeological science, these cults and isms and their accepted "revelations" float in the misty atmosphere of nebulosity.

c) The mystical view. Proponents of this idea feign great reverence for the authority of the Bible; but they also maintain that God still speaks to men apart from, and independent of, the Bible. This view is often referred to as "the inner light." Each soul may receive from the Deity a "revelation" of God's will for his life for the immediate present. One need not laboriously investigate the historical revelation in the Bible when one has a much quicker and surer contact with God. Mysticism has flourished in all periods of church history and is found also in non-Christian religions. Perhaps the most striking example of it within the Christian fold is Quakerism. That this system is inimical to the truth of God is evidenced by the following considerations.

(1) Mysticism confuses spiritual illumination with its false concept of an inner "revelation" to the soul. The Bible most certainly teaches that Christians can be enlightened in the knowledge of God's truth (cf. Eph. 1:18; I John 4:1-6). As we submit ourselves to God and humbly beseech Him to open our minds as to the meaning of His Word, God's Spirit does illuminate our hearts so that we are able to

understand the Word of God properly. This privilege is open to all Christians. It exists in varying degrees in all believers — some more, some less. In none, we may rightly suppose, is it found in perfection. We all "know in part" (I Cor. 13:12).

(2) Nowhere in the Bible is there promised to believers a revelation from God apart from, and independent of, the written Word of God. "To the law and the testimony! if they speak not according to this word, surely there is no morning for them" (Isa. 8:20). The Bereans are commended because they searched the Scriptures daily to see if Paul's teachings were true (Acts 17:11).

(3) The whole principle of mysticism is too subjective. Ignoring or repudiating the finality of Biblical revelation, mystics make each man his own little infallibility. When a man has an infallible utterance from the Deity in his own heart, why should he bother himself about a dubious revelation in the misty past?

(4) Finally, mysticism has always been accompanied with features which make it highly repugnant. We mention but a few of these here. In the first place, by the very nature of its belief, it relegates the Bible to a very minor place in the Christian life. It has a shorter and quicker way of reaching God. In the second place, it encourages pride and self-conceit. If Paul needed a thorn in the flesh to keep him humble because of the great revelations committed to him, how much more should finite men, who pretend to receive revelations, need something to keep them humble! In the last place, as is true of all who repudiate the final authority of the written Word of God, mystics have been historically prone to justify practices, contrary to the Bible, on the basis of a supposed revelation directly to their soul from God. John Bunyan repudiated the Ranters (a mystic and antinomian sect of his time) because he found in their beliefs and practices things that were antagonistic to the Word of God (see his *Grace Abounding*).

d) The modern, liberal view. Because this view is widely held in the modern church and because a vast literature about the Bible advocates this position, it will repay us to deal with it fully, delineating its chief characteristics. Since the present volume is written largely against the modern view of the Bible, it becomes necessary to know exactly what this new view really is. What we give below as the chief features of this position must be understood in the light of the most prominent propounders of this view. There are those who would object to some of the descriptions given below of the modern view of the Bible, but, on the whole, chapter and verse could be cited in reputable liberal books to substantiate each one of the following points.

(1) The modern view repudiates absolutely the idea of verbal inspiration. It speaks derisively of such a concept as "bibliolatry" — the worship of a book! The dogma of an infallible book is abhorrent to the liberal mind.

(2) As a corollary to the foregoing, the modernist rejects entirely the idea that the Biblical writers were inerrant. It is repeatedly affirmed in liberal works on the Bible that the Bible is "full of mistakes." These "mistakes" are found in the historical statements, the scientific descriptions, the prophetic announcements, and even in the moral and dogmatic pronouncements of the Bible. No part of the Bible is absolutely exempt from the possibility of error. And the liberal is confident that no amount of harmonizing attempts can rid the Bible of its errors. The writers of Scripture were, like other men who write, subject to the same tendency toward error.

(3) Different parts of Biblical revelation differ in the degree of their "inspiration." The early parts, written in the immaturity of the race, are less reliable than the subsequent portions; and the "inspiration" of the New Testament is on a higher level than that which belonged to the Old Testament. In fact, the high-water mark of "inspiration" is found in Christ. But even in Him we do not find absolute infallibility. He is not to be cited as an authority in matters of the authorship of books in the Old Testament from which He cites.

(4) "Inspiration," according to the liberal, is determined largely by the principle of evolution. How much is "revealed" to Israel at any time is determined by the stage to

which Israel has arrived in her gradual evolution. Certain truths, therefore, which the Bible seemingly puts at an early date are relegated to a much later time so as to put Israel's development on a level with the contemporary nations of antiquity. And, to make Israel's religion even more natural, it is dogmatically asserted that many of her best ideas were taken over from Egypt or Babylon or Greece or some other nation.

(5) The Bible, it is said, contains the Word of God but is not identical with the Word of God. The Word of God is centered in the thought about some event in the history of redemption; but since the writers of Scripture were not infallible in their statements, we must not, it is affirmed, accept every historical and scientific statement that they make. The accounts of the creation and the fall of our first parents in the Garden of Eden are not to be taken as literally true; they are myths or legends handed down to us with their crude and pre-scientific ideas still in them. But, nevertheless, we are told, those primitive myths still "contain" a message from God if we can but (as the liberal can!) separate the useless husk from the corn. Then we will find a true utterance of God!

(6) "Inspiration" did not cease, we are informed, when the canon of Scripture was finished. It is stated that many books written since the age of the Apostles are to be considered as "inspired" in the same sense as the books of the Bible. Thus the Bible's uniqueness is leveled off and its authority considerably truncated. The Bible may accordingly be emended, revised or disregarded if the reader supposes he has found a higher authority in a later author.

(7) Some books in the accepted canon of sixty-six should not be in the list of "inspired" books, according to the liberal standard of judgment. Harsh words are said especially against Esther and the Song of Solomon. Neither of these would be in our canon if the liberals had their way about such matters. And it is claimed that some of the apocryphal books which Protestants commonly disown should be included in the canon; in fact, it is said that some such books have a better right to canonicity than some (like Esther) that are

actually included. It has even been suggested that in some pagan writers will be found higher insights of spiritual truths than those which the Bible contains.

(8) Finally, the modern liberal makes the "modern mind" or experience or human reason or scientific discovery the test or criterion as to what in the Bible is, after all, "inspired." Rejecting an infallible book, they turn to the (fallible) mind of the scholars they consider most competent to pass judgment on such matters. We have thus a "consensus" of the opinion of modern scholars. It is taken for granted, of course, that conservatives, who believe the Bible to be the infallible Word of God, are not to be classified as scholars!

We have thus surveyed the main elements entering into the modern, critical idea of Biblical inspiration. It is obvious that such a position is utterly irreconcilable with the historic church view of Scripture. Without attempting here a full-scale rebuttal of the liberal position, we will, nevertheless, point out some of the most devastating weaknesses of their view. Let us note the following:

(a) The modernist view of Biblical inspiration, as set forth above, leads automatically, as cause and effect, to the ultimate repudiation of the Bible as a final authority for Christian truth and morals. This has been the whole tendency of the liberal movement in the modern Church. When inspiration is denied to the Biblical writers in any other sense than that which is common to non-Biblical writers, we have no final court to which appeal may be made. We are lost on a sea of uncertainty without any compass or pilot.

(b) The modernist view likewise makes man his own bible. If the "modern mind" can sit in judgment on Scripture, it can easily take the next step of dispensing with Scripture entirely. Why go back to ancient times, consulting men with only the crudest kind of knowledge about the world we live in, when we today, with all of the vast knowledge of modern, scientific research at our disposal, know much more than a provincial seer or prophet of a benighted past age? Thus the modern view of the Bible results in man's becoming his own bible, that is, his own authority in matters of belief and practice.

(c) The liberal view of the Bible destroys the very essence of the Protestant faith and thus repudiates the Reformation. It is crystal clear that the Reformers believed the Bible to be the Word of God. Their belief was based on the conviction, common to all of them, that the Bible alone is our only rule of faith and practice. They cast overboard all the impedimenta of tradition, decrees of councils, dogmas of popes, and the like. The authority of the Bible to them was supreme. The modern Protestant who tries to hold on to the Reformation faith, without subscribing to the Reformer's view of the Bible, is in an illogical position and loses his birthright to the Protestant name. Rejecting an infallible Bible, he becomes an easy prey of a church which holds that its pope is infallible. Paradoxically as it may appear on the surface, a modern Protestant, holding a modern view of the Bible, is a very likely candidate for the church of Rome! Protestantism can remain Protestant only as it holds on to its cardinal and fundamental belief that the Bible is the very Word of God.

(d) The old, orthodox view of the inspiration of the Bible, which the modern liberal scoffs at and contemns, is not as contemptible as he supposes. One does not risk intellectual suicide by accepting it. In fact, to tell the whole truth, a Christian risks intellectual and moral suicide if he does not accept it, for no other view will square with the plain words of Scripture. And, with the rise of the science of archaeology, the Bible has more defenders in the scholarly world in the realm of its historical accuracy than it had before that science made its terrific assaults against the bulwarks of higher criticism. Instead of being behind the times and an obscurantist, the believer in the historical accuracy of the Bible is really much more up-to-date than his modernist contemporary, who still wants to put on the fashion of the Graf-Wellhausen-Driver age. Such clothing is outmoded today and makes nothing but an intellectual freak of the one who is still stubborn enough to wear it.

(e) Furthermore and finally, the liberal's denial of Biblical inspiration makes the modern scholar a fulfiller of the very Scriptures whose divine inspiration and infallibility he so emphatically repudiates. There is no realm where inspiration is so compelling as in the fulfillment of prophecy. Was it not for this reason that Christ and the Gospel writers so repeatedly cited Old Testament passages to prove that Christ was indeed Israel's Messiah? But the same Divine Spirit, who guided the Old Testament seers in their descriptions of Messiah's advent, energized and guided the New Testament writers as they described the course and outcome of the present age of grace. In their predictions we find the announcement that a great turning away from the faith would take place before the second advent (cf. II Thess. 2:1ff; II Tim. 4:3, 4). Without attempting to set dates for the Lord's return, we must acknowledge, as a matter of common knowledge, that there has been a great apostasy in modern Christianity and, in that apostasy, the inspiration of the Scriptures has been a principal target. Thus the very inspiration that is scoffed at as being intellectually dishonest is confirmed by the very scholars who deride it.

V. OBJECTIONS TO INSPIRATION

It is quite natural, since the Bible obviously claims to be God-inspired, that men should try to find reasons to invalidate the Bible's claim. It will be in order, therefore, for us to deal briefly with some of the major objections to the Bible's inspiration made by those who do not accept its claim. It will hardly be necessary for us to add the thought that our treatment here is anything but exhaustive.

A. *No Autographs*

One objection that seems formidable, at least on the surface, is found in the contention that inspiration cannot be established because we lack the evidence (that is, the autograph copies) by which to test such a doctrine. Since it is admitted by all that no original copy of any book of the Bible is now extant, and since even our earliest manuscripts do not go back to the times of the Biblical writers, it is claimed that it is foolish to try to prove something about the autographs, that is, their inspiration, when we do not possess the copies for which inspiration is claimed. Although this objection appears potent, it is really weak — and that for the following reasons:

1. The science of textual criticism. It is now possible to reconstruct the original text of Scripture on the basis of the available data which we possess in such abundance today. By means of numerous manuscripts — some of which are quite ancient — and by means of ancient versions and quotations found in the Church Fathers, it is possible to ascertain what was in the autograph copies themselves. The passages about which textual criticism is still uncertain, as to what the original text actually was, are approaching almost the zero number. Most of the variant readings are insignificant and do not affect a fundamental doctrine of Scripture. Futhermore, the variations, for the most part, can be easily explained as some scribal error in transmission.

2. No evidence of undiscovered corruption of the text. It is true that some of the early heretics attempted to mutilate the text of Scripture in the interest of their dogmatic presuppositions. Notorious in this list is Marcion's disfigurement of the Gospel of Luke to support his disbelief of Christ's virgin birth. Others followed his example. But in practically every case, modern textual authorities are able to detect such attempted mutilations of the original text. That there is any essential difference between what the apostles wrote and our best edited texts of Scripture today (such as Westcott and Hort's or Nestle's) no competent scholar would dare to assert.

3. Inspiration is an integral part of the historical process. By this we simply mean that the doctrine of the Bible's inspiration does not rest on the lone fact of possessing, or not possessing, the original copies in which that doctrine is taught. If one should claim that we cannot hold that the autographs were inspired because we do not have them and, therefore, cannot ascertain what they actually taught, then we must assert that that person annihilates all history at one stroke. In the world of ancient literature outside the Bible, we know what a Plato or an Aristotle taught about many things even though we do not possess an autograph of either

of them. And, in some cases, an ancient pagan writer has but a scanty bit of his writings which have survived down to the present time. But the part that has survived, even though it is represented by late manuscripts, is usually accepted by the classical scholar as representing what the writer actually said centuries ago. By the same method we accept the far more abundant evidence confirming the original text of Scripture. There is nothing left, if this is not done, except skepticism — a skepticism that puts a question mark about anything in the past, whether it be in the Bible or in some pagan author.

4. Why no autographs have survived. No one can give an entirely satisfactory reason why all the writings penned by the sacred writers have perished. It may be said that the material upon which they were written could not survive the ravages of time. But we do have papyri that come down from Biblical times. Or, it may be said that the early Christians had no planned program for the preservation of the original copies of their sacred books. One could think of even other reasons. But undoubtedly God's providence had a hand in this whole affair. God may have allowed the autographs to drop out of sight for one of the following reasons: If they had survived, men might have made them objects of worship or veneration or attributed miracles to their presence.

If they had survived, the whole science of textual criticism would have been unnecessary. God inspired originals of Scripture but left the transmission of the text from one generation to another to man. That is in line with God's method generally. Christ, before leaving the world, commissioned His disciples to go to the uttermost parts of the earth; but he left the carrying out of that commission to His Church in every generation.

Finally, in all of God's purposes, there is always some room left for the exercise of faith. In the question under consideration it appears that we must believe even though we do not have the original. If a man does not believe that the Bible is God's Word because we do not have the autographs, then it is hardly likely that he would believe even if we discovered some original copy of Paul's letter to Philemon. There must be faith, and autographs do not necessarily engender faith.

B. *Mistakes and Contradictions*

One of the most characteristic charges made against the Bible's inspiration is that it is full of mistakes and contradictions. This accusation has been hurled so often against the Bible that it is sometimes accepted as true on the grounds of mere assertion alone. The mistakes attributed to the Bible are manifold and are often made by those who pose as defenders and teachers of Christian truth. Since this subject will be dealt with again when we deal with the modern view of the Bible, it will not be necessary here to do more than indicate the method by which this attack on the Bible may be handled.

1. Some "mistakes" are due to our ignorance. Here it is not the Biblical writer who is at fault but rather our inadequate information. It is undoubtedly true that the writers of Scripture possessed knowledge of certain things that we no longer have today. They were far nearer the source of the facts than we are today and many of the writings of ancient times have long since perished from the earth. Paul, for example, mentions by name the two Egyptians who withstood Moses (II Tim. 3:8), although their names are nowhere recorded in the Old Testament narrative. In Matthew 27:9f it is asserted that a statement made by Jeremiah was fulfilled when Judas took the thirty pieces of silver, although the prophecy cited is actually found in Zechariah (11:11ff). On the surface this looks like a terrible mistake. It has been cited constantly as "Exhibit No. 1" for the fallibility of the Biblical writers. It is possible, however, that Jeremiah himself was the original author of the prediction. If this be so, Zechariah is citing the same prediction as originally given by (but not recorded in) Jeremiah. Matthew knew of the original source and properly cites it as coming from Jeremiah. In a somewhat similar manner Paul cites a blessing pronounced by Jesus (Acts 20:35) which is nowhere found in the four Gospels. It is impossible to

say that Jesus Christ never uttered the word attributed to Him by Paul. Paul had a source of knowledge about such things that we no longer possess.

2. Some "mistakes" and "contradictions" are imputed to Biblical writers where none actually exists. It is commonly affirmed, for example, that John contradicts the Synoptics when he puts the cleansing of the Temple at the beginning of Christ's ministry (John 2:14f). The Synoptics put this event at the close of His earthly life. Neither source makes mention of another cleansing. But it is surely proper for us to suppose that the event took place twice. There is nothing forced or unnatural about such a possibility. More than one thing in history has been repeated with somewhat the same circumstances. Rome and Carthage fought three deadly wars within a little more than a century. In our generation Germany has twice attempted to bring the world under her dominion, and the nations lined up against her in each war were largely the same ones.

Under this heading may be put a long list of apparent "contradictions" found in the Gospels. Included here are such items as the two genealogies of Christ, the differences in the order of Christ's temptation, the time of the institution of the Lord's Supper and the day of our Lord's death (Wednesday or Friday), the inscription on the cross, and the different accounts of the resurrection. No one can categorically assert in any one of these cases (or many others which could be mentioned) that we have a flat contradiction. It is possible, for example, that the inscription on the cross is given in the four Gospels either in part or in one of the three languages used in the inscription. It is likely that the full inscription read somewhat like this: "This is Jesus of Nazareth, the King of the Jews." Biblical inspiration does not demand absolute uniformity in such matters. In fact, if we had such uniformity, there would be no need of four Gospels.

3. Some "mistakes" and "contradictions" are due to a faulty method of interpretation which we impose upon the Scriptures. This matter will come before us again in a later chapter on criticism and interpretation. Suffice it here to

cite a few instances to illustrate what we mean. The Bible surely does not teach the theory of evolution, and nothing but disharmony and conflict will ensue if it is interpreted from that angle. The Bible does not teach that Christ came into this world to inaugurate an earthly kingdom; those, therefore, who hold to such a notion cannot but make the Bible self-contradictory. The Bible does not teach that Christ's natural father was Joseph, but those who teach such a foreign idea will create a multitude of conflicting statements about the person of Christ and the gospel record. Those who exclude the supernatural from the Bible and make everything square with their naturalism will find it very difficult, if not impossible, to accept what the sacred writers say about miracles, prophecy and revealed truths. If Isaiah 7:14 does not refer to the virgin birth, as Matthew explicitly says it does (1:22f), it is not because we lack Biblical evidence for such application, but rather because a theory of naturalism is imposed upon the Bible, making it contradict itself. And so we could go on with many other illustrations of difficulties, arising out of a false system of interpretation into which everything in the Bible is made to fall in line.

4. Some "mistakes" and "contradictions" especially concern the realms of science and history. These matters will be dealt with more adequately in later chapters of this book. Let us but mention in passing a few things that will strengthen our faith. First of all, if our view of inspiration is right, that is, if the Bible is fully and verbally inspired, we must believe that God safeguarded the authors of Scripture against the inclusion of any kind of error — whether in morals, science or history. It is unthinkable that the Biblical writers gave us pure morals but incorrect science. To say that they were men of their day in the matter of science and thus were capable of many erroneous concepts about the natural world amounts to the same thing as saying that they were men of their day in their ideas about God, sin and salvation.

5. Some "mistakes" and "contradictions" will doubtlessly remain as problems of faith even after the best solution is

attempted. This does not mean that we are yielding one point in the Bible's inspiration and infallibility. It does mean, however, that we must believe the Bible is true, even if there are a few places which we cannot satisfactorily explain to an unbelieving world. In fact, it is hardly likely that the Bible would be a divine book if there were no difficulties in it at all. The very fact that there are "some things hard to be understood" (II Pet. 3:16) in the Scriptures is an evidence of their divine origin.

C. *The Morality of the Bible*

From antiquity down to the present day, the unbelieving world has accused the Bible of inculcating moral principles unworthy of the best interest of society. Instead of the Bible being the source of all that is good and wholesome in life, these critics affirm quite dogmatically that it is the polluted spring from which flows all that is evil. The moral teaching of the Bible is particularly held up for contempt and ridicule. The Freethought Press Association publishes *The Bible Unmasked* (authored by Joseph Lewis), which by 1943 had gone through eighteen editions. In that book are to be found every obscene story which the author thinks he finds in the Bible. The Bible is also criticized severely by liberals for its account of the slaughter of the Canaanites, the imprecatory Psalms, and other such things. Without attempting here a full treatment of this subject in the light of the Bible's inspiration, let us note carefully the following factors:

1. The Bible never describes a man's sin for the sake of enticing men to the same sin; it rather recounts the sin of a Jacob or a David to show how that sin brought punishment as a consequence. The men of the Bible were real men and had temptations similar to the rest of mankind. The records of their yielding to temptations are written down that others might not yield to similar temptations in their lives (cf. I Cor. 10:1-13). The Bible never justifies the sins of a child of God; but it does show repeatedly how God is justified in the punishment of the sins of His children.

2. In dealing with the moral problems of the Bible we

should remember that God is a God of justice. He is long-suffering and kind, but is also a God who executes vengeance upon evil-doers. He allows the Canaanites to continue wilfully in their immoral practices until the iniquity of the Amorite is full; then He sends the Israelites as the executioners of His vengeance. In His forbearance and mercy, God allows the rebellious Jews forty years to repent of their national sin of killing their Messiah; then He sends Titus, the executioner of His wrath (Matt. 22:7; I Thess. 2:14f), to destroy their wicked city. It is God who is the moral governor of the universe and He will execute vengeance on all who do evil (Ex. 20:5; Rom. 12:19). If we had a greater sense of justice, we would have a greater detestation of sin and those who commit sin. The imprecatory Psalms (e.g., 58:6; 109:10; 137:8, 9) may seem harsh and severe to us, but let us remember these facts: Men instinctively feel repulsion at some heinous crime and cry out to God for justice to be executed. Let a child be kidnaped and then murdered, and the whole nation cries out that the perpetrators of the crime be dealt with to the full extent of the law.

Even in the New Testament, which our critics claim is on a higher moral level than the Old Testament, we find expressions similar to those in the older revelation. Paul could remember that God will execute vengeance on Alexander, who did him much evil (II Tim. 4:14). Christ (Matt. 23:13-36) as well as Jude (5-16) could pronounce woes upon workers of iniquity and those who pervert the way of truth. The persecuted of all ages cry out to God for vengeance upon their cruel tormentors (Rev. 6:10).

3. Those who accuse the Bible of teaching a low moral standard or of containing impure accounts of man's wickedness have characteristically lived after the manner of the thing they criticized in the Bible. Quite often it happens that the man who is concerned as to where Cain got his wife is not too much concerned about his own moral life. Or, to put it otherwise, he criticizes the Bible in order to justify his own immorality. *The Bible Unmasked* or the *Age of Reason* is not inappropriate in a brothel or a saloon, but the Bible in either place makes the occupants uncom-

fortable. For an excellent discussion of the moral problems of the Bible one will find R. A. Torrey's *Difficulties in the Bible* (1907) still helpful.

D. *The Non-Superiority of the Bible*

In modern times, especially since the advent of the comparative religious school of criticism, it has been felt by some scholars that Christianity can no longer claim a book that is superior to the sacred books of other religions. We are now told that it is a mistake for missionaries to call attention to the mistakes and low moral teaching found in the sacred books of other religions (cf. Charles A. Briggs, *The Study of Holy Scripture* [1899], pp. 608ff). The missionary, we are told, must admit that there are similar things in the Bible. Although the Bible may not be as bad as some of the other sacred books are, yet we cannot claim uniqueness or superiority for it. On this subject let us make the following observations:

1. It cannot be proved in any single case that the Bible has borrowed its moral ideas from other great religions of the world, but it can be proved that some of the Bible's teachings have been borrowed by other religions. It is undoubtedly true (as we shall show later) that Zoroastrianism got its essential ideas from the Jews during their exile in the land of the Medes. Since Mohammedanism arose centuries after the birth of Christ, it is clearly obvious that that religion borrows heavily from the Christian's Bible. The same can be said about the other religions of the world.

2. No other religion except Christianity can make the claims for its sacred books equal to the claims made for the Bible. These other sacred books know nothing of real miracles, of fulfilled prophecies, of a Messiah who rose again from the dead, and of faith that is real and vital. The fruits of Christianity surely show that its Book is from God; the fruits of the other great religions show that they are not of God. When the true teachings of the Bible prevail in any society, we find peace and order; when the Bible is corrupted and perverted, even by its supposed friends, disorder and wickedness abound.

3. The toning down of the Bible's superiority in our modern age is due to an acceptance of the modern view of the Bible rather than to any change in the Bible's essential nature. The presumed mistakes and low moral teaching found in the Bible are the result of the critical reconstruction of the Bible in the light (?) of the naturalistic theory of evolution. By his very nature, the believer in evolution will not allow any uniqueness to the Bible among the religions of mankind. All religions, according to his theory, are groping toward the truth; no religion, not even Christianity, can claim a monopoly on the truth. In his view truth is always relevant — never to be obtained as long as man is in his upward climb on evolution's ladder. But the Bible will not stay put among the books of other religions. It will not be classified as co-equal. It will always, either explicitly or implicitly, assert its God-given authority and uniqueness.

VI. How to Deal with Biblical Difficulties

In closing this chapter it will be well for us to consider how Bible problems should be dealt with by the believer in the divine origin of Scripture. Our suggestions are designed to be helpful to those who may be in honest doubt about the Bible's inspiration and uniqueness. Let us carefully note the following points:

A. *Absolute Honesty and Fairness*

Let us be willing to admit that there are difficult places and problems in the Bible. No one who is at all conversant with the Bible will deny such a fact. Let us face the difficulty fairly and let us insist that the skeptic use the same measure of fairness that he demands of the Bible-believer. Let us make no claim for the Bible that cannot be substantiated by the facts in the case. And it is absolutely imperative that we know, as far as possible, what the facts are so that we might not have thrown at us something which we are unprepared to handle. This will mean, of course, that we must be just as diligent in investigating the facts as the skeptic is in creating difficulties. Long hours of arduous study must sometimes be given to a Biblical prob-

F

lem before a solution is arrived at which is reasonable and satisfactory.

B. *Prayer for Guidance and Illumination*

If the Holy Spirit is the real Author of the Bible, as we believe He is, and if that blessed Person is available at all times, according to Christ's promise (John 14:16; 16:13f), then it is important that the child of God go to the Author of Scripture when any difficulty arises in his study of the Bible. This does not mean, however, that we are to neglect the helps that are available, written by devout men, to explain Bible problems. The Spirit of God has undoubtedly used such men to defend the Bible against its adversaries. The Bible has never lacked defenders in any age and these men have been the intellectual peers or superiors to any on the side of unbelief. After all, however, we must seek the mind of the Spirit in prayer, beseeching Him to illuminate our minds with His truth and dispel our doubts.

C. *Humility and Teachableness*

The Bible will not unfold its secrets to men who approach it in an arrogant or know-it-all spirit. It is possible that our difficulty with the Bible lies not in the Bible but in ourselves. And it is also possible that some theory to which we tenaciously hold creates the problems and difficulties from which we seek relief. A man, who will not give up an erroneous interpretation of Scripture when he has been convinced by every reasonable means that his view is wrong, is a rebellious spirit and cannot expect peace in his mind or heart. It behooves each one of us to examine ourselves and our interpretation in the light of God's revelation as a whole. If we have given the wrong meaning to certain passages of Scripture and have now come to see the error of our way, it is well that we acknowledge our mistake and turn from it. If a man says, for example, that Christ could have sinned when He was tempted or else His temptation was nothing but a sham, he really has not seen what dangerous ground he is on theologically; but if he says that Christ, being God incarnate, could not sin, then he is on safe ground even if he cannot explain fully or satisfactorily to the unbeliever how a holy being could be tempted as we are and yet not be able under any circumstance to yield to the temptation.

D. *Some Methods in Dealing with Bible Difficulties*

We wish here to put down just a few more suggestions regarding the troublous problems that arise from a study of the Bible. If these are consistently followed, most of the vexing difficulties will vanish.

1. Let us assume as a working hypothesis that the Bible writers were honest men intent on proclaiming the truth and that they were just as reasonable as we are today. Let us try to put ourselves in their situation and look at the facts from their perspective. Let us not impute mistakes and contradictions to them when we cannot prove them. In any case where there is more than one explanation, let us accept that explanation that makes sense and allows the Biblical writer at least to be consistent. Let us suppose that we were there at the time when the incident or fact was recorded and then see if we cannot visualize the whole situation.

2. Let us always be willing to wait for further light. It is a bad sign when a man is always ready to jump to the conclusion that a statement in the Bible is in error just because he cannot give an immediate solution to the problem. If we are really out to know the truth and not to find fault with the Bible, then God will surely lead us eventually to the truth (cf. John 7:17). If some of the negative critics had had patience to wait for further light before they passed judgment on the Bible's truthfulness, they would appear in much better light today.

3. No solution of the Bible should be adopted if it brings the Bible into conflict with itself. The Bible is a harmonious Book which is self-consistent. If an erroneous interpretation is accepted in one place, it will affect many other like places in the Bible. If a man says that there is no hell simply because he interprets a few rather difficult passages that way, then he brings chaos into the Bible and produces confusion and doubt where there was none before;

for it is plainly evident that no sound exegesis would support the theories connected with annihilationism, second probationism or conditional immortality.

4. Finally, let us use all sound hermeneutical principles which are available today for the better understanding of the Bible. We mention a few of them here: a) The original languages should be consulted where any difficulty has arisen. Let us be sure that we have properly translated the Bible. Illustrations of faulty translations will be given in a later chapter. b) The study of the context of a passage is an important step in the solution of any problem. What is the writer speaking about? Sometimes the context must include the whole book in which the debated passage is found. c) All of God's Word must be taken into account in dealing with any single portion of it. In the light of all of God's revelation we find the proper meaning of any individual passage. It is still true that "no prophecy of scripture is of private interpretation" (II Pet. 1:20). d) And, as stated above, let us be willing to consult books written on the subject of Bible difficulties to see what solutions have been discovered by men more capable than we are. Such solutions should always be tested against the light of God's inspired Word. If the solution helps toward faith, it should doubtlessly be accepted; if it tends toward doubt and unbelief, it should be rejected. Let us remember the apostolic injunction: "prove all things; hold fast that which is good" (I Thess. 5:21).

In conclusion, let us remember that we are in a great conflict today over the inspiration and infallibility of God's Word. On which side of this gigantic battle will we stand? Will we be among those who use their influence and their scholarship to undermine the Bible as God's Word, or will we be among those who seek to defend and establish the Bible as the Word of the Eternal God? Our prayer is that you will place your name among the latter group.

CHAPTER THREE

REVELATION AND CRITICISM

In the present chapter we propose to deal with what is called "revelation." This is a large subject in present-day theological discussion and has engendered quite a bit of heat. Our purpose shall be to consider revelation in its larger aspects as it affects the Bible and the Christian faith. It will be necessary, therefore, to define what revelation is, to distinguish it from inspiration, to differentiate its twofold aspects, and to prove that God's revelation is now a unified whole in what we speak of as the Bible.

I. DEFINITION

In order that we may get a clear picture of what revelation is, it will be necessary, first of all, to ascertain what the Bible says about this concept. Then it will be in order to distinguish it from inspiration and closely related concepts.

A. *The Biblical Idea*

Our English word "revelation" comes from the Latin *revelatio,* which designates an unveiling or uncovering. In the literal sense it is applied to anything that was formerly hidden by a covering. The Greek word *apokalupsis* (from which we get "apocalypse") covers practically the same idea as *revelatio.* A word study of *apokalupsis* as used in the New Testament reveals the following facts:

1. *Apokalupsis* used in connection with the first advent of Christ and its resulting truths. Here we have such facts as these: a) It is used of the "unveiling" of the mystery of redemption (Rom. 16:25; Eph. 3:3). b) It is used of the "unveiling" of Jesus Christ to the Gentile world (Luke 2:32; cf. Isa. 42:6; 49:6). c) It is used of the "unveiling" of knowledge to Paul regarding the content of the Gospel

(II Cor. 12:1, 7; Eph. 3:3). d) It is used of the "unveiling" of knowledge about the Gospel to a Christian congregation (I Cor. 14:6, 26). e) It is used of the "unveiling" of knowledge about Paul's apostleship (Gal. 1:12) and subsequent guidance (Gal. 2:2). f) It is used of the "unveiling" of knowledge to a reader of the Scriptures (Eph. 1:17). g) It is used of the "unveiling" of Jesus Christ concerning the present age of grace (Rev. 1:1).

2. *Apokalupsis* used in connection with the second advent of Christ. In seven places this word appears to be used of the "unveiling" connected with the parousia or second advent of Christ (Rom. 2:5; 8:19; II Thess. 1:7; I Pet. 1:7, 13; 4:13). Christ is now hidden from our view, but when He returns there will be a glorious "revelation" or "unveiling" of His presence.

It should be remarked that the Greek verb *apokalupto* (which comes from the same root as *apokalupsis*) has practically the same meaning and is used in about the same sense (cf. Brooke Foss Westcott, *An Introduction to the Study of the Gospels* [1872], p. 9, n. 1). There are, of course, other Hebrew and Greek words that designate the concept of revelation.

B. *Revelation Defined by Contrasts*

It is obvious that the concept of revelation does not stand alone but is vitally related to other expressions involved in the total conception of God's revelation to man. Here we want to deal primarily with its relationship to inspiration and illumination.

1. Revelation and inspiration. Revelation, in the restricted sense in which we are now using it, is the unveiling of truth to man which he could not otherwise know by natural reasoning. That there is a sun in the sky is not a revelation; but that God exists as triune is a revelation. It is impossible for man to figure out who or what God is unless God reveals His nature to man. Much that is in the Bible is not a revelation, since many of the facts were matters of common observation and investigation (cf. Luke 1:1ff). And here is where inspiration is necessary. All of the Biblical

writers were agents of the Spirit of God and thus their writings were God-breathed whether they concerned matters of history, which could come under the supervision of any competent investigator, or whether they concerned supernaturally revealed truths which no man could discover by natural reasoning. It is proper, therefore, to say that the Bible contains a revelation from God, but it is improper to say that the Bible contains inspired writings. This latter assertion is improper because the Bible *is* inspired throughout; it is God-breathed in every part. Revelation assures us that we have in the Bible a knowledge of God, which God has given to man; inspiration assures us that that revelation has been accurately and truthfully transmitted to us through prophets and apostles chosen by God to be His spokesmen. In the special sense to be described in a moment, revelation ceased with the last writer of Scripture; at the same time inspiration also ceased. There are today no agents chosen of God to reveal new truths; and there are likewise no inspired prophets.

2. Revelation and illumination. A prophet may receive a revelation from God but not understand the import of what he receives. It is clearly evident that Daniel did not understand the significance of the visions committed to him until he received illumination as to their meaning (cf. Dan. 9:22; 10:12-14). The seer of Patmos needed the interpreting angel to give the meaning of the visions he saw. Sometimes a subsequent revelation was necessary to give definiteness and meaning to a previous revelation (I Pet. 1:10-12). Peter received a wonderful revelation from God concerning Christ's person (Matt. 16:16f), but what immediately followed (Matt. 16:22f) showed plainly that Peter's mind had not yet comprehended the purpose of Christ's mission. Compare also Luke 24:32, 45.

C. *Two Types of Revelation*

It has been quite customary to divide revelation into two aspects — the revelation of God in nature (the universe, providence, history, man's conscience) and the revelation of God in the Scriptures of the Old and New Testaments.

Although this division is intensely debated and totally rejected by some modern theologians today, we shall, nevertheless, follow this twofold division in the ensuing discussion.

II. NATURAL REVELATION

For several reasons it will be best to present the revelation of God in nature first. For one thing, it appears that the natural precedes the supernatural, or spiritual, in the order of history and redemption (cf. I Cor. 15:45). And, furthermore, the glory and wonder of God's supernatural revelation can be seen to greater effect against the background of natural revelation. We shall, therefore, attempt to present in orderly outline the essential elements in natural revelation first.

A. *The Content of Natural Revelation*

This revelation, as indicated above, is that which is discoverable about God from nature — whether it be nature viewed externally (in the creaturely world, including God's providence and man's history) or internally (in man's conscience). It has been maintained that this revelation includes at least five concepts about man's relationship to his Maker. In each case we give the passages in supernatural revelation (that is, the Bible) that sustain these concepts.

1. Belief in a supreme Being (Ps. 19:1f; Rom. 1:19f). This concept is universal among all mankind in spite of their polytheism and animism.

2. The supreme Being is the Creator and Governor of the visible world (Acts 17:24-28). He provides rain and sunshine and the changing seasons for the well-being of His creatures.

3. The supreme Being is to be worshiped in a becoming manner (Acts 17:24, 27; Isa. 40:18-26). Man knows instinctively that idolatry is wrong. God is not to be worshiped by images of the deity.

4. Men should conform their moral conduct to the light they have from nature (Rom. 2:1-16; Luke 12:47f). Their conscience will never be satisfied in sin; it will either excuse or accuse them.

5. The sins of men incur the just punishment inflicted by man's Maker. Because of this sense of sin, man attempts to appease the wrath of God by rites, ceremonies, and sacrifices (Isa. 40:18-22; 44:9-22; 46:5ff).

B. The Certainty of Natural Revelation

That there is a natural revelation is proved by the following considerations, the first of which is, of course, the most important of all.

1. Natural revelation proved from the Bible. It has been believed by conservative theologians that the Bible explicitly supports the idea of a natural revelation. In the Old Testament the "Nature Psalms" (19, 29, 104) affirm that the heavens declare the glory of God. Since the Hebrew construction here is paraphrastic, a more accurate translation would include the idea that they continually declare the glory of God. In Romans 1:18 we are told that God's wrath is being revealed (present tense) from heaven against all of man's unrighteousness. In the verses that follow (1:19ff) it is stated that man had a knowledge of God from the very beginning of his creation but that, because of his sin, he perverted and corrupted that knowledge. The corrupt heart of man refused to have the knowledge of God (1:28, 32). In his perverted state, man did those things that are "against nature" (1:26), that is, contrary to the light that nature affords. Paul can even appeal to nature in support of a matter about woman's hair (I Cor. 11:14, 15). All these passages, and others, appear to support the view that there is a revelation of God in nature and man's conscience.

2. Natural revelation proved by archaeology. Since this matter will be referred to again in the chapter on archaeology, we need not here anticipate the argument presented there. For the present we simply mention the fact that leading archaeologists (particularly Dr. S. Langdon) have come to the conviction that the earliest inhabitants of ancient Sumer were monotheists (see his "Monotheism as the Predecessor of Polytheism in Sumerian Religion" in *The Evangelical Quarterly* [April, 1937], pp. 136-146). Consult also Sir Charles Marston's *New Bible Evidence* (1934), pp.

50-64. This discovery is in line with what Paul said in Romans 1:19ff.

3. Natural revelation proved by anthropology. Since, again, this subject will be dealt with later, we need not go into detail here. Suffice it for the present to affirm what P. Wilhelm Schmidt has so conclusively proved, namely, that a belief in a Supreme Being is to be found among all peoples — even those in the most uncivilized state. A popular summary of this argument will be found in S. M. Zwemer's *The Origin of Religion: Evolution or Revelation* (1945). The facts there presented support the view that even savage tribes today retain, as a remnant of the image of God in them and also as a remnant of the revelation made to man in his original state of innocency, some of the basic concepts (prayer, sacrifice, immortality) revealed far more clearly in the light of supernatural revelation. God has not left Himself without a witness (Acts 14:17) in the pagan world, having written His law upon man's heart (Rom. 2:15).

C. *The Corruption of Natural Revelation*

Even a casual observer of the heathen world will readily admit that man is corrupt before God and that "the dark places of the earth are full of the habitations of violence" (Ps. 74:20; cf. Gen. 6:5, 11f). Let us, therefore, consider the causes and the effects of this corruption of natural revelation.

1. The causes of this corruption. Undoubtedly the paramount cause of this corruption of natural revelation is found in man's apostasy as recounted in Genesis 3. In that rebellion against his Maker, man's nature as made in God's image was seriously affected. Man became a rebel, blind to spiritual things, a servant of his evil passions, dead in his sinful nature, and unable to change his corrupt heart (Rom. 3:10-18; Eph. 2:1ff). Thus man began his devolution, not stopping until he worshiped "creeping things" (Rom. 1:23). It was man's self-inflicted blindness which incapacitated his mind by the noetic effects of sin so that he could no longer read aright the revelation that God had given to him. This revelation could be objectively "clearly seen" (Rom.

1:20); but subjectively, because of his darkened understanding and hardened heart (Eph. 4:18f), man serves "vain things" and walks in his own way (Acts 14:15ff).

2. The effects of this corruption. Dr. Edward J. Jurji (in an article on "The Science of Religion" in *Theology Today* [July, 1950], pp. 194-205) shows that there are three results of man's perversion of natural revelation. They are: a) Primitiveness (which includes such things as ancestor-worship, animism, cannibalism, secret orders, worship of sun, etc.). b) Anthropocentricism (which includes the deification of man — whether in ancient or modern times, or among primitive or civilized peoples). c) The great world religions (excluding, of course, the Christian religion). This means that the great ethnic religions (Mohammedanism, Buddhism, Hinduism, Confucianism, Taoism, Shintoism) are man-made perversions of the truth of God found in natural revelation. The non-Christian peoples "hinder (or, hold) the truth in unrighteousness" (Rom. 1:18).

D. *The Characteristics of Natural Revelation*

God's revelation in nature has a number of aspects which we must now briefly set forth. On some of these much more could be said, but our purpose forbids a detailed delineation.

1. Natural revelation is universal. First of all, it is universal in time. At no time in the world's history has God left Himself without witness (Acts 14:17). Then, it is universal in scope or territory. Wherever man is found, the heavens keep on declaring the glory of God (Ps. 19:1f). Paul appeals to Psalm 19:4 to show how God's message 'went out into all the earth" (Rom. 10:18). Paul told pagans that "they should seek God, if haply they might feel after him and find him, though he is not far from each one of us" (Acts 17:27).

2. Natural revelation is objectively real. Though man has wilfully incapacitated himself so that he cannot read God's glory in nature (which is His handiwork — Ps. 19:1; 104:13, 24), the testimony of nature to nature's God is still there. Man's subjective state of sin hinders him from

knowing the truth. But the truth is there just as much before man's sin (Gen. 3) as afterwards.

3. Natural revelation therefore is judicial. This fact is emphasized three times in the first chapter of Romans (1:24, 26, 28). Because men, contrary to the light that they had (Rom. 1:19f), "exchanged the truth of God for a lie, and worshipped and served the creature rather than the Creator" (1:25), God "gave them up" to a degenerate state; but in that state they are "without excuse" (1:20), their conscience testifying against them (2:12-16).

4. Natural revelation in man's present state is insufficient. This, in the light of the foregoing, may appear like a contradiction. But it is not if we consider the following facts: God gave to man a revelation in nature; this we have already shown. Man, because of his sin and rebellion against God, is not able now to read that revelation aright. His vision is blurred. God graciously gave to man another reve-lation of Himself (supernatural revelation) which man (by the new birth and the spiritual illumination that follows) is able to read aright. In addition, the regenerate man is also able to read aright God's natural revelation. But the unregenerate man — pagan or civilized — needs something more than the light of nature to satisfy his need. Natural revelation, therefore, is inadequate for the following reasons:

a) Men in their present state of sin are unable to know God as they ought to know Him. A supernatural revelation is needed to correct and rectify the effects of sin on man's mind and heart (cf. I Cor. 1:21; 2:13f).

b) When men are deprived of the light of supernatural revelation, they degenerate further and further into idola-try, sensuality, and the like. No people has ever developed a higher form of religion under the light of natural revela-tion alone. All heathen countries today bear witness to this fact.

c) Natural revelation does not give to man in his present state an answer to the problem of sin. From nature man can discern that God is powerful, just, orderly, and that He punishes sin; but where is grace and mercy found? Man's self-inflicted punishments, designed to appease a wrathful God, can never satisfy man's heart or conscience.

d) Finally, natural revelation does not reveal how a sinful man can be saved. It is only supernatural revelation that tells us the story of how God sent His own Son into the world that we might live through faith in Him (John 3:16). Christ is the only way to the Father (John 14:6); and there is no other name than His whereby man must be saved (Acts 4:12). A Buddha or a Confucius can never take away our sins or give peace to the sinful soul.

E. The Contribution of Natural Revelation

In view of what we have just said it may appear strange that we now speak of the contribution of natural revelation. But actually it is not so strange if we take into account the following factors:

1. Natural revelation renders man inexcusable. This is so plainly stated by Paul (Rom. 1:20; 2:1) that it need not be emphasized further. No man can ever justify his misdeeds on the ground that he had insufficient light to discern between the right and the wrong.

2. Natural revelation makes imperative the need of the supernatural light of the Gospel. Stated perhaps more clearly, the Gospel, because of man's present state of spiritual blindness and impotence, must be sent to those who have only the light of nature. Men without Christ are lost; only He is the way to God (John 14:6). Buddha, Confucius or Mohammed can never save a soul from hell. No modern "re-thinking missions" can ever rid the Church of its great commission to preach the Gospel to all peoples (Matt. 28: 19f).

3. Natural revelation is a point of contact for the Christian missionary. Like Paul in his speech to the Athenians, the missionary can start with the "unknown God" and proclaim the true God (Acts 17:22ff). As we showed previously, all men, even the most primitive, have still a remnant of a Supreme Being (Schmidt's "Sky-God") in their background. That knowledge that "lighteth every man as he cometh into the world" (John 1:9, margin) can be the

point of contact that will lead the heathen, when he hears the Gospel-message, to Christ (cf. Acts 8:27-35).

4. Moreover, natural revelation brings down a double guilt on those who share its light and the much fuller light of supernatural revelation. The man who rejects Christ in a land where the Gospel is proclaimed will receive greater punishment than the man who never had the light of the glorious Gospel of Christ. The rejection of double light means double punishment. See Romans 2:1-16.

5. Finally, natural revelation is a servant of special revelation. The servant is never independent of his master. So it is with natural revelation. It says: "I receive my orders and instructions from my master, special revelation; if you want to know more about me, go to my master and he will tell you fully what I am and what I can do." Imperfect as natural revelation is because of man's subjective blindness to spiritual truth (I Cor. 2:14), it, nevertheless, bears a willing testimony to its master. In a real sense it is a *preparatio evangelica.* In Addison's famous lines:

> In reason's ear they all rejoice,
> And utter forth a glorious voice;
> Forever singing, as they shine,
> "The hand that made us is Divine."

III. SUPERNATURAL REVELATION

Having considered some of the main points regarding God's natural revelation, we are now prepared to deal with the elements belonging to God's supernatural revelation. Our subject will be dealt with along the same general lines as in the previous discussion.

A. *The Content of Supernatural Revelation*

It will be necessary, for a right understanding of our subject, to define and limit the content of supernatural revelation. In order to do this adequately, we call attention here to two specific things that must be included, we believe, in circumscribing the content of special revelation.

1. God's entire revelation in the Bible. This is the broadest interpretation we are permitted to put on supernatural revelation. It includes all of His written Word now in-

corporated in the sixty-six canonical books of the Old and
New Testaments. Each of these books, even that which
might appear the most insignificant, is a total part of God's
supernatural revelation. Of course, in this delimitation we
are looking at this revelation from the standpoint of the
present time — not from the viewpoint of prophets and
apostles as they received it from the mouth of God. To
the Church, there is but one supernatural revelation and
that is found in our inspired Bible.

2. God's plan of redemption. More specifically, we can
affirm that God's special or supernatural revelation is that
which He unfolds in His Word concerning the plan of
redemption. Supernatural revelation finds its reason for existence in redemption. Had man remained in his state of
integrity in which he was created, there would have been
no need for a special revelation written in a book. As far
as we know, the holy angels never had a special or supernatural revelation committed to them. Among such creatures, even as among God's redeemed in heaven, the distinction between "natural" and "supernatural" has no meaning. In heaven the supernatural becomes the natural.

B. *The Contradicters of Supernatural Revelation*

It is quite natural that, man being what he is (I Cor.
2:14), there are some who deny the reality of any supernatural revelation. It will be profitable, therefore, for us
to spend a moment on the causes and consequences of this
denial of supernatural revelation.

1. The causes of the denial. Primarily there are but two
causes:

Man's philosophy. Deism is a classic instance of this.
That system, as is well known, denied that there is any
supernatural revelation given to us by God. The only revelation man has, it affirmed, is that which is found in nature.
Thus, everything that breathes the supernatural (prophecy,
miracles. revealed truths) was categorically negated. Much
of English Deism has imperceptibly infiltrated into the modern view of the Bible and thus dominates the liberal approach toward the Scriptures. But Deism is not alone in

its denial of supernatural revelation. All anti-theistic systems (Atheism, Agnosticism, Materialism, Idealism, etc.) repudiate such a revelation.

Man's heart. Significantly the Bible informs us that the deniers of God's existence are "corrupt" (Job 19:1ff) — in fact, man's heart is "exceedingly corrupt" (Jer. 17:9). Man does not want to hear Gods voice in supernatural revelation (the Bible), telling him in plain words about his sin and his need of a Saviour. He stops up his ears and will not listen (cf. Acts 7:57; 22:22).

2. The consequences of this denial. There are a number of consequences that follow in sequence when supernatural revelation is rejected. We mention here briefly some of the most important:

a) One of the characteristic signs that betrays those who repudiate supernatural revelation is the intensity of their efforts to minimize the Bible and magnify the sacred writings of the ethnic religions. The attempt is made to show that the Bible is, after all, on practically the same level with other religious literature and any apparent superiority it may possess is due to the religious genius of the Jewish people. Just as the Greeks gave us (naturalistically) an appreciation of beauty in art and the Romans gave us (naturalistically) a concept of righteousness and law, so the Jews gave us (naturalistically) the best expression of man's religious yearnings.

b) A second sign follows: these deniers of supernatural revelation immediately set out on their task of de-supernaturalizing the Bible. Every conceivable effort is made to denude the Bible of its supernaturalism. Miracles are explained away in a fashion that taxes the ingenuity of the most credulous; prophecy is likewise emptied of all prediction in a manner that must sear the conscience of the critic (instances of their manner will be presented in a later chapter). Revealed truths are likewise explained in such a way as to make Israel the borrower rather than the custodian of such truths. When all of this is done (when the operation is complete and all the vital organs are removed), then the critic exclaims, "See, the Bible is just like any other book!"

But when a man's heart is removed he dies; so when the supernatural is cut out of the Bible by the critic's knife, there is no Bible left!

c) Finally, a third consequence ensues. Deniers of supernatural revelation see no need why the Christian Church should be concerned about the lost state of the heathen world. We are told that the pagan has his religion (Buddhism, Islam, Hinduism, etc.) and that he is satisfied with it. And we are told that the critics in Christian countries have so riddled the Bible and de-supernaturalized it that we have nothing to offer to the pagan above what he already has. It would be an act of presumption, we are informed, for us to pose as custodians of a revelation from God which the heathen must receive or die in his sins.

C. *The Contribution of Supernatural Revelation*

Surely here we reach the well of inexhaustible truth. In God's written Word we have the acme of supernatural revelation made to man in his present sinful state. Our remarks here are indebted somewhat to Richard Watson's *Theological Tracts* (1791), Vol. 6. pp. 360-368.

1. Supernatural revelation confirms those truths that man could ascertain from Reason's voice or the light of nature. Here stands out the truth concerning the being and nature of God — the unity of God, His personality, and His attributes (such as power, goodness, holiness).

2. Supernatural revelation confirms those principles of truth that man might assume as probable but still not quite certain. Such concepts as the following belong here: a) The forgiveness of man's sins when he truly repents (cf. Luke 24:47; Acts 2:38ff; 17:30f; 26:18). b) The immortality of the soul (cf. Luke 16:19-31; II Cor. 5:1-10; Phil. 1:21). c) Future rewards for the righteous and future punishments for the wicked (cf. Matt. 25:31-46; Rev. 20:11-15).

3. Supernatural revelation reveals those things to man which man could not possibly have conceived by the exercise of his reason. These are the truths which the Gospel especially makes known to us, such as: a) God's love for us in sending His own Son to be our Redeemer (John 3:16).

Here must be placed also all those facts concerning the person and work of the Redeemer which man could never have discovered, such as Christ's unique (virgin) birth, His humanity and deity joined in one person, His temptability and yet impeccability, His substitutionary death for the sinner, His resurrection with an incorruptible body, His ascension to God's right hand where He officiates as our High Priest until He comes again in glory. b) God's sending the Holy Spirit into the world to carry on and complete the work which Christ began (cf. John 16:7-14). c) The union of the believer with Christ in an indissoluble union which can never be broken (cf. John 10:27ff; Rom. 8:10; Col. 1:27). d) The consummation of redemption in the resurrection of the body and the inheritance of a kingdom which has no end (I Cor. 15:12ff; Phil. 3:20f; Jas. 1:12; I Pet. 1:3ff; II Pet. 3:11-14). The distinctive mysteries of the Christian faith are excellently presented in a classic little work by T. J. Crawford, *The Mysteries of Christianity* (1874).

D. *The Characteristics of Supernatural Revelation*

The nature of supernatural revelation is such a simple, and yet at the same time such a complex, subject that it will be necessary for us to look at it from a manifold viewpoint. God's revelation in His Word is like the rainbow — it has many colors, yet it is the same rainbow of promise. Let us now consider some of its characteristics.

1. It is a possible revelation. No one who is a theist will deny its possibility from God's side. Surely the God who made the world can reveal Himself to man in a way that transcends the order of nature. If we believe in a direct creation of man in the image of God (which image gave to man innate powers far above those given to animals), then we must allow that man has the capacity to understand God's revelation. Make man a product of naturalistic evolution and you automatically deprive him of the ability of knowing God; you put him, in fact, on the same level with animals.

2. It is a probable revelation. By this we simply mean

that if God is a God of love and compassion, as the Bible abundantly shows He is, and if man, His image-bearer, is in the terrible plight described so realistically in the Bible (cf. Rom. 3:10-18), then it is highly probable that God would make a further revelation of His will and purpose than that which man had in nature and his own conscience.

3. It is a God-initiated revelation. This is so self-evident that it hardly calls for further comment. It was not man who sought God, but rather God who sought man, after man's rebellion turned him away from God (cf. Gen. 3:9ff; Isa. 55:1ff).

4. It is a necessary revelation. This also is abundantly clear. The history of man since his apostasy shows the utter inability of man to arrive at ultimate truths about God or about himself. Man is ever learning but never able to come to the full knowledge of the truth (cf. II Tim. 3:7). No man can know the Father actually and savingly except through Christ (Matt. 11:25ff; John 14:6; Acts 4:12). It is imperative, therefore, that a revelation be made to mankind above that which nature affords or else we are lost eternally. Our groping without this Light can but lead us to eternal night (II Pet. 2:17; Jude 13).

5. It is an authenticated revelation. This simply means that God has accompanied His supernatural revelation with supernatural signs so that any reasonable soul must acknowledge its supernatural origin. These signs are such things as miracles and the fulfillment of prophecy (as well as other distinctive marks of supernaturalism), which prove conclusively that "the finger of God" (Ex. 8:19) is in this business. To reject such signs of the supernatural is to make one guilty of the unpardonable sin (Matt. 12:24-32).

6. It is a purposive revelation. It is not a hit-or-miss affair, but one that is carefully planned by the Triune God from eternity. The one great purpose that runs through all of God's supernatural revelation concerns the redemption of sinful man through Christ (cf. John 3:16). All other purposes are secondary to this one.

7. It is a historical revelation. Events in this revelation take place in a temporal context and are linked together

with the objective facts of history. These events did not take place secretly "in a corner" (Acts 26:26), but are written plain and large on the page of history. This revelation mentions persons, places and things whose existence in their historical context can be indubitably proved (as we shall see in a later chapter) by archaeological research.

8. It is an interpretative revelation. In no other place except in Bible history can we find a line of prophets and apostles who had a message from God to interpret the events of time. Neither Egypt, Babylon, Greece nor Rome had anything of this sort. But the inspired prophets and apostles of Israel and the Church had messages pregnant with meaning for all of time. No one in ancient times except the inspired Isaiah (44:28; 45:1-3) knew the purpose behind Cyrus' life and mission. And to the heathen, the rainbow is simply a physical phenomenon of nature; but to the recipients of supernatural revelation, it is a constant reminder of God's faithfulness to His covenant promise (Gen. 9:13). God's supernatural revelation shows that history has meaning and is replete with spiritual significance. It shows also that all things fulfill the eventual design that God has in our present existence in this world (cf. Rom. 8:28).

9. It is a manifold revelation. It has come "in divers manners" (Heb. 1:1). God has not used a uniform method but has varied the ways by which He has revealed His will to man. Sometimes He has spoken directly to man (as when Moses met God on Sinai), sometimes He used dreams, sometimes visions, and sometimes other modes (see James Orr, *Revelation and Inspiration* [reprint ed.; 1952], pp. 78ff).

10. It is a progressive revelation. It has come in various stages. There was first the original revelation made to the human race, then the revelation made to the Patriarchs, then the revelation made to Moses and Israel and the prophets; finally, the revelation made in and through Jesus Christ. There is a real "progress of doctrine" in this revelation. Note, in particular, how the Messianic hope is increasingly explained from Genesis 3:15 down to the time when Christ came in "the fulness of time" (Gal. 4:4). It is not a progress from error to truth (as presented in the

modern view of the Bible), but rather a progress from truth to a greater expression of the same truth.

11. It is a written and inspired revelation. God's revelation (as we showed in the first chapter) has been committed to us in words inspired of the Holy Spirit (cf. II Tim. 3:16; II Pet. 1:21). Apart from supernatural inspiration, it is impossible to conceive how God's supernatural revelation could be transmitted to us without error.

12. It is a complete and final revelation. All that God intended to reveal to man of His nature and plan is now incorporated in the revelation given to us in the sixty-six canonical books of Scripture. This revelation has been "once-for-all" (Jude 3) committed to the saints of God and no additions or subtractions are to be made by later hands (Rev. 22:18f). All who pretend to receive revelations beyond the Bible are frauds and impostors (cf. Matt. 24:24).

13. It is an exclusive revelation. By this we mean that it is the only revelation given to the race of mankind. Christianity has a unique Book and a unique Saviour. The Bible is not to be compared with the sacred books of ethnic religions; it can only be contrasted with them. The Bible is not one of several equally valid revelations from God; it is the only supernatural revelation which we have.

14. It is a unified revelation. This characteristic will be dealt with more fully under a later heading. We list it here as one of the features of God's revelation. In the Bible we have a harmonious presentation of God's truth, each part of which, like the stones in a building, fits perfectly in its right place in the total structure.

15. It is a Christo-centric revelation. Christ is the center of all God's revelation and the fulfillment of all His promises (Rom. 15:8; II Cor. 1:18-20). Christ is in all the Scriptures and they are meaningless without Him (Luke 24:27, 45ff). One who rejects Christ as the Son of God must reject the Bible as the Word of God; and one who rejects the Scriptures as God's supernatural revelation must logically reject Christ as Saviour and Lord.

E. *The Coherence (Unity) of Supernatural Revelation*

There is hardly any problem connected with Biblical revelation that has been more the center of attention and debate
than that which concerns the unity of revelation. In the
last century the theological world has witnessed a complete
retreat from the position held by negative critics of the Graf-
Wellhausen type. In fact, it is only within the last generation that liberals have been emphasizing the unity of the
Bible. That we may see this subject in its modern context,
let us note the following things:

1. Deniers of the unity of supernatural revelation. Under
this heading we place those who, for one reason or another,
reject the total unity of God's revelation. In putting these
together, we do not mean to imply that they all share the
same view about the Bible.

a) Deniers because of philosophy. Here we place Deists
and all like them who reject entirely and absolutely all
supernatural revelation. To them there is but one revelation from God — that contained in nature and man's conscience. Many of those who take the liberal view of the
Bible undoubtedly belong in this same category, for implicitly their anti-supernaturalistic viewpoint leads them to
the same conclusion.

b) Deniers because of blindness. Here we place all un-
converted Jews who, because of their spiritual blindness (cf.
John 9:38-40; 12:39f; Rom. 11:25), have rejected the entire
New Testament as a revelation from God. To them only
the Old Testament is a revelation of God's will.

c) Deniers because of misinterpretation. Here are to be
placed certain evangelicals called dispensationalists who will
not allow that the New Testament is the intended fulfillment of the Old Testament revelation. To them the whole
present age of grace is but a "great parenthesis" which was
unknown in the Old Testament. They insist that the Church
Age is not in the prophetic forevision. Theoretically, at least,
they teach that if the Jews had accepted Jesus as their
Messiah and King, the present age of grace would have
never materialized — yet the Old Testament would have been
fulfilled as intended! This same group also teaches that the

older concept of the one covenant of grace, covering the Old and New Testament dispensations, must be surrendered in the interest of their view which holds that all of time is divided into seven great dispensations with an equal number of covenants and that, theoretically, if not actually, man's way of salvation is on different terms in each.

d) Deniers because of compromise and prejudice. Under this heading we place three groups: (1) Those like Marcion in the early church and Harnack (and those who follow him) in modern Christianity who reject the Old Testament in favor of the New Testament. To some in this category (like the ancient Gnostics) the God of the Old Testament was more of a demon than a God. In their hatred of the Jews, the Nazis of Germany rejected the Old Testament. (2) There are those, especially of the comparative-religion school, who, rejecting the Old Testament, would engraft the New Testament on the ethnic faiths of the various pagan nations. To this group the Old Testament is an obstacle to one world-wide faith. The Christian missionary, if he followed the behest of this party, would leave his Old Testament at home. (3) There are those who would make the New Testament a product of Hellenistic mysticism and thus would divorce it from the Old Testament. The ideas found in Paul, according to this school, are part and parcel of the syncretistic faith of the pagan mystery-religions. Thus the Old Testament is not the basis and background of New Testament theology. They divorce the New Testament from the Old Testament that they might wed it to Greek mysticism.

2. Deniers of the unity of New Testament revelation. This subject is so broad and intricate that we can barely think of covering it adequately in this brief survey. The lines are not always drawn as sharply as our outline might indicate, and there is, in some cases, considerable overlapping. However, a poor outline in this case is perhaps better than none at all.

a) Those who deny unity largely on textual grounds. In this field are found all those critics who endeavor to find a number of different sources, especially in the Gospels, for the New Testament record. These critics are not satisfied until they have pinned down "Q" and all the other imaginary sources of the Synoptics. And, as is to be expected, they find discrepancies and contradictory statements in the various sources.

b) Those who deny unity largely on grounds of historical and literary criticism. Here are to be placed those who find a conflict between the Synoptics on the one hand and the Fourth Gospel on the other hand. It is (or has been) affirmed that the Jesus of the Synoptics is different from the Jesus of the Gospel of John. It has been maintained that there are a number of conflicting differences between the life of Christ in these two sources. To cite just one, the cleansing of the Temple takes place at the beginning of Christ's ministry in John, but in the Synoptics it is at the close.

c) Those who deny the unity of the New Testament on theological grounds. We divide this group into two sections that are theologically miles apart. (1) There are those in the liberal group who make a clash between the simple Jesus of the Synoptics and the theological Christ invented by Paul. The idea here is that Jesus was a good man but that this man, at the instigation of Paul's keen intellect, was glorified and deified by the Early Church. Thus we have the contrast between the Jesus of Nazareth and the God of Chalcedon. There are, of course, many variations of this disunity that is forced upon the New Testament. (2) From an entirely different viewpoint there has arisen, among evangelicals, a group called dispensationalists, who have brought disunity into the New Testament. Very briefly put, their system runs about like this: Christ came to establish an earthly kingdom, but when He was rejected as Israel's King, He changed His plan and went to the cross. Morally this rejection of Christ took place at Matthew 11:20-24; officially it was consummated by His trial before the Sanhedrin. Up until His moral rejection, Christ was announcing the sooncoming of the earthly kingdom; when He perceived that the Jews had rejected Him as their King, He began to announce a new message concerning His death. In line with this disunity of Christ's mission, we have the novel notion that "the gospel of the kingdom" (which was proclaimed by John the Baptist, Christ, the Twelve and the Seventy) is something entirely different from "the gospel of the grace of God" which we are to proclaim in the present age. The former "gospel" concerned the near-arrival of the expected earthly kingdom; the latter "gospel" concerns the salvation offered through Christ's atonement. Naturally, on the grounds just outlined, dispensationalists make a distinction between the legalistic (or Jewish) portions of the New Testament (which usually include up to Matt. 11) and the evangelic portions. Some ultra-dispensationalists find the break between these portions as late as Paul's arrival in Rome (cf. Acts 28:25-28) and thus leave only a fragment of the New Testament (such as Paul's letters to Ephesus, Colosse, and Philippi) for the New Testament Church to claim.

3. The unity of the Old and New Testament. It is quite evident that if both the Old and New Testaments originate in the mind of God, they must be unified in content, purpose and scope. Admittedly there are differences between the two Testaments or dispensations that are due to one's being prior to, or preparatory for, the other. The differences lie on the surface; the unity is deep and fundamental. We present here a simple digest of the underlying unity of the Old and New Testament revelations of God's will to mankind.

a) The unity of prediction and fulfillment. One of the most obvious facts that confronts the student as he approaches the New Testament is the way it cites the promises of the Old Testament as fulfilled in, and by, the later revelation. The Gospel of Matthew, in particular, repeats the refrain of fulfillment quite often (cf. 1:22; 2:5; 4:14; 8:17, etc.). Christ came specifically to fulfill the Old Testament promises (cf. Rom. 15:8). Throughout the New Testament, in every aspect of its teaching, the Old Testament is appealed to as confirmatory evidence (cf. Acts 2:16ff, 25ff; 4:25ff; 13:40f, 47; 15:16ff; Rom. 3:4f, 10ff; 4:6f; 9:25f, 29; 10:16ff; 11:9f, 26f; 14:11; 15:9ff, 21; etc.).

b) The unity of the Messianic promises and their fulfillment. This is, of course, another aspect of the preceding head. It should be particularly noted how the promises concerning Christ are fulfilled in the New Testament. Christ evidently saw in all the major portions of the Old Testament (Law, Prophets, Psalms), predictions concerning His advent to earth (cf. Luke 24:26f, 45ff). The same is true of all the New Testament writers — John (I John 3:8); Peter (I Pet. 1:10ff); James (Acts 15:15ff); Paul (Acts 26:6, 22f; Rom. 15:8).

c) The unity of type and antitype. The following are among some of the Old Testament types that are reported in the New Testament as illustrative of some truth: Jonah's experience (Matt. 12:39ff); the lamb of sacrifice (John 1:29); the brazen serpent (John 3:14); Israel's experience at the Red Sea and in the wilderness (I Cor. 10:1-11); Melchizedek (Heb. 7:1-25), etc.

d) The unity of the people of God in both Testaments. The line of faith is traced from Abel right down through the Old Testament and it finds its culmination in the New Testament Church (cf. Matt. 8:11; Heb. 11:4-40). Membership in the kingdom of God depends upon a new birth (John 3:1-12) — not being a physical descendant of Abraham (Matt. 3:8, 9; John 8:52ff). He is a true Jew who is one inwardly (Rom. 2:28f). Isaac represents the children of God's promise (Rom. 9:6ff; Gal. 4:21-31). Abraham is the type of faith and the father of believers (Rom. 4:1-25; Gal. 3:6-18, 29). The New Testament Church is God's "people" (Rom. 9:25f; 10:19f), God's "royal priesthood" (I Pet. 2:9), God's "elect race" (I Pet. 2:9), etc. Compare Exodus 19:6.

e) The unity of the covenant of grace. The New Testament is so integrated with the Old Testament in its teaching regarding the covenant of grace that one cannot be torn from the other except by the complete destruction of both. It would require a volume to deal with this subject adequately. We confine our attention here to a presentation of the most important points: (1) The present age of grace is the fulfillment of the Old Testament prediction concerning "the last days" (Joel 2:28ff; Acts 2:16ff). From the New

Testament standpoint we are now living in eschatological times (cf. Heb. 1:1). (2) The present age is the fulfillment of "the new covenant" promised in the Old Testament (Jer. 31:31ff; Heb. 8:8ff). Christ introduced this covenant by His death (Luke 22:17-20; I Cor. 11:23-25). (3) The sacraments of the Old Testament period were the Passover and circumcision; the sacraments of the New Testament — the Lord's Supper and Baptism — largely correspond to them in meaning and significance. (4) The New Testament period is the fulfillment of the promised "outpouring" of the Holy Spirit (Joel 2:28ff; Acts 2:16ff). (5) The "everlasting kingdom" announced in the older period of God's revelation is introduced by Jesus Christ (Isa. 9:6f; Dan. 2:44; 4:3; 7:14, 27; Luke 1:33). (6) Jesus Christ Himself is, in the New Testament, equated with the Jehovah of the Old Testament revelation (cf. Isa. 40:3; Matt. 3:3; John 1:23). The one who calls on the name of Jehovah (Jesus) shall be saved (Joel 2:32; Rom. 10:13). Many other such parallels could be cited to show the unity of the Old and New Testament revelation.

4. The unity of the New Testament revelation. That the New Testament as an organic unity is an article of our faith can be easily proved. We shall first look at this unity externally and shall then present it internally.

a) The external unity of the New Testament revelation. The following points enter into the outward unity of the New Testament: (1) The common use of the Greek language. There is no absolute evidence that any other language than Greek was used in the writing of the New Testament. The theory that the Gospels and other portions of the New Testament were written in Aramaic has practically no support. (2) The period in which written. All of the New Testament, we believe, was composed within the first century and thus arises out of the same historical situation. (3) The authorship is unified. All of the writers of the New Testament were men who had had a common experience and background. They were either apostles or else men who were closely associated with one or more of the apostles.

b) The internal unity of the New Testament revelation. The proof for this is so convincing that it is hard to understand how anyone acquainted with the evidence could possibly come to a different conclusion. Without attempting to be exhaustive, we set forth here a brief survey of the facts that bear on the subject.

(1) One view of Scripture. The New Testament is unified in its view of Scripture in the following particulars (compare also the first chapter): (a) All the New Testament documents appeal to the Old Testament uniformly, as inspired and authoritative. There is no dissension among them as to which books are in the canon; and there are surely no schools of criticism among them, doubting or denying the traditional authorship of certain Old Testament books. Paul quotes from the first part of Isaiah (6:9f; Acts 28:26f) and the second part of the same book (65:1; Rom. 10:20) and attributes both to the same author. (b) All the New Testament authors look upon the Old Testament revelation as representing actual history. There was not among them (as there is among us today) those who took part of the Old Testament as mythical and legendary and part as historical. To Paul, Adam (Rom. 5:14), Abraham (Rom. 4), Isaac (Gen. 4:21-31), etc., were real persons whose lives were definitely connected with the history of redemption. (c) The New Testament writers consistently appeal to the Old Testament revelation as fulfilled in the New Testament. They all considered it as prophetic and Messianic — reaching its consummation in Christ. Christ taught this doctrine (Luke 24:27, 44ff) and He was followed by Peter (Acts 2:25-36; 3:24f; I Pet. 1:9ff), James (Acts 25:15ff), Paul (Acts 26:22f) and others.

(2) One view of theology. This is such a comprehensive subject that we can but touch the most significant points. At the outset, let us say that we cannot find among the New Testament writers such parties or divisions as we have in modern Christianity. There were not among them some who believed the virgin birth of Christ and some who denied it, or some who affirmed the impeccability of Christ and some who denied it, or some who held to the substitutionary

view of the atonement and some who held another view. One consistent teaching runs through the New Testament on every essential doctrine of the Christian faith. This will be more easily seen in the following details.

(a) The New Testament Christology is unified. Let us note the following truths about Christ. First, His incarnation. The New Testament teaches (Matt. 1; Luke 1) that He was born of the Virgin Mary without a human father. There is nothing in all the rest of the New Testament that would make one take a different view of Christ's incarnation. Although Paul does not mention the virgin birth as such (cf. Gal. 4:4), his whole Christology is based upon such a foundation. It is unthinkable that a Jew like Paul could attribute to Jesus the glorified and deified position which he gives Him if He were a mere man born of human parents like the rest of the race. Second, His sinlessness. Paul (II Cor. 5:21; Heb. 7:26) and Peter (I Pet. 1:19) and others speak of Him as sinless. Third, His deity. Paul calls Him "the great God" (Titus 2:13); John calls Him "the true God" (I John 5:20); Peter calls Him "our God" (II Pet. 1:1, margin); and Thomas confesses the same (John 20:28). Fourth, His death. Paul affirms that Christ died for us (Gal. 2:20; Eph. 5:2, 25). Peter states that He died for the unrighteous (I Pet. 1:18f; 3:18). John tells us that we are loosed from our sins by His blood (I John 2:1f; 4:10; Rev. 1:5). Fifth, His resurrection. All the New Testament writers bear witness to the fact that the Lord Jesus is the risen Lord. Peter affirms it (Acts 2:25-35; 3:14f); Paul believes it (I Cor. 15: 4; Col. 3:1); John teaches it (Rev. 1:5, 18). Sixth, His present session at God's right hand. He is there according to Peter (Acts 2:34ff; 3:21; I Pet. 3:22), according to Paul (Col. 3:1; Heb. 1:3; 8:1), according to John (Rev. 3:21). Seventh, His return in glory. So Paul teaches (I Thess. 4: 13ff; Titus 2:13), and Peter (I Pet. 5:4; II Pet. 3:10ff), and John (I John 3:2; Rev. 19).

In the references cited above we have not given passages from the four Gospels, although such passages could have been cited easily. There is complete unity between the teaching about Christ in the four Gospels and what is said about Him by Peter, Paul, John and all the New Testament writers.

(b) The New Testament soteriology is unified. The New Testament teaches the same doctrine regarding the plan of salvation. First, it teaches that all are sinners in God's sight — Paul (Rom. 3:10ff); Peter (I Pet. 4:1ff); John (I John 5:19). Second, all men must repent — so write Peter (Acts 2:38; 3:19), Paul (Acts 20:21), John (Rev. 2:5, 21; 3:3). John the Baptist and Christ taught the same (Mark 1:4, 15). Third, men must believe in order to be saved. This is affirmed by Peter (I Pet. 1:5; 2:7), Paul (Rom. 10:9f), and John (I John 5:5). James (2:14-26), when properly understood, does not conflict with this doctrine. Christ, of course, taught that men must believe on Him (John 5:24). Fourth, men must be born again in order to enter God's spiritual kingdom. The basic passage here is what Christ Himself said to Nicodemus (John 3:1-12). But His apostles teach consistently the same truth. Witness Peter (I Pet. 1:3; 2: 1, 2), John (I John 3:9), James (1:18), Paul (Rom. 8:14ff). Fifth, sanctification and good works must accompany the new life. Christ, of course, laid the foundation for this doctrine (John 15:1ff). His apostles taught the same; note, for example, Paul (I Thess. 4:3; Titus 3:1, 8, 14), Peter (II Pet. 1:5-11), John (I John 3:17), James (2:14ff). Sixth, the perseverance of believers to the end of life. Here, again, Christ laid the foundation of this doctrine when He affirmed that His sheep would never perish (John 10:28f). But the same truth is taught by Paul (Rom. 8:35-39; Phil. 1:6), Peter (I Pet. 1:5), Jude (24), and John (I John 3:2, 9, 24). Seventh, the final glorification of believers at the second coming of Christ. Again, Christ laid the foundation of this doctrine (John 14:1-3; 17:24). But it is also taught by Paul (II Cor. 5:1-10; I Thess. 3:13; 5:23), Peter (I Pet. 1:7; 5:4), Jude (24f), John (I John 3:2).

(c) The New Testament eschatology is unified. The foundation of this unity, of course, is found in the parabolic teaching of our Lord (Matt. 13) and in His eschatological discourses (Matt. 24 and 25; Mark 13). Here we will state what Christ taught and then show how the apostles repeated the same truths in their writings. First, Christ taught that the present age ends in apostasy — wars, pestilences, false prophets characterize the whole period (Matt. 24:1-14; Luke 18:8). Peter (II Pet. 3:3ff), James (5:1-8),˙ Paul (I Tim. 4:1ff; II Tim. 3:1ff; 4:3f), and John (I John 2:18; 4:1-6; Rev. 13, 17, 18) taught the same truth. Second, Christ taught that believers ought always to be waiting and ready for His coming, although they cannot know the exact time (Matt. 24:32-51). Paul also tells us to look for His coming (Titus 2:13); Peter tells us that the Chief Shepherd will appear (I Pet. 5:4); John reminds us that it is a purifying hope (I John 3:2f); James˙ affirms that the Judge is at the door (5:9). Third, the end of this age takes place when Christ returns in glory — so Christ affirms (Matt. 24:14). Paul teaches the same (I Cor. 15:24; II Thess. 1:5-11); and so does Peter (II Pet. 3:8-15); and John (Rev. 19). Fourth, Christ taught a resurrection and a separation of the righteous from the unrighteous (Matt. 13:40-43, 49f; John 5:28f). Paul held the same truth (Acts 17:31; 24:15; II Thess. 1:5-11). So did John (Rev. 20:11-15) and Peter (I Pet. 4:5, 6; II Pet. 3:7).

We have thus traced the unity of the New Testament revelation concerning the Scriptures, Christology, soteriology, and eschatology. Other great departments of divine truth (such as ecclesiology) could also have been considered; but what has been presented on the several themes discussed has abundantly proved the thesis that there is complete unity in the New Testament revelation regarding every aspect of revealed truth.

IV. CONCLUSION

Our study in this chapter has led us to some definite conclusions which we must set down here in concise language. In the first place, we have seen that there are two great revelations which have the same Author — natural revelation and supernatural revelation. In the second place, the deposit of supernatural revelation committed to us is now found in the Bible. No other book can claim to be a revelation from God. In the third place, God's supernatural revelation is unified in all of its parts and in all of its teachings. We have shown that there is complete harmony between the Old and New Testaments and that there is perfect harmony between what Christ and His apostles taught. Lastly, how much we should glorify God for such a revelation as He has given to us in His Word. Like the Psalmist we can exclaim: "Oh how love I thy law! It is my meditation all the day. Thy commandments make me wiser than mine enemies; for they are ever with me. I have more understanding than all my teachers; for thy testimonies are my meditation. I understand more than the aged, because I have kept thy precepts" (Ps. 119:97-100).

CHAPTER FOUR

PRINCIPLES OF CRITICISM

Practically every science has its accepted canons of research and investigation. This statement applies to the physical sciences as well as to the non-physical. As there are accepted laws in the realm of biology, so there are recognized principles of historical and literary study. These principles or laws are the expression of those factors that should govern or guide the student in his investigation of the subject. They are the bounds or limits beyond which he must not go if his results are to be legitimate and valid. This means that as the mathematician acknowledges the eternal validity of the multiplication table as the basis and limit of his investigation, so the student of literary and historical subjects must recognize that there are established principles determining and limiting his results. It is our purpose, therefore, to give in the present chapter a brief survey of the subject indicated by our title.

I. WHAT IS CRITICISM?

It will be necessary at the outset to ascertain what criticism really is. Unless we have an understanding of the import and significance of this term, we will find ourselves on a shifting sea of changing opinions. It shall be our purpose, then, to define this word, give some illustrations of its use in extra-Biblical materials, and show its two main spheres of investigating Holy Scripture.

A. Definition

Our English word "criticism" comes from a Greek word (krino) which means "to judge." The original meaning of the Greek word meant "to separate." Then it came to mean "to choose"; and finally "to decide" — that is, "to judge." The person who made the decision was called the *krites,* which corresponds to our English "judge." These ideas are still all latent in our use of the term "criticism." For that word connotes, first of all, a separation (of truth from falsehood), then a choosing (that which corresponds to reality), and finally a decision or judgment (which is final and definitive). In all criticism there must be at least three elements: the thing criticized, the standard by which it is criticized, and the judge who makes the decision. Let us look at each of these briefly.

1. The thing criticized. This may be anything that is the subject of criticism. In the literary world it would be something like a book, a play, a poem. In the artistic world it would be something like a building, statue, painting or the like. In the realm of Biblical criticism it would concern some book of the Bible, seeking to ascertain its date, authorship, unity, etc.

2. The standard used in judgment. This feature refers to the fact that there is an accepted standard by which to judge a thing. If the thing to be criticized is an ancient document, then the document should be carefully tested with reference to what is already known about such documents. The script used, the character of the material upon which the writing is recorded, and other such factors should enter into the question regarding the age of the document. The recently discovered *Dead Sea Scrolls* give a significant illustration of the method of criticism that is applied to an ancient document to ascertain its probable age.

3. The judge or critic. Here is introduced the most uncertain factor in criticism. The human element is the most variable and uncertain. Different critics will look at the same material from different angles or backgrounds. To one biologist a fragment of a skull is a conclusive proof that evolution is true. To another scientist it is sheer nonsense to base such a theory on such inconclusive evidence. We need but cite again the *Dead Sea Scrolls* as an illustration of how violently different are the conclusions of different critics. This situation explains why it is that, in the criticism of the Bible, one set of scholars will firmly believe that "the

assured results" of criticism lead them to accept the non-Mosaic, composite authorship of the Pentateuch. Another group of scholars, equally competent, will be as firmly convinced that Moses wrote the Pentateuch. The Pentateuch is the same Pentateuch; the principles of criticism are (presumably) the same; but the critics arrive at opposite results. The question naturally arises whether there is any absolute judge who will decide which one of the conflicting views is right. This question must await a later discussion.

B. Some Extra-Biblical Illustrations of Criticism

We propose here to look at two illustrations of the application of critical principles to non-Biblical material. The first is called *The Apostles' Creed*; the second has been called *The Pseudo-Isidorian Decretals*. Let us look at each briefly.

1. *The Apostles' Creed.* Here we will ask our reader to consult P. Schaff's *Creeds of Christendom* (4th ed.; 1884), Vol. 1, pp. 12-23, from which our material here given is gathered. Let us note these things about this *Creed*:

a) From the standpoint of textual criticism, it can be determined that the present text can hardly be traced back earlier than the sixth century of our era. Older forms of the *Creed* are found in Rufinus (about A.D. 390) and in Marcellus (A.D. 336-341). Furthermore, the famous *Descensus ad inferos* clause is undoubtedly an interpolation from the Aquilejan Creed (cf. W. G. T. Shedd, *Dogmatic Theology* [1891], vol. 2, pp. 604-608). Thus a number of additions and changes have been made in this *Creed* since its origin.

b) From the standpoint of higher criticism (that is, the investigation regarding the date, authorship, unity, etc., of the document), we are in the realm of objective certainty that this *Creed* is not the composition of the twelve apostles (as traditionally believed) before they scattered. The reasons for this judgment are the following (summarized from Schaff):

(1) The intrinsic improbability of such a mechanical composition. It is highly improbable that such a unified work arose after the manner indicated by the legend of its origin.

(2) The silence of the New Testament. There is no reference there describing such an occasion or such a document. The last great council of the apostles together was at Jerusalem (Acts 15), but nothing is said there about this *Creed*. There is no allusion to it as such in the New Testament.

(3) The silence of the Early Church. None of the Church Fathers or Synods makes any reference to such a creed. It is unlikely that the Council of Nicea would have drawn up a creed if one already existed in the Church and was considered apostolic.

(4) The great variety of form that this *Creed* has experienced (indicated briefly above) is indicative of the fact that it was not considered apostolic. If the New Testament had received the same treatment, the textual problems in it would perhaps be ten times as great as they actually are.

Thus there is every reason to believe, on the basis of internal and external evidence, that *The Apostles' Creed* is not apostolic in origin and, therefore, should not be put on the same level with the New Testament. This means that this *Creed* is not inspired, but is rather on the same level as other creeds produced in later periods of church history. This result is arrived at, of course, by the application of sound canons of criticism to the document.

2. *The Pseudo-Isidorian Decretals.* These *Decretals*, coming actually (as now generally accepted) from the middle of the ninth century, purport to be a genuine collection of decisions of popes and councils from the second century down to the eighth century. In this collection is found the notorious Donation of Constantine, which pretended to be a genuine writing of Constantine himself, although actually written four centuries after his time. In this Donation, Constantine (out of gratitude to Pope Sylvester I, who had healed the Emperor of his leprosy) granted to the pope and his successors the city of Rome and a large surrounding territory. The *Decretals* were used during the uncritical Middle Ages to back up the popes in their claim to temporal power. Now it should be noted that the fraudulent character of these *Decretals* was uncovered by the application of critical principles. Let us hear a resumé of the argument as

presented in the *New Schaff-Herzog Encyclopaedia of Religious Knowledge* (1911), vol. 9, pp. 344f: —

> The falsity of the Pseudo-Isidore's fabrications is now admitted, being proved by incontestable internal evidence (e.g., anachronisms like the use of the Vulgate and the *Breviarium Alaricianum* — composed in 506 — in the decretals of the older popes), by investigations concerning the sources and methods of the fabricator . . . and by the fact that Pseudo-Isidorian letters were unknown before 852.
>
> The fabrications of the Pseudo-Isidore are not expressed in his own language, but consist of sentences, phrases, and words taken from older writings, genuine and apocryphal, set together into a mosaic of about 10,000 pieces. The excerpts are freely altered and are sometimes given a sense directly opposite to the original, but by his method the Pseudo-Isidore sought to give to his ninth-century product the stamp of antiquity. The labor involved was enormous; etc.

We have quoted the statement above to show how principles of literary criticism were used to establish the fraudulent character of these notorious *Decretals*. There is, by the way, a rather significant contrast between these *Decretals* (whose forgery is now generally admitted) and the Book of Deuteronomy, whose fraudulent character ("pious fraud") is claimed by the modern school of criticism and whose real, or non-fraudulent, character is maintained by the conservative school. In the former case, conservatives and liberals unite in condemning the *Decretals* as a "pious fraud" or deception manufactured for a definite purpose (that is, to advance the claims of the papacy); in the latter case, conservatives loudly reject the critical view that just principles of criticism require Deuteronomy to be called a "pious fraud" also.

C. *Types of Criticism*

Biblical criticism is usually divided under two heads — higher and lower criticism. We shall now attempt to differentiate between these briefly.

1. Textual criticism. Lower criticism is often called textual criticism. The word "lower" does not indicate an inferior position with reference to "higher" criticism. Rather, lower criticism is the foundation upon which higher criticism is based. The first work on any document is the ascertaining of the true text, and this is the primary work of the textual

critic. Much labor has been expended by competent scholars to get at the exact text. Such men as Tischendorf, B. Weiss, Westcott, Hort, Nestle and others have spent years of research in order to give us the correct text of the Bible. The means by which this investigation is pursued consist of the use of (a) ancient manuscripts whose particular value in every case must be carefully ascertained, (b) quotations of the Bible in writings of the Church Fathers, and (c) ancient versions into which the Bible was translated. By observation and experience, textual critics have arrived at certain canons by which to determine whether a reading is genuine and true to the original or autograph or, on the other hand, is an interpolation or scribal error (due to some physical infirmity of the scribe) or an intended change in order to alter the meaning of the original. By the application of their canons the textual critic is able to give us, except in a few cases still disputed, what was in the original Bible. Thus our Westcott-Hort's or Nestle's Greek Testament represents what was (except for possibly a fraction of one per cent) in the original autographs. Textual criticism is a laudable science and the Christian Church is indebted to those who have spent their lives in an investigation of this subject. It has been on the side of true faith in that its constant effort has been to ascertain what were the *ipsissima verba* (the very words) of Scripture in the original manuscripts.

2. Higher criticism. When the textual critics have finished their work and have prepared a copy of a document which they can claim represents what the original author said, then the higher critic begins his job. This task takes into account the following factors (among others) regarding a document whose text is now established.

a) Authorship is of paramount importance. One of the first things we want to know about a writing is its author. The higher critic searches throughout the document to see if it throws any light on its authorship. If there are no internal signs of authorship, then the critic calls into the investigation the external evidence of authorship. This usually means that he will take into consideration what contemporaries say about the writer of the book under investigation. If there are no contemporaries that refer to the work, then he will try to find if it is quoted, or alluded to, by those who follow in later ages.

In Biblical criticism the authorship of a book is considered to be of great importance. However, it must be admitted that this is one point which differentiates the modern view from the older, conservative view. The modern view has in many places rejected the traditional authors of books of the Bible. Numerous examples of this fact could be cited. Suffice it for us here to mention the Pentateuch in the Old Testament and the Pastoral Epistles in the New Testament, in both of which cases the traditional authorship is rejected by the modern view. It can be said that there are three classes of books with reference to their authorship. In the first class are those whose traditional authorship (as indicated above) is rejected by the modern school of critics. In the second class we put those books whose traditional authorship is accepted and defended by the conservative school. In the two classes just mentioned would be included practically all the books of the Bible. There is, however, a third class which would include those books, about whose authorship neither conservative nor liberal is absolutely sure. The most outstanding book in this category is undoubtedly the Epistle to the Hebrews.

It may be pertinent to ask here if the authorship of a particular book has any bearing on one's faith. This is a question upon which conservatives and liberals disagree. The former class usually maintains that the question of authorship affects one's faith; the liberals, on the other side, affirm that there is no necessary connection between one's faith and one's view about authorship. On this subject it will be well if we consider the following:

(1) Books whose divine authorship may not be doubted. According to the conservative this group would include all the books in the canon of Scripture. He would argue that the Epistle to the Hebrews is surely of divine origin (and thereby has a right in the canon), although we cannot establish dogmatically its human author.

(2) Books whose human authorship may not be doubted if one of the following tests is met: (a) Internal evidence: is there evidence from the book itself that indicates its real authorship? Here practically all of Paul's epistles would be placed, for there are many internal signs (references to himself and to historical situations, language and style, etc.) that betray their common authorship by Paul. Internal evidence is one of the chief tests used by conservatives to ascertain the authorship of a book. (b) External evidence: are there sufficient evidences outside the book under question to ascertain its authorship? Here the scholar would ask himself such questions as the following: Does some contemporary or later person refer to the book or quote from it as coming from a known person? Does the book agree with the known historical facts of the time when the author is supposed to have lived? Let us cite a case in point. It is well known that the liberal view rejects the Danielic authorship of the book bearing Daniel's name. Is there evidence, external to the book itself, teaching us to believe that Daniel was the true author of this book? Of course, it is evident that our Lord quotes from Daniel and applies the prophecy which he quotes (Matt. 24:15) to the historic Daniel. Did our Lord actually know that Daniel was the author of the prophecy? The conservative scholar will reply in the affirmative; and, because of this fact, he assures himself, on the basis of the Lord's infallible testimony, that the authorship of the historical Daniel must be accepted. The only way to get around this evidence is to assert that our Lord's words must not be taken at their face value or that, in this case, the modern critic has more evidence or knows more than the Lord Jesus Christ.

And right here we see the bearing of the authorship of a book on one's faith. If my Lord affirms that David uttered the words of the one hundred tenth Psalm (cf. Matt. 22:43-45), and yet I (in line with most liberals today) deny that David wrote that Psalm, then I am saying that my Lord was in error or mistaken or did not have sufficient information upon which to make His statement. Dare I, a creature sinful and finite, make such an accusation against the Lord of Glory? Thus the conservative has always felt that there is a direct connection between our attitude toward the authorship of a book and our personal faith.

b) Date. Criticism seeks to know the time when a particular book originated. Various factors enter into the question of a book's date. These we shall mention in a subsequent treatment of our subject.

We call attention here to the fact that almost all conservatives, accepting the traditional authorship (for the most part), put the books of the Bible in the time that corresponds to the dates of the author's life. For example, practically all conservatives accept the Pauline authorship of the Pastoral Epistles. If this be so, then a place must be found in Paul's lifetime for these epistles. If Moses wrote the Pentateuch, then those books must be placed within the life of Moses. If we know when Moses lived, then we know when the Pentateuch was written.

Most liberals, rejecting many of the traditional authors of Scriptural books, lean toward a later date for many books of the Bible. As an illustration, few (if any) conservatives place any of the Old Testament books later than about 400 B.C.; but, on the other hand, the modern liberal will put a number of these books after that date. The tendency in the modern view is to bring the books of the Bible down to a later date. In some cases this simply cannot be done, for the facts cry out too loudly against a change. For this reason such books as Amos, Hosea, Jeremiah, and Habakkuk have been allowed to stand in their traditional places in history.

c) Unity. Criticism must ascertain whether a particular book is unified or composite. Here again there is a great divide between conservative criticism and liberal criticism. Conservatives have unitedly held for unified authorship of Biblical books; in contrast, the liberal has, in many cases, introduced composite authorship into the writing of the books of the Bible. There is hardly a more striking case at hand than that which the Pentateuch affords. Here the liberal school rejects the Mosaic authorship and substitutes what they call the composite authorship of the Hexateuch.

The liberal believes that the first six books in the Bible were written by unknown writers or schools (commonly called J, E, D, and P) and that these separate documents (written from about 850 to 550 B.C.) were not welded together into a unified whole until the time of the Babylonian Captivity.

Outside of the Pentateuch (Hexateuch), there is hardly any book of the Bible that has been more fragmentized than Isaiah. While conservatives accept the book as coming from the prophet Isaiah (living in the eighth century, B.C.), the liberal school has broken this wonderful book up into fragments. The moderate section of the modern view (including such scholars as Driver, G. A. Smith, Skinner, A. B. Davidson) would give Isaiah about forty-four of the sixty-six chapters. The radical school of modern scholars (including such names as Cheyne, Duhm, Gray) reject about four-fifths of the book as Isaiah's (cf. George L. Robinson, *The Book of Isaiah* [1938], pp. 59f).

d) Genuineness. This word really applies to authorship. It means simply that a work is written by the person whose name it bears. If, for example, Daniel actually wrote the book that bears his name, then that writing is genuine; if that be not the case, then Daniel is a non-genuine or spurious or counterfeit writing. If the events recorded in Daniel actually took place, that book can be described as authentic. If they did not take place as described but are the invention of the author, the book can be called fictitious or apocryphal.

In conservative scholarship genuineness is always attributed to a book. There is no such thing as a "pious fraud" in the conservative's vocabulary with reference to a Biblical book. Likewise there is no such thing as a book which relates fictitious or imaginary things. This is not so with reference to liberal scholarship. In that school we find cases where a book is described as ungenuine in authorship and unauthentic (at least in significant parts) in its description of events. There is hardly a more notorious example of the critical view on this subject than that afforded by their treatment of Daniel. The liberal tells us that it was not written by the real Daniel (but was written by a pseudo-

Daniel) and does not actually relate the facts of history correctly. Thus Daniel is at least ungenuine (that is, it is spurious) in its claim of authorship and it is unauthentic (at least in parts) in its description of events.

e) Destination. Criticism investigates the destination of a book to determine who the readers of the book were or to whom it was first addressed. In many cases this is perfectly obvious from the content of the book. There is hardly any question, for example, that the church at Rome was the recipient of the Epistle to the Romans. The references that Paul makes in the epistle to the church there (cf. 1:7, 15; 15:22-29) make it impossible to entertain any other view of its destination. It would seem most likely, too, that the Book of Revelation was addressed to the seven churches of Asia.

In some cases, it is rather difficult to determine exactly who were the original readers of a particular document. Scholars have argued back and forth since ancient times regarding the readers of the Epistle to the Hebrews. Perhaps the question will never be settled entirely. However, this uncertainty should in no wise jeopardize the inspiration and value of the epistle for us today.

Liberals and conservatives are likely to have more agreements with reference to the destination of particular books than in any other category of their relationship to one another. However, it must be noted that when a book's date is changed to a later time (as is done so often among the liberals), it cannot but affect the destination of the book. Let us again use Daniel as an illustration. According to the conservative view, this book was written by the historic Daniel at the close of the Babylonian exile and was addressed to the returnees to inform them that it would be some time (that is, 490 years, on the basis of the prophecy of the seventy weeks: Dan. 9:24-27) before the new covenant announced by Jeremiah (31:31ff) could be fulfilled. According to the liberal view, the Book of Daniel was addressed to some persecuted Jews during the time of Antiochus Epiphanes in order to encourage them to stand up under their persecution because the expected deliverance from God was shortly at hand.

f) Place of writing. It is also within the province of criticism to ascertain where the writer was when he wrote a particular book. It is quite evident, for example, that John was on the island of Patmos when he received the revelation of Jesus Christ (Rev. 1:9). Sometimes the place mentioned in a document has given rise to different opinions as to which place was meant. The "Babylon" mentioned in I Peter 5:13 has been applied to three different places — the city of Rome mystically called Babylon (which certainly helps out the Roman Catholic claim that Peter was the first bishop in that city), the ancient city on the Euphrates, and the Babylon on the Nile (now known as Old Cairo). The first mentioned place seems to be the least likely (cf. G. T. Manley (ed.), *The New Bible Handbook* [1948], pp. 398f). Sometimes the place of origin of a document is not any one particular locality. It is impossible, for example, to affirm that Acts was written by Luke at one single place. The "we"-sections in Acts (16:10-17; 20:5-15; 21:1-18; 27:1-28:16) show unmistakably that Luke's eye-witness accounts originated at different places as he accompanied Paul on his journeys. Undoubtedly Moses wrote the books of the Pentateuch at different places. Although Jeremiah delivered most of his messages in Jerusalem, yet it is certain that some of his prophecies were uttered in Egypt (43:9-11; 44:30).

g) The nature of a document. It is also the duty of the critic to ascertain what is the nature of a particular document which he is investigating. To which literary type does the writing belong? Is it historical? Is it legendary and fictional? Is it prophetic? Does it use plain prose or is there a figurative or symbolic meaning that must be dis covered by some key? All these questions (and others) concern the nature of a document.

On this subject there are vital differences between the conservative and liberal approach to the Bible. On more than one book these schools divide in their conception regarding the nature of a book. Let us use a few illustrations. Is Esther historical or mythological? The conservative replies that it is good history. The liberal, accepting the historical character of some elements in the book, throws considerable doubt on the historical trustworthiness of the book as a whole. Is Jonah history or an allegory? Here again the two schools divide. To the liberal it is allegory; to the conservative it is history. Is the Book of Revelation a true prophecy or is it a crude attempt of some early Christian to depict pictorially certain things about a Nero-myth? Here again the conservative stands on different ground from his liberal contemporary. The right solution to many of these problems is discovered when true principles or accepted canons of criticism are used. These canons will now be presented.

II. CANONS OF CRITICISM

Every science, as we have already said, must have a set of rules by which its investigation is governed. One could not make progress in mathematics if he began by discarding the multiplication table. Chemistry has its definite laws regarding the composition of solids and gases. Physics must abide by its laws. So it is of every science. And this is just as true in literary research and investigation. In the following discussion, therefore, we shall deal with some of the basic canons of investigation as they concern the critic himself, his standards of research, and the document which he is investigating.

A. *Canons of Criticism for the Critic*

Every one who studies the Bible is, in a certain sense, a critic. This simply means that he makes some judgment regarding the Bible. The judgment may be favorable or unfavorable. It may be made by a person of no learning or it may be made by an erudite scholar. Every man has the right to exercise his judgment with reference to the Bible (cf. John 7:17). In our presentation of this subject we are taking criticism as a legitimate science.

We are well aware of the fact that in our modern era the word "criticism" has fallen into disrepute in many quarters. Especially is this so when "higher criticism" or "higher critic" is spoken of with reference to those who take a naturalistic approach toward the Bible. Because so much of modern criticism has been destructive of the traditional views that have been entertained for centuries, it is quite the common thing, in our mental associations, to equate "higher criticism" with "destructive criticism." In the present book we often use the term "critic" or "critical" as designating the modern, anti-supernatural approach. Those who hold such negative views often complain against the application of "destructive" to their approach. They grant, of course, that their position, in many points, contradicts and invalidates the position held by the Church down through the ages. But they maintain that there must be the destruction of erroneous views before the temple of truth can be erected. And it is their firm conviction, for the most part, that they have been called of God to overthrow the inherited traditions about the Bible which the Church has naively received.

Our present concern, however, will be to present the critic in terms of what he ought to be if he is true to his calling. We are speaking more particularly, of course, about those who make it their business to investigate the Bible with reference to critical problems (authorship, date, unity, etc.). For such we believe that the following principles will apply.

1. The critic must have adequate knowledge of his subject. He will thoroughly train himself in every department of learning that concerns his subject either directly or indirectly. Some scholars have pursued this principle so rigidly that they have literally learned dozens of languages in order to handle at first-hand any phase of their field of research. Dr. Robert Dick Wilson was a good example of what we are here speaking about, for he felt no one could know too much when it came to investigating the Bible. In carrying out this principle the real critic must have a knowledge of the original language of the document which he is investigating. No definite judgment can be based merely on some translation — whether it be ancient or modern. He must also be able to investigate original sources that have a bearing on his field of study. Secondary sources — such as modern books

in the field of criticism — have their place and value; but they can never take the place of the primary sources for a definitive judgment.

Too many modern critics have been willing to take the views of a Wellhausen or a Driver as final without subjecting them to the scrutiny of the original sources. It is indeed possible that a modern critic may have omitted a significant bit of information from antiquity or may have given it a particular slant suitable to his own views.

Scholarship today is in desperate need of young men who will dedicate their lives, under God, to the laborious acquisition of such knowledge as shall enable them to investigate the field of Biblical criticism. This need is more than desperate in conservative circles, where there has been a noticeable tendency to neglect this necessary field of study. There are far more books today written from the liberal standpoint than from the conservative position in the realm of introductory questions about the Bible. It is hoped that this situation will be speedily corrected as a younger generation of conservative scholars takes up the torch.

2. The true critic must be able to do his own thinking. This is simply an extension of what has just been said. It does not mean that the critic will ignore the research and investigation of competent scholars in his own field. Nor will he refuse to read the literature produced by scholars of a view different from his own.

Too many scholars follow some great name in their department of Biblical studies. Such names as Barth, Brunner and Niebuhr are in some circles held in almost as high esteem as Peter, Paul and John. No name in modern criticism is more outstanding, perhaps, than Wellhausen's. Yet it is possible, even probable, especially in the light of discoveries made since his time, that Wellhausen led several generations of scholars astray with his naturalistic principles. Because his name is so great and his influence so strong, few men have been able to break away entirely from his anti-supernaturalism.

There is (yes, it is true!) such a thing as traditionalism among scholars who reject the traditional view of the Bible.

Their viewpoint becomes fixed and few dare to differ from it. To do so — at least in any significant detail — would perhaps declassify them as scholars, for only those who follow the Graf-Wellhausen-Driver-Pfeiffer line belong to the party. Scholarship is tolerated and called scholarship as long as it agrees with the basic principles of the founders (just mentioned) of modern criticism. But that man, regardless of his erudition, who holds to the Mosaic authorship of the Pentateuch no longer qualifies himself as an independent thinker, for he has adopted the traditional view of the Church! Scholars, of course, can be terribly inconsistent. A man is not a scholar because he follows the traditional view of the Church regarding the authorship of the Pentateuch (although his view is not here based on tradition alone), but he is a scholar if he follows the "traditional" view propounded by Wellhausen (against many facts that militate against his position) regarding the non-Mosaic authorship of the Pentateuch!

3. A true scholar must have an adequate comprehension of what constitutes real evidence. There are laws of evidence that any lawyer would recognize. Such laws would be recognized instinctively by a jury of common men. Real, objective evidence must be clearly distinguished from what is circumstantial or conjectural. And too much emphasis cannot be put on the thesis that the critic does not manufacture his evidence. Evidence belongs to the realm of facts as they have actually happened.

When an ancient document is examined with reference to its age and authorship, we cannot conjecture, apart from concrete facts, when it was written or who wrote it. The facts are in the document itself or in contemporary documents that have been transmitted to us. Any one who has a fair knowledge of evidence can make a decision with reference to the facts.

Too much of modern criticism has built elaborate theories regarding the Bible on the scantiest kind of "evidence." Will one hold today that the intricate hypotheses concerning Christ and the Gospels associated with the rationalism of Paulus, or the development-system of Baur, or the na-

turalism of Schleiermacher, or the mythicism of Strauss had
any substantial foundation or justification on the basis of
objective facts? (Compare F. W. Farrar, *The Witness of
History to Christ* [1871], pp. 55ff.)

4. A true critic must guard against unproved assumptions.
The history of modern criticism is characterized by one
wrecked hypothesis after another. When one critic or theory
is discarded as untrue, another critic arises with a more
devastating theory. One of the principal contributions made
by Dr. Robert Dick Wilson was his insistence that unproved
assumptions should be subjected to the closest kind of
scrutiny and, if found wanting, should be rejected. If one
will examine his two-volume work on Daniel, he will see
how often Dr. Wilson first quotes from some modern critic
at length, then states as propositions the critic's assumptions, and finally subjects each assumption to the careful
examination of the relevant facts.

Quite often assumptions are made when the reader is
not aware of such. Whenever a critic uses such language
as "maybe," "perhaps," "let us assume," "it may be supposed," "it is quite unthinkable," or the like, it may be supposed that he is defending a weak case and, in place of
evidence, is laying before his reader a barrage of unproved
suppositions.

One of the most characteristic assumptions found in modern books about the Bible is that "all scholars" agree on a
certain conclusion. That is, of course, pure fiction invented
to confuse the reader as to what is scholarship. "All scholars"
do, of course, agree that Daniel was not written by the
historic Daniel if you exclude such men as R. D. Wilson,
E. J. Young, or Charles Boutflower. But these men are as
well qualified from the standpoint of scholarship as any on
the other side.

Assumptions change from generation to generation just
as styles in clothing change. About one hundred years ago
it was quite the thing in some quarters to assume that Moses
could not have written the Pentateuch because writing was
not known at such an early time. That assumption would

I

be intolerable today. Or it was assumed in the same quarters that the patriarchs were mythical or fictional characters invented by a later age and reflected back to an earlier period. Such an assumption could not be entertained today except by risking one's scholarship or knowledge of modern archaeology.

Assumptions can, of course, be repeated so often and by so many that even they are counted as facts. But no matter how often an assumption is repeated or how many acclaim it as true, it still must be called an assumption if that is really what it is. There is no assumption more often taken for granted in modern criticism than the theory of evolution. The theologian of the modern type is more than likely to accept this scientific theory as true and apply it to the development of Israel's religion. Compare, for example, H. E. Fosdick, *A Guide to Understanding the Bible* (1938).

5. A true critic must use all the facts that are available. This statement means that he is not to neglect or ignore any aspect of his problem that might be essential to its solution. Sometimes critics are guilty of using certain factors that produce a very plausible argument for a theory. However, the conclusion is invalidated because one bit of evidence is ignored or slighted.

A striking case is found in the modern criticism of the Pentateuch. The literary argument for composite authorship of this portion of the Bible has been magnified to such an extent that other arguments have been neglected or minimized. Psychological, historical, archaeological, and theological aspects of this problem have been toned down in the interest of divisive authorship. However, these neglected aspects are being given greater weight today.

If there is a solution to a problem that is consistent with the historical trustworthiness of Scriptures, it must not be rejected simply because it helps us to understand the Bible. We may not have the final solution today regarding the census described by Luke as taking place when Quirinius was governor of Syria, but we know enough of Luke's proven historical accuracy elsewhere to say that it is hardly likely that he made a mistake on this point. It is very probable that Quirinius may have been governor twice — a possibility that was not taken into account in the earlier criticism. Consult H. S. Gehman (ed.), *The Westminster Dictionary of the Bible* (1944), pp. 505f.

6. A true critic must be willing to follow the truth wheresoever it leads him. No critic worth his name, whether conservative or liberal, is in his work just to support a pet theory. He must be willing to pursue the facts wherever they lead him. His aim is to know the truth. Nothing else will satisfy his soul.

The critic, therefore, must have a high regard for what is true in contrast to what is untrue. If his study shows him that he must give up some conception of the Bible which he has been taught by his teachers or read in some book, then, if the view taught him does not agree with facts, he must relinquish it in the interest of truth. He may no longer be called a scholar by his associates, but what is that when' one knows he has followed the truth.

The true critic will never cover up some bit of information that might affect a cherished view. If he has held a view that is now proved to be erroneous, he must be willing to acknowledge his error and re-examine his premises or presuppositions that led him into the error. At one time it was quite the common thing in some critical circles to depreciate the references in the Bible to the Hittites. Such a low estimate of the Bible's historical value on this subject is impossible today in the light of modern discoveries that have unveiled a great Hittite Empire that the modern critic knew practically nothing about until the archaeologist began his work.

7. A true critic must have a willingness to wait for further light before he imputes untruthfulness to an ancient document. Those who have obeyed this principle have had far less to retract than those who disobeyed it. It is quite likely, in view of what archaeology has done in the past one hundred years to illuminate and confirm the pages of

the Bible, that practically all of the remaining historical problems may soon be solved.

There was a time when the historical character of the fourteenth chapter of Genesis was called in question by negative critics. Even today some die-hard liberals doubt the historical accuracy of the account. But no one can dogmatically assert that that chapter is out of accord with the known facts that have been discovered (cf. W. T. Pilter, *The Pentateuch: A Historical Record* [1928]). At one time distinguished critics doubted the very existence of Sargon, who is mentioned only once in the Bible (Isa. 20:1) but not in any other source coming down to us from ancient times. Since 1843, when the French excavated the ancient palace of Sargon, the critical doubt about Sargon has evaporated like mist before sunshine. With these lessons before us, all critics should think more than twice before they impatiently impute error to Biblical documents.

8. Every critic must have a spiritual sympathy with the subject he is investigating. We must enter understandingly into the situations of ancient times. To write a true history of a people, we are being told today, one must understand the people about whom he is writing. The customs, habits, characteristics must be appreciated. Certain facts of history are automatically hidden to the man who writes from a preconceived viewpoint of what a person ought to have said or done in a given situation.

The modern critic is unable to understand Paul unless he shares the faith that dominated Paul's life. This is why so many critics go astray in their understanding of the Bible. They cannot understand its supernaturalism simply because their "faith" does not include supernaturalism. And by this exclusion they are disqualified as true critics. If an actor is to make his part real and vital in a play, he must enter sympathetically into the life of the person he represents in the play. If a singer is to sing "I know that my Redeemer liveth," the words must come from the heart before they come from the lips.

B. *Canons of Criticism Concerning a Document*

In addition to the critic himself, whom we have just discussed, there are certain standards which must govern his research. We are, of course, dealing primarily with Biblical subjects in the realm of literary investigation. The following principles, we believe, will apply here.

1. Tradition must be accepted as valid testimony unless it can be proved that the tradition is untrue to facts. Often in critical matters tradition enters as one of the contributing factors in the final decision. Some critics, especially those of the liberal school, attach little or no value to a tradition respecting a book's authorship or date. Others, however, consider traditions in such matters as one among several factors. Most conservatives belong here, but no conservative would make a final judgment in critical matters on the basis of tradition alone. The conservative is not — contrary to the idea held by some — a "mere traditionalist."

The application of this principle is manifold. For instance, a tradition exists that the men of the Great Synagogue (120 members presided over by Ezra) edited and fixed the canon of the Old Testament. Some accept this tradition as probably right; others reject it as absolutely untrue. Neither conservative nor liberal feels justified in using this uncertain tradition as if it settled once and for all the date when the canon was fixed. That the Old Testament existed in its threefold form (Law, Prophets, Writings) rests upon solid evidence (Philo, the New Testament, Josephus); but that the canon was fixed by the men of the Great Synagogue is a matter of uncertain tradition. However, since most conservatives believe that the Old Testament canon was completed in the early post-exilic period, this tradition is accepted as probably right since it seems to be confirmed by other circumstances (cf. J. H. Raven, *Old Testament Introduction* [1910], pp. 32f).

There is a tradition concerning Peter's residence at Rome and his being the first bishop of the church there. However, since the New Testament does not corroborate such an idea but rather offers some insuperable problems (the fact, for instance, that Paul makes no reference to Peter in his epistle to the church at Rome), it is extremely hazardous to build the idea of the 'papacy upon such an insecure tradition. Tradition undoubtedly has its place in critical matters, but its trustworthiness must be supported in every case by unimpeachable evidence.

2. The argument from silence has a valid place in critical investigations. This argument is resorted to by both liberals and conservatives, as the occasion may demand, to support some position. It has its place if it is used wisely and properly; but it also has some serious defects. We give here some of the ways in which it affects critical studies.

a) This argument has no weight at all if it can be shown that a certain thing existed even though it is passed over in silence by those who undoubtedly knew about it. To illustrate this, we mention the fact that the whole Christ-myth conception of modern times appeals to the silence about Christ among contemporary, pagan writers. But this fact obviously has an explanation. Those writers undoubtedly looked upon the movement introduced by Christ as too contemptuous to justify their attention. In the second century, when Christianity assumed a significant size, it is mentioned by pagan writers. One can cite the fact that the whole Rabbinic literature does not contain one reference to John the Baptist, but Josephus, a contemporary, considered him important enough to mention him (cf. Jakob Jocz, *The Jewish People and Jesus Christ* [1949], p. 58). The New Testament does not mention anywhere as an accomplished event the destruction of Jerusalem (A.D. 70), although parts of the New Testament were undoubtedly written after that event.

b) The argument from silence has significance when it can be shown that a writer should have mentioned a certain thing. It is incredible, for example, that Peter was founder and first bishop of the church at Rome in the light of the fact that Paul makes no allusions to Peter in his letter to the church there. It is unthinkable that Paul would have desired to impart to the Christians some spiritual gift to establish them if Peter had been there for years already (cf. Rom. 1:11). And it is still more unbelievable that Paul, in view of his clear-cut policy expressed in Romans 15:20, would have dared to build on Peter's foundation — if Peter had been the founder of the Roman church!

c) Facts cannot be twisted to give the argument from silence more plausibility. Modern critics, for example, have used the argument from silence to prove their theory that the Priestly Code of the Pentateuch did not exist prior to the Babylonian Exile. But this theory can be maintained only by calling the few references to the priestly legislation "interpolations" of a later hand. This is a simple device but it is not valid as objective criticism. If one can delete from a document what is contrary to one's theory, then Bible history can be made to read in as many different ways as there are critics with a theory. Negative critics use the fact that Jesus ben Sira does not mention Daniel among his worthies in Ecclesiasticus as an evidence that the Book of Daniel was written after Ben Sira's time. But this is by no means a conclusive argument (cf. R. D. Wilson, *Studies in the Book of Daniel* [1938], pp. 76ff).

d) The argument from silence can rarely, if ever, be used as the only or conclusive argument in literary studies. It has its value, but there should be confirmatory lines of evidence in addition to it. If this argument were conclusive in itself, it could be proved that the Israelites were never in Egypt as slaves because the monumental evidence is practically nil on this subject. Many a history has been written that leaves out a particular subject because it was not in the writer's plan or because he was prejudiced against it. There is a history of the American people that practically ignores the Christian Church. We all know, of course, that the Church has played an important part in the history of the United States.

3. Literary style has a bearing on critical questions. Quite often the stylistic argument is appealed to by critics to prove their point with reference to a book's authorship. No

group of scholars has used this argument more than those who belong to the liberal school. We cite here some typical illustrations. One of the basic arguments appealed to for the composite authorship of the Hexateuch is found in the supposed difference between the J-document and the E-document, as well as between D and P. Style enters into the argument concerning the unity of Isaiah. In the New Testament the un-Pauline authorship of Hebrews and (especially) the Pastoral Epistles is based supposedly on style. The writer of the Fourth Gospel is taken to be different from the person who wrote Revelation, on the basis of style. On this subject we may make the following generalizations.

a) All scholars admit that there are stylistic differences in the Bible. Not even conservatives believe that the Holy Spirit pre-empted the individual writers of their stylistic differences. Although John expresses purpose frequently, he never employs a syntactical method that is common with Paul. This does not mean, of course, that John did not know the idiom that Paul uses so frequently. It simply means that John's mental characteristics were different from Paul's and the Holy Spirit employed both idioms. One cannot possibly read John's writings and Luke's without seeing stylistic differences of syntax and vocabulary.

b) The use of the stylistic argument in matters of literary criticism is subject to definite limitations and qualifications, among which we mention the following:

(1) It is often difficult to determine the extent of a man's style. No man uses all his vocabulary in any one document and undoubtedly has in reserve many words that could be used if the subject demanded their use. We know a man's style and vocabulary only by the documents which have come down to us. If we could find the many letters that Paul sent to his parents as a university student, our estimate of the extent and variety of Paul's style and vocabulary would undoubtedly be considerably enlarged.

(2) It follows that a man's vocabulary and style may differ according to the subject about which he is writing

and the persons to whom he is writing. It is known, of course, how negative critics object to the Pauline authorship of the Pastoral Epistles on the basis of stylistic and vocabulary differences between these three letters and the rest of Paul's writings. In the Pastorals Paul uses a number of words which are not found elsewhere in his writings. Elaborate tables are constructed to prove these differences. Thus a very plausible argument is built on the basis of vocabulary and style. Conservatives do not deny these differences, but maintain that they are consistent with Pauline authorship if we take into account three factors: (a) Paul is writing to young ministers (Timothy and Titus) who ought to be better educated than the average member of a church. (b) Paul is writing about ecclesiastical organization and as such his vocabulary ought to include other words than those formerly used. (c) The larger number of words in the Pastorals are in line with Paul's vocabulary elsewhere and the syntactical expressions are consistent with Paul's idiom in earlier letters. Giving due weight to these three factors makes it almost impossible to build a conclusive argument against the Pauline authorship of the Pastorals on the basis of style.

(3) In the consideration of the argument from style all the facts that enter into this problem should be taken into account. Liberal critics have, for example, called attention to the stylistic difference between the first part of Isaiah (1-39) and the second part (40-66) and, on the basis of this difference, they have taught that the book is of dual or triple authorship. On the other hand, conservatives have emphasized the undoubted similarity of style running throughout the book. The unique title "The Holy One of Israel" runs throughout Isaiah, being found 14 times in the earlier part (1-39) and 16 times in the latter part (40-66). It is even more significant when we remember that this title is not used elsewhere. It would seem as if it were Isaiah's "trade-mark" showing unity of authorship. Even liberal critics who accept the dual-authorship theory admit that the whole book breathes the spirit of Isaiah,

(4) We must recognize that a writer's style may change during his span of life. Deuteronomy, for instance, is separated from the previous Mosaic legislation by a period of about forty years. This difference in time could at least be one factor in the difference in style. Isaiah's public ministry covered a period of about forty years, during which time his style could have changed some.

(5) Style in itself is never an absolute proof of authorship, especially if other factors tell a different story. Let us admit that there are, for example, certain stylistic differences in Isaiah; but, on the other hand, there are facts that militate against dual or triple authorship. One such fact is found in the quotations from Isaiah found in the New Testament. These quotations are taken from all parts of the book and are uniformly attributed to Isaiah. Evidently our Lord and His apostles had no trouble, from style or otherwise, in attributing the whole book to Isaiah. Let us admit that there are certain stylistic differences between the Pastorals and Paul's earlier writings; on the other hand, there are some potent arguments for Pauline authorship. In fact, up until the nineteenth century there was never a question about Paul's authorship of these epistles. If the stylistic argument is valid here, why did those who lived nearest the Apostle Paul never discover that the Pastorals were (as claimed by some moderns) second-century forgeries?

(6) The weakness of the argument from style is illustrated by the fact that modern scholars are quite incapable of detecting different writers in documents that are known to be composite. Some books in modern times have gone through several editions with changes made in each edition (for example, *The New Standard Bible Dictionary*), and yet it is quite impossible (even when the names of the several writers are appended to an article) for a modern critic to separate one author from another. If this is impossible in a language that is our mother-tongue, it approaches asininity when we try to differentiate a J-writer from an E-writer in the Book of Genesis

4. A book almost invariably betrays the time of its authorship. It so happens that everything bears the marks of the age in which it came into existence. Pottery and manuscripts, automobiles and clothing, weapons of war and bathtubs — all these change from generation to generation and bear the indelible impress of the age that gave them birth. The critic is like a detective as he investigates a document for signs, often microscopic, that put it in its right place in history. Some of these signs are the following:

a) References to known events. For instance, the reference to the destruction of No-amon (or Thebes) in Nahum 3:8 puts the prophecy of Nahum not earlier than 664-3 B.C. Since Nahum predicts the downfall of Nineveh (which took place in 612 B.C.), his prophecy must come between these two dates. Haggai gives the date for each of his four messages (1:1; 2:1, 10, 20), placing them in the reign of Darius (who reigned from 521-486 B.C.). Therefore, Haggai's discourses are to be placed in 520 B.C.

b) References to a document by external sources. This simply means that we accept as valid what contemporaries say about a book's origin. They were surely in a better situation than we are today to know who an author was and when he lived and what he wrote. External evidence is a very valuable asset, and the more we have of it the more certain we are usually regarding its testimony. A good illustration of the use of external evidence is found in the criticism of the Gospel of John. As early as A.D. 150 this Gospel was used by heretics (Marcion) and the faithful (Irenaeus). Thus its existence can be traced to a very early date by external references to it (cf. for many details, H. P. V. Nunn, *The Authorship of the Fourth Gospel* [1952]).

c) Seemingly insignificant things in a document often betray its date. Only a contemporary that knows the little niceties of speech and customs can put a book in its right context in history. Let us use a modern illustration. In the nineteenth century schools for the training of women were called "female." So far as we know, such a description is not used today. We have "women's colleges," but not "female colleges." A man writing a thousand years from now could hardly know this subtle difference between the nineteenth and twentieth century; but we know it very well today. Let us apply our illustration to the Bible. In the Pentateuch no king of Egypt is called by his name. He is rather referred to as "Pharaoh" or "the king of Egypt." However, in the later, historical books of the Old Testament we have the kings of Egypt called by their names — Shishak (I Kings 11:40; 14:25; II Chron. 12:2, 5, 7, 9); So (II Kings 17:4); Pharaoh-necho (II Kings 23:29, 33-35). A foreigner living in the time of Abraham or Moses (when Egypt was a great nation) would have referred to the head of Egypt as "the king of Egypt" or (more deferentially) "Pharaoh"; but a person living in the time of Isaiah (when Egypt was no longer a great power) could call the king of Egypt by his name. If, therefore, the Pentateuch had been written where liberal critics put it (J — 850; E — 750; D — 621; P — 550), these fictitious writers would have had in Genesis and Exodus the actual names of the kings of Egypt with whom Abraham, Joseph, and Moses came in contact. But the fact that the Pentateuch conforms to the customs of the time of its origin is a clear proof that it was not written five hundred or more years later when no one would have known the subtle differences which had long since passed out of man's usage (cf. W. T. Pilter, *The Pentateuch: A Historical Record* [1928], pp. 377-389).

5. The authorship of a document is determined by a number of factors of an internal and external nature. The following remarks will give us the gist of what must be taken into account here.

a) We must give due weight to statements in a book indicating its authorship. Surely the statements in Revelation (1:4, 9f; 22:8) indicate that the Apostle John was the author. This same principle applies in many cases in the Old and New Testaments. For example, the Book of Deuteronomy would surely appear to be the work of Moses from the references in the book itself (31:9-12, 24).

b) The witness of contemporaries, or those who shortly followed, must be accounted very strong evidence. In the early days of Christianity there was a consistent testimony (Justin, Irenaeus, Hippolytus, Tertullian, Origen) that the Apostle John was the author of Revelation. With the internal evidence just referred to, this ought to give a conclusive argument for the Johannine authorship. In the Old Testament the Law is attributed to Moses from the time of Joshua (1:8) down to the close of the canon (Mal. 4:4).

c) Unified authorship is proved by various internal and external facts. We have already dealt with these in our discussion concerning style. Style, as we saw, is not always a reliable test regarding authorship. In the Book of Isaiah style is appealed to, as we have shown before, to prove diversity of authorship; but style can also be used as an evidence of unity of authorship. In addition, we have the testimony of the New Testament, which cites many parts of Isaiah as coming from the prophet. To the conservative scholar this is sufficient evidence for believing in the unity of Isaiah. In the New Testament, external evidence is strong for the Johannine authorship of the Gospel of John and the Revelation. However, some liberal scholars object on the grounds that the style of Revelation is different from the style of the Fourth Gospel. On the other hand, conservatives appeal to the fact that there are strong stylistic affinities between the two works. If the difference in nature of the two works is taken into account, the stylistic differences practically explain themselves away.

d) Pseudepigraphy does not properly belong to canonical books. This appears as a bald statement of fact rather than as a principle of research. Pseudepigraphy enters into Biblical criticism in two ways. On the one hand, it is claimed by the liberal school that certain books of the Bible are now discovered, by literary investigation, to be pseudepigraphical. Two of the chief works placed in this category are Deuteronomy and Daniel — both of which are called "pious frauds." The Pastoral Epistles are also put in this class by liberals. Of course, conservatives object vehemently to this classification and advance valid reasons against such a view. The other way by which pseudepigraphy enters into Biblical criticism is found in the contrast made between the Biblical literature on the one hand and the known pseudepigraphical literature that flourished in the early days of Christianity. We have dealt with this subject at length in the first chapter and need not repeat what was said there.

CHAPTER FIVE

THE HIGHER CRITICAL POSITION STATED AND REFUTED

There is today a well-defined view of the Bible that can be called the liberal, higher-critical position. This view, which is opposite to almost everything in the conservative viewpoint, is held almost altogether by those who have adopted a modern, naturalistic approach to divine revelation. It includes in its rank scholars of all shades of unbelief. One thing, however, is held in common by all proponents of this school: the rejection of the Bible as the infallibly inspired Word of God.

I. PRESENTATION AND REFUTATION OF THE MODERN VIEW

It will be our purpose in the present chapter to state carefully and refute adequately the main principles that dominate and characterize the modern approach to the Bible. These principles will be found in profusion in books written by exponents of the modern, rationalistic view. In some cases we shall cite such references, but we do not consider it necessary to document every statement. The following, then, are among some of the most outstanding characteristics of the modern critical approach to the Bible.

A. *The Modern View Questions Bible's Historicity*

In order that we may understand the critical position we shall state the main points held by such scholars and shall then show how, on conservative grounds, such points are invalid.

1. The modern view. So extensive and radical is the critical reconstruction of Biblical history that it is impossible to state all the details that enter into it. It will be sufficient, however, to show where this reconstruction leads one.

a) Genesis (1 to 11) is described as mythological and legendary. In these early chapters we are not to find true history. The accounts of the creation, the fall, the first civilization, etc., are not to be taken as actual historical events. They are simply traditions handed down and borrowed from other nations. They are myths which contain a true lesson for us, and they are superior to the myths of the Greeks and other pagan nations. One need only read A. Richardson's *A Preface to Bible Study* (1944) to see that this description represents the modern attitude toward these early chapters of Genesis.

b) Later books of the Bible contain historical inaccuracies. Such books as Daniel and Esther are especially cited as excellent examples of the historical inaccuracies of the Bible. But the inaccuracies are by no means limited to these books — nor should we leave out the books of the New Testament.

c) Historical mistakes nullify the idea of an infallible book. We are confidently informed by the modern view that the old doctrine of verbal inerrancy must now be given up. Sir Frederick Kenyon (*The Bible and Archaeology* [1940], p. 26) tells us such a concept cannot stand the slightest examination.

d) Christianity does not rest on the historical credibility of the facts recorded in the Bible. Spiritual facts, we are told, belong to a realm above history. To prove a miracle like the virgin birth of Christ is irrelevant. The essence of Christianity survives historical investigation because the essence is not bound to this or that objective fact of history. So there is no absolute connection between the objective facts of history and the subjective faith of the believer in eternal realities. (See H. F. Rall, *Christianity* [1940], pp. 300-312.)

2. The refutation of the modern view. In a later chapter we shall show the confirmatory proof of the Bible's historical accuracy which is now available from archaeology. We shall, therefore, not present here an elaborate refutation of the charges hurled against the Bible by modern critics. Let the following remarks suffice for the present.

a) Much of the Bible is conceded to be true history, even by the most extreme of radical scholars. The older skepticism that had its day before the rise of modern archaeology is now largely abandoned by more sober critics and it is increasingly felt that there is a far greater residuum of real history, even in the earlier parts of Scripture, than was thought possible in the heyday of Graf-Wellhausenism. Such archaeologists as Albright, though by no means conservative, are calling for a retreat from the earlier skepticism regarding the Bible's historical trustworthiness.

b) One after another of the "mistakes" of the Bible in historical matters has been cleared up by subsequent study and investigation. In some cases we probably do not have at present sufficient knowledge to explain satisfactorily all the historical problems in the Bible. We must still, for example, wait for further light on the question regarding the identity of "Darius the Mede" (Dan. 5:31; 6:1; 9:1). We can affirm that there is today hardly a single historical problem in the New Testament that has not been solved by archaeology or further study. See A. T. Robertson, *Luke the Historian in the Light of Research* (1920).

c) The historical character of Biblical revelation is such a fundamental element that it cannot be sacrificed, except at the loss of all that is necessary to our faith as Christians. Biblical revelation is essentially a historical revelation; it cannot survive in the atmosphere of myth and legend. In fact, it is yet to be proved that the Bible contains either of these or anything like them. No one can demonstrate objectively that either Ruth or Esther or Jonah belong to the realm of fiction, romance or allegory. Our faith is intertwined with the facts of history. Destroy the facts and you ultimately destroy the faith which the facts engendered. Christianity is not a nebulous cloud that has no body or substance or is disconnected with the facts of history.

d) The Bible is so unified in its construction that, if the facts in one part or area are questioned or denied, another part likewise is endangered. One cannot, for example, undermine the account of the fall of our first parents in Gen-

K

esis 3 without at the same time undermining the doctrine
of sin as outlined by Paul in Romans 5 and elsewhere. If
Adam was only a myth, it is hard to understand how Christ
can be considered real (Rom. 5:14, 15; I Cor. 15:45).

B. *The Modern View Undermines the Bible's Uniqueness*

One of the most important factors found in the modern
view of the Bible is that the Bible is not unique as was
once supposed and taught. We shall show how the critics
de-emphasize the uniqueness of the Bible and then shall
present the conservative refutation.

1. The modern view. If one reads very much in critical
literature about the Bible he will be surprised, if he really
believes the Bible as the Word of God, at the manner of
treatment given to the Bible by modern scholarship. The
Bible is treated, in fact, worse than other literature. One
would suppose that the only interest one should have in the
Bible is that which finds its ultimate expression in denials
and negations. Here, then, are some of the ways the Bible's
uniqueness is impaired by the modern school.

a) The first eleven chapters of Genesis are traditions that
have come into Hebrew literature from other sources. In
these chapters are found the traditions about the world's
beginning, written from the crude standpoint of antiquity,
which came to Israel when some Jewish scholars during
the Babylonian Captivity borrowed them from Babylonian
sources.

b) The whole sacrificial system is said to have been borrowed from either the Egyptians or the Babylonians. Some
critics prefer one source; others prefer the other.

c) Furthermore, it has been contended by the modern
view that Israel borrowed her concept of monotheism from
the heretic Egyptian king, Ikhnaton (Amenhotep IV).

d) It is common practice among those of the liberal viewpoint to affirm that Israel got her ideas about Satan, the
resurrection and the judgment, and the Messiah from the
Zoroastrian religion during the time of her Babylonian Captivity. This is taught as absolute truth in textbooks on
history (e.g., J. H. Breasted, *Ancient Times* [1935], p. 259)

and comparative religions (e.g., R. E. Hume, *The World's Living* [1946], p. 191).

e) In the New Testament some liberal scholars have advocated that the concept of the virgin birth was borrowed from paganism and others have tried to find in the mystery-religions the sources of Paul's theology.

2. The refutation of the modern view. Without attempting here a complete refutation of each point enumerated under the critical heading above, we limit ourselves to certain matters that prove unquestionably the Bible's superiority.

a) We make the categorical statement that, in no single case, can it be proved that the Bible has borrowed any of its basic or fundamental truths from pagan nations. As proof for this statement one could cite the massive learning and argument found in Bishop Stillingfleet's *Origines Sacrae* (1836), or the brilliant essay on "The Wisdom of the Ancients Borrowed from Divine Revelation" found in volume 5 of Daniel Waterland's *Works* (1843). All who belong to the modern school should be required to read these old works. Briefly put, the argument runs something like this.

(1) The pagans themselves confess that their best ideas were derived from Moses and the prophets. This is extremely likely because of the fact that the best of the pagans (Plato, Aristotle, etc.) did not arise until Old Testament revelation had come to a close. Even if we should accept the critical dating of Old Testament books (which we surely do not), we would still have the major part of the Old Testament books prior to the rise of Greek literature. Another fact should be noted. It is that from the time of Jeremiah onward there was a large Jewish colony in Alexandria, which city was second to Athens in pagan philosophy and second to Jerusalem in Jewish learning. It was in this city that the Old Testament was translated into Greek and this translation undoubtedly contributed to the spread of Jewish ideas among the pagans. Everything, therefore, is in favor of the supposition that the Greeks borrowed from the Jews.

(2) Converted pagans, who were formerly philosophers,

confessed to the fact that their basic ideas were not original but borrowed. Such men used this knowledge to show the uniqueness of the Biblical revelation. The only answer the pagans could give was that which made the Bible a patchwork of errors. Celsus and Porphyry are notorious examples of this hostile attitude among the pagans. But the philosophy of these ancient pagans has been adopted as true in much of modern criticism.

(3) It can be shown that the pagan world borrowed and corrupted the thoughts and ideas found in the Bible. Instead of the Jews being the world's arch-borrowers (as the modern view would have it), it turns out that the pagans are the ones who did the borrowing. The account of creation, for example, was not borrowed from the Babylonians and then purified of its polytheism by some Jewish scribes; it is rather the case that the pagans borrowed and corrupted with their polytheism (cf. Rom. 1:18-23) the basic concepts of Biblical revelation.

b) The arguments advanced on the critical side for the Bible's borrowing will not in any case hold up when subjected to careful scrutiny. Let us note here some of the cases mentioned above and see how weak the "evidence" actually is.

(1) Israel's monotheism. It has been claimed, as we saw above, that Israel's monotheism came from the Egyptian king, Amenhotep IV. This view is usually associated with the name of Prof. J. H. Breasted and his *The Dawn of Conscience*. Regarding the supposed originality of Ikhnaton's (Amenhotep IV's) "monotheism," let us observe the following facts. (a) This Egyptian king was essentially a sunworshiper and his heliolatry, though extravagant, was not particularly different from all such worship of the sun in the ancient world. (b) The titles he applied to his god were also applied to other gods and to men. (c) The attempt to find a parallel between his Hymn to the Sun and the one hundred fourth Psalm is far-fetched and inconclusive. A few scattering similarities between the two documents cannot possibly justify the conclusion that the Psalm-

writer borrowed from Ikhnaton's Hymn. (d) There is not the slightest kind of proof that Israel borrowed her monotheistic belief from the Egyptian. As far as we know, Israel was the custodian and guardian of monotheism from the beginning. See Solomon Goldman, *The Book of Books: An Introduction* (1948), pp. 58-103.

(2) Israel's sacrificial system. It has been held by some modern scholars that Israel derived her sacrificial system from either the Egyptians or the Babylonians. On this we make the following remarks by way of refutation. (a) Dr. M. G. Kyle, after a thorough study and investigation of the Egyptian religion, comes to the conclusive opinion that it differed from Israel's religion on four basic points (substitution, redemption by blood, dedication and fellowship). There could be no possible derivation. Thus Israel is not indebted to Egypt for her religion. See Dr. Kyle's *Moses and the Monuments* (1920). (b) Dr. W. Lansdell Wardle, in his *Israel and Babylon* (1925), shows that Israel's religion is not derived from the Babylonians. It cannot be shown, he asserts, that monotheism, the creation accounts, her basic religious ideas or any other essential feature of Israel's religion had its birth in Babylonia. Thus it cannot be proved that the chosen people got their sacrificial system or other religious truths from either the Egyptians or the Babylonians.

(3) Israel's ideas about Satan, angels and the resurrection. It is almost universally accepted among negative critics that Israel got her ideas about Satan, angels and the future life from the Zoroastrians during her sojourn in Babylonia. It is said, for example, that before Israel went into captivity in Babylonia, there is no record that such ideas prevailed among the Jews. But while the Jews were in captivity they borrowed these concepts from the Zoroastrian religion and incorporated them in the books (such as Chronicles and Daniel) written after the Babylonian Captivity. This seems plausible and persuasive on the surface but cannot, as the following will show, bear up under careful scrutiny.

(a) There is absolutely no evidence, either internally or externally, that Israel borrowed these concepts from the

Zoroastrians. Let us look at several facts. On the one hand, it is uncertain as to what the exact date of Zoroaster's life was. Probably 590 B.C. is near the date of his birth. That is shortly after the deportations to Babylonia had begun. But, on the other hand, let us note here the fact that the Northern Kingdom (Israel) had been conquered and deported to Assyria as far back as 722 B.C. We are definitely told that the Jews of the ten tribes were settled in the cities of the Medes (cf. II Kings 17:6). These Jews, though belonging to the apostate Northern Kingdom, had been instructed in the true religion by such prophets as Amos, Hosea, and Micah. It is highly improbable that these Jews never said anything about their faith or beliefs in the land of their captivity. And let us remember that these Jews had been among the Medes (the country of Zoroaster's birth) more than a century before the most probable date assigned to Zoroaster. Thus Israel's faith had had a century of contact with the Medes before Zoroaster arose among them. It appears far more likely, therefore, that Israel contributed to Zoroaster's faith than the reverse. Critics are prone to cover up the line of evidence that points to the priority of Israel's faith among the Medes before Zoroaster arose on the scene.

(b) It cannot be proved, except by the most arbitrary re-dating of Old Testament books, that Israel did not possess such concepts as Satan, angels, the resurrection and judgment until the Jews contacted the followers of Zoroaster. Such ideas were the common possession of ancient peoples long before the time of Zoroaster and are found in their pure form in the literature of the Hebrews prior to the Babylonian Captivity, as Dr. R. D. Wilson shows in his *Studies in the Book of Daniel* (Second series; 1938), chapter 5.

(4) Paul's borrowing from the mystery-religions. It has been claimed by some critics in modern times that Paul borrowed the main concepts of his religion from the pagan mystery-religions. There are several powerful facts that militate against this theory, such as:

(*a*) The time-element completely destroys this theory. It can be shown, from a chronological standpoint, that Paul's faith and theology antedate the mystery-religions. If there was borrowing, it is far more probable that the mystery-religions borrowed from Paul (as they actually did).

(*b*) More and more scholars are realizing that the basic concepts of Paul's religion go back to the Old Testament, rather than to Judaism or the mystery-religions. The great theological words of Paul's epistles find their original home in the Old Testament. Without that part of God's revelation it is practically impossible to understand Paul's teaching.

(*c*) Moreover, there were radical differences between the mystery-religions and the religion of the New Testament. Let us note these: First, Christianity is not properly a mystery-religion. It is indeed true that it has its mysteries, but these mysteries rather refer to secret things that God has now revealed in the Gospel. Christianity is not esoteric like a Masonic organization. Second, Christianity is based squarely on the historic mission and death of a real person, Jesus Christ; there is nothing of the nebulous character of an Attis, an Osiris, or a Mithras in it. Third, Christianity was an intolerant religion. When one became a Christian, he must come out of pagan worldliness (cf. II Cor. 6:14-18). But this was in no wise true of the mystery-religions. See *History of Civilization* (1947), Vol. 1, pp. 332f, by Hutton Webster and John B. Wolf. Also consult J. Gresham Machen's *Origin of Paul's Religion* (1923).

In our brief survey of this subject we have proved that the Bible does not borrow from pagan sources for its basic, theological concepts. It is true, of course, that Israel often followed the heathen practices around her and often fell into the worst kind of idolatry. But to use such apostasies from the true faith as proof that Israel borrowed her concepts of monotheism, sacrifice, and other important subjects is to completely misunderstand the subject under investigation. No one will deny that Israel borrowed paganism from paganism; but that is not our subject. What we are contending for is that Israel as represented by the true faith and the true prophets of the Lord never secured her basic concepts from the surrounding paganism. God Himself is the source of her knowledge of God and God kept His revelation pure and true through the inspired men to whom He committed this revelation. And this fact is borne out by the investigation which we have now finished.

C. The Modern View Rejects Supernatural Prophecy

If there is anything that distinguishes and characterizes the modern view of Biblical revelation it is found in its attitude toward what we call prophecy. We shall, therefore, detail and document somewhat this modern attitude. In each case we shall give a brief reply from the conservative viewpoint.

1. Prophets were preachers rather than predictors.

a) Critical view presented. It is affirmed that prediction was an insignificant part of the prophet's ministry. Some deny that it had any part at all in his message. The prophets were essentially preachers of righteousness for the people of their times, calling men from their sins and idolatry back to the worship of Jehovah. Such men as Amos and Jeremiah were interested, we are told, far more in the social evils of their age than in what was going to happen a hundred or thousand years in the future. When such men did make "predictions" they confined themselves to events near at hand that almost anyone conversant with the prevailing currents of world history (like a modern news-reporter) could foresee as about to happen. In some cases these guesses concerning the future (such as Daniel's forecast of early deliverance from Antiochus Epiphanes) did not actually come to pass. Such a view as just described may be found in H. H. Rowley, *The Rediscovery of the Old Testament* (1946), p. 256; and I. G. Matthews, *The Religious Pilgrimage of Israel* (1947), pp. 130f, 153f.

b) Conservative refutation. The following elements enter into our reply: (1) One must admit that the prophets were preachers of righteousness to their generation. One cannot understand them unless he understands their message in terms of their relationship to their times. When we have admitted this, we have admitted what is self-evident. (2)

There is, nevertheless, much in the prophets that must be understood as predictive. And this predictive part concerned things near at hand (as Amos' prediction of the Assyrian captivity; 7:9, 11, 17), and things far off in the future (as the same prophet's prediction of Messianic times; 9:11ff; cf. Acts 15:16-18). Jeremiah could tell the length of the Babylonian Captivity (25:11; 29:10) just as well as the introduction of the new covenant in Messianic times (31:31ff; cf. Heb. 8:8-12). Daniel could tell about Antiochus Epiphanes in chapters 8 and 11 just as well as about the much later advent of King Messiah in chapters 2, 7 and 9. Isaiah could tell the name of Cyrus (44:28; 45:1) just as well as the name of King Immanuel (7:14), who was to come centuries later. Micah could foretell the destruction of Jerusalem (3: 12; cf. Matt. 24:2) just as well as the lowly advent of Jesus Christ (5:2f; cf. Matt. 2:6). (3) We cannot, of course, admit that the prophets made mistakes in their predictions. We reject totally the critical insinuation that the prophet's predictions did not come to pass. Our first reason is that no such case has been proved. It is only on the premise that the critical theory about Daniel is right that a case can be made out for his mistaken notion that the kingdom of God was just about to come. We do not accept the premise upon which this theory is built. Our second reason is this: If it can be proved that the prophets were wrong in their predictions, then there is no reason why we should accept them as right in their other statements. If they were limited in their forevision, they were equally limited in their insight into spiritual truths. If we reject their prophecy, we must likewise reject them as teachers of righteousness.

2. God's words transmitted to us through fallible man.

a) Critical view presented. It is claimed that God's words have come to us through the personality of the prophet and that the divine words may have been misunderstood by the prophet. As rumor grows and is considerably modified as it goes from one person to another, so God's words have been modified somewhat as they have come to us clothed in the prophet's finite understanding of them. The prophecy failed because the human vehicle failed to comprehend its true meaning. Thus we should not blame God for the failure which was due to the fallible prophet.

b) Conservative refutation. The idea just presented is utterly detestable from the conservative viewpoint. The following observation can be made against it: (1) The critical view, if carried out logically, would lead us to absolute agnosticism in regard to anything the prophets uttered. We have no assurance that any statement, prophecy or moral truth, is accurately reported to us as it comes through the erring personality of the prophet. This critical view is of the same nature as "Form-criticism" in modern New Testament criticism. If it is true, we could have but a whisper of the voice of God in the prophets. (2) The Bible makes the distinction between a prophet's illumination and the revelation committed to him by God (cf. I Pet. 1:10-12; Dan. 9:20-23). It is perfectly true that the prophets did not always clearly understand the full import of what they were given to write; nevertheless, what they wrote under the influence of the Spirit of God came "from God" — not themselves (II Pet. 1:21). Even the disciples did not understand altogether what the Lord taught (cf. Luke 24:45; John 2:21f).

3. Prophecies called later interpolations.

a) Critical view presented. If one will consult a one-volume commentary of the Bible (e.g., the one edited by Bishop Gore) and will read the notes on Amos in that commentary, he will frequently come across such statements as "interpolation," "gloss," or "later hand." These terms are applied to passages in Amos and other Biblical writers that the modern critics consider to be insertions by a later person who incorporated them in his revised edition of the prophet's book. For example, Amos 9:11, 12 (which James applied to the call of the Gentiles; Acts 15:15-18) is said to be the work of a later, post-exilic writer or scribe. The idea back of this is the naturalistic view that the prophet could never have had such a wonderful concept at such an early date. Not only in Amos but, as we said, in the prophets generally, we will find this critical device used to get rid of the predictive nature of a prophecy.

b) Conservative refutation. Our answer to the critical method just outlined is this: (1) There is absolutely no textual evidence to support the claim that the prophetic passages are an insertion of a later hand. There are no manuscripts that do not contain the debated verses. Therefore, the method employed is as arbitrary as anything that could be conceived. If a scholar has the right to cut out a passage of Scripture on the pretext that it is a later "gloss," and yet cannot produce the proof to show that it is a gloss, then he can make the Bible read any way he wants it to read. Any objectionable material can easily be excised on the supposition that it is the addition of a later hand. (2) This whole idea is based on the naturalistic theory of development of religious thought. It is contended that certain ideas cannot arise until late. Thus a glowing description of Messianic times (as in Amos 9:11f) must necessarily come in post-exilic times. Amos, therefore, can not really be its author. If one adopts the theory of development just referred to, he will find, of course, a congenial argument for his textual excisions; but if one rejects such a theory (as we do), then there is no ground for that nefarious business. (3) Do the critics, after all, accomplish their desired aim in all the glosses they impute to Scripture? Not at all. If Amos 9:11f is placed in post-exilic times, it is still a great prophecy of Messianic times. If Joel is put in the same period, he is still a great predictor of the outpouring of the Holy Spirit at Pentecost (Joel 2:28ff; Acts 2:17ff). We do not mean here to admit that such post-exilic dates are justifiable; all that we mean is that the critics by their lowered dates cannot exclude the prophetic character of the passages under debate.

4. Prophetic books and sections dated after the event.

a) Critical view presented. Characteristic of the critical viewpoint is the constant tendency to date a prophetic book or section after the date of the predicted event. Two notorious examples of this tendency are seen in the critical dating of Daniel and what they call "Second Isaiah" (chapters 40 to 68). There are, of course, other examples of this approach to prophecy from the critical viewpoint.

b) Conservative refutation. Our reply must be necessarily brief and inadequate, but we believe that the following propositions show the insufficiency and folly of the critical position. (1) On purely objective grounds of historical research and investigation, we believe that it is impossible to defend successfully the late date (around 165 B.C.) of Daniel or the post-exilic date of Second Isaiah. It is not possible here, of course, to give all the facts that conclusively support the traditional dates of these books. That has been done by competent scholars on the conservative side in regard to Isaiah (e.g., O. T. Allis and G. L. Robinson) and in regard to Daniel (R. D. Wilson and E. J. Young). In a later chapter in the present work the Book of Daniel will be considered. (2) Without imputing motives, we believe that the late dates assigned to these books would never have been advanced had it not been for the obvious fact that they contain predictions of an unusual nature. In Isaiah (44:28; 45:1) we have a prophecy which names Cyrus by name as the one whom God has raised up to let Israel return from the Babylonian Exile. Now on naturalistic grounds such a thing is utterly unthinkable. How can a man be named over one hundred years before his birth? In fact, it would approach very near a century and a half before Cyrus came on the scene that the historic Isaiah, on conservative grounds, made his prediction. Naturalism, of course, will not allow such a thing to be possible. It follows, therefore, that the critics must invent a "Second Isaiah" who lived in the early post-exilic era and who, as a contemporary of Cyrus, knew very well the name of the Persian king who permitted the Jews to return from Babylonia. Of course, Cyrus was not the only king or person called by name before his birth. We have other cases such as Josiah (I Kings 13:2; II Kings 23:15f) and Immanuel (Isa. 7:14; Matt. 1:23). Such a thing is not at all out of place or to be unexpected, if we accept the supernatural as our premise. So, after all, it boils down to an acceptance or a rejection of the supernatural.

5. Prophecies have been miscalled prophecies.

a) Critical view presented. Here the critic informs us that we have misunderstood some statements in the Bible and called them predictions when in reality they were not predictions at all. Let us cite one of their examples by way of illustrating their meaning. We are told that the classic statement in Isaiah 7:14 (see the comments in the one-volume commentary edited by Bishop Gore) was not really a prediction of the virgin birth of Christ (as Matt. 1:23 affirms), but was a reference to some young woman of marriageable age (not necessarily a virgin) who lived in Isaiah's time. The Early Church, looking around in the Old Testament for texts supporting its high Christology, found this passage in Isaiah and naively (through a slavish reliance on the Septuagint, which wrongly used, we are dogmatically told, the Greek word for "virgin") applied it to the birth of Christ, thus making a plain historic statement into a prophecy.

b) Conservative refutation. The patience of conservative scholarship is considerably taxed as it deals with critical theories like this. We give here but a gist of what could be said in reply: (1) It is a serious thing to call in question or reject the application of prophecies made by inspired men (II Pet. 1:21). If Matthew was inspired at all, he surely knew that Isaiah 7:14 applied to the virgin birth of our Lord. In this case we would rather stand with Matthew than with the most learned scholar who rejects Matthew's application and interpretation. Scholars who pose as great teachers of Christian truth and yet reject Matthew's use of Isaiah 7:14 must stand before God's judgment-seat and give an account of their stewardship as teachers. We are most definitely sure that God will judge them severely for rejecting His Word and putting their own word in its place. See Matthew 7:21-27. (2) Furthermore, if one rejects the Scriptural application of a prophecy, he must flounder around in a mire of man's ever-changing theories. There is hardly anything more conclusively certain than that the great "servant-passages" in Isaiah 52:13 - 53:12 apply to, and was fulfilled by, our Lord Jesus Christ. Yet there are many of the critical school that tell us that the prophet had in mind, either the pious remnant of Israel in the post-captivity period, or some outstanding saint (such as Jeremiah), or he may have had in mind the Jewish nation as a whole. Any interpretation, it seems, will satisfy the critic except the one which the Bible so clearly presents as the real one. The conservative can cite three facts that confirm his interpretation. First, the New Testament cites this great prophecy in a number of places (e.g., Matt. 8:17; John 12: 38; Acts 8:32ff; Rom. 10:16; I Pet. 2:24f) and applies it uniformly to our Lord. In the second place, this has been the consistent interpretation of the Christian Church down to the rise of modern rationalism. Thirdly, no other interpretation will fit all the facts. When liberals reject the Messianic interpretation of this passage, they have nothing certain to present in its place. One scholar says the servant is Jeremiah; another says it is the pious remnant; and a third tells us it is Israel as a whole. And the end is not in sight, for another scholar will arise and tell us that someone else is in mind. But God's truth is unified and consistent; man's errors are legion, complex, and intricate.

6. Prophecy mere guesswork like the oracle of Delphi.

a) Critical view presented. At the bottom of all the attempts of negative criticism to empty the Bible of its prophetic chraracter is that view (propounded, for example, by I. G. Matthews in his *The Religious Pilgrimage of Israel* [1947], p. 225, notes 16 and 18) that the prophets were as vague, mysterious and ambiguous as the notorious oracle at Delphi. Theorizers have found a dozen different "keys" that will fit different crises in history down to the modern date-setters who find here predictions concerning the Antichrist. Such, in brief, is the critical view of a book like Daniel. Its apocalypticism is put on the same level with the apocalyptic literature that prevailed in the first two centuries before and the first two after the advent of Christ.

b) Conservative refutation. Such a view as outlined is really so naturalistic that it is hardly conceivable that any one holding to the barest kind of theism could entertain it at all. It is appropriate in the mouth of a Celsus or

Porphyry but utterly inconsistent with any kind of supernaturalism. We offer our reply as follows: (1) There is obviously a great gulf which separates Biblical apocalypticism (as in Daniel or Revelation) and its nearest rival among the non-canonical literature that flourished among the Jews and early Christian sects. In the later chapter on Daniel we specify some of the most outstanding differences. To put Daniel or Revelation on the same level with Jewish or Christian apocalypticism of the non-canonical sort is to reveal one's utter incapacity to judge between that which is real and from God and that which is an imitation and from man. (2) That Biblical prophecy was not of the same sort as heathen divination can be proved conclusively if one will honestly investigate the subject. For such an investigation we invite the liberal, in these modern days of perverted scholarship, to examine again such a work as *Hale's Analysis of Chronology* (1830), Vol. 4, pp. 109-118, where he will find a just evaluation of pagan divination. Let us not despise the scholarly works of a past century which were written to confirm the truth of God's Word!

We have covered now the most important objections offered by the liberal viewpoint against predictive prophecy. We believe that in every case there is a valid and reasonable defense against the critical objections. We offer here several general propositions against the whole critical evaluation of prophecy. In the first place, prediction is an integral part of the Word of God that is woven into every part of the Bible. To pull out this important thread would be to unravel the very foundation of God's Word. If the predictive element is taken out, the rest will not hold together. In the second place, it can be proved, beyond a shadow of a doubt, that the Biblical writers themselves and the Lord Jesus Christ in particular, firmly held to the predictive nature of the revelation committed to them. That they were mistaken in their conception here could be held only by sacrificing the authority which we attach to their writings and their teachings. If they were mistaken about prediction and fulfillment, they could just as well have been mistaken about all the other matters of revelation of which they were recognized spokesmen. In the third place, we believe that every reasonable soul will admit that there are at least some Biblical instances of absolute prediction that cannot be explained away by any kind of manipulation. As one such instance, we cite Christ's prediction regarding the fall of Jerusalem as given to us in Matthew 24; Mark 13 and Luke 19 and 21. Note these facts: Even the most liberal critics will admit that Christ uttered such a prediction. Moreover, the prediction was circumstantial enough to preclude mere guess. Christ affirmed that the fulfillment would be within the lifetime of some to whom he spoke these words. Furthermore, it should be noted that no Jew, speaking as a Jew, would have uttered such a prediction. The Jews were proud of their city and their Temple and were certainly not anticipating any destruction of either. In fact, they were expecting the soon arrival of the time when the city and the Temple would flourish as never before. That the Jews did not expect such a destruction is evidenced by the fact that they brought Christ's prediction up as a significant charge against Him at His trial. Thus it is demonstrably true that Christ uttered a prediction regarding the fall and destruction of Jerusalem and that the prediction was literally fulfilled within forty years. Though the New Testament does not record its fulfillment (although some of the New Testament was written after A.D. 70), we know from Josephus the details of its accomplishment. If there is one such prophecy in God's Word, as the one just cited, we have every reason to suppose that there are many other instances of the same. And our supposition is well confirmed by the facts of Holy Writ.

D. *The Modern View Rejects Traditional Authorship*

One will not read far in critical literature about the Bible until he realizes that the traditionally accepted authors of the books of the Bible are generally rejected. That we may see the critical view more fully on this subject we present the following reasons, with conservative answers, why they reject the traditional authors of Holy Scripture.

1. Disregard of tradition.

a) Critical view presented. It would be a mere truism for us to assert that the critical view places little value on tradition. Critics seem to delight in proving that traditions are wrong when they are used as arguments against their viewpoint. This has gone so far in their total conception of Scripture that they contemptuously refer to those who hold to traditional views regarding the authorship of certain books as mere traditionalists. One writer has the audacity to call tradition the bastard of history.

b) Conservative view. It is absolutely not true that conservatives accept the traditional authorship of Biblical books merely on the grounds of tradition alone. Conservatives are not slavish followers of traditions. They recognize that all traditions must be carefully scrutinized on the basis of historical investigation. This investigation shows that some traditions are to be totally rejected; others are to be accepted partially or with modifications; and others have every right of being accepted as true. We need not here cite instances of each class. It will suffice to note two illustrations. On the one hand, conservatives do not accept the Mosaic authorship of the Pentateuch purely on the basis of tradition. It is true that tradition does support the conservative here; but he relies more upon the internal evidence in the Pentateuch and the external witness of the rest of the Old Testament and of our Lord and the New Testament generally. When other evidences support the tradition here, he sees no reason why he should reject the tradition or why he should be called a traditionalist, when tradition is only one — and that not the most important — evidence upon which he comes to his conclusion. As another illustration, conservatives as a class accept the Pauline authorship of the Pastoral letters. It is undoubtedly true that one evidence upon which this view is based is found in the tradition, found in some early extra-Biblical writers, that Paul was released from his first imprisonment at Rome and had an extended ministry, including a visit to Spain (cf. Rom. 15:24), before he met death in a second imprisonment (cf. II Tim. 4:6ff). But this is not a mere tradition that conservatives eagerly grasp after in order to save the Pastorals for Paul. Even in Paul's last letter (cf. II Tim. 4:16ff; and compare T. Zahn, *Introduction to the New Testament* [2nd ed., rev.; 1917], vol. 2, pp. 59ff) there is sufficient evidence to make a good case for the acceptance of the tradition. This is not a mere matter of desperation, seeking to save the Pastorals at all cost; it is rather a fact that can be corroborated with a good evidence, as is accepted on many other issues, about which there is no controversy.

2. Disregard for the authority of the New Testament.

a) Critical view presented. Modern liberals as a class simply will not accept as decisive the authority of the New Testament in regard to the authorship of Old Testament books. If we tell them that Jesus Christ accepted the Mosaic authorship of the Pentateuch or the Davidic authorship of the Psalms or the Danielic authorship of Daniel, they inform us that such statements, coming from an uncritical age, cannot be accepted as binding upon modern scholarship. Not only that, but we are told that Christ did not pose as an authority in the field of historical research and that His views about such matters are not to be considered as final.

b) Conservative view. We need not again enter into a defense of our Lord and the New Testament in general against the critical attacks made on His and its authority. Suffice it to say: (1) It cannot be proved in any case that our Lord or the New Testament writers were in error in their statements about authorship. For one thing, they were surely closer to the sources of information than the modern scholar is today. For that very reason their word should carry considerable weight. (2) There is never any controversy in the New Testament between Christ and the Jewish leaders regarding the authorship of their Old Testament books. They were staunch believers in the Mosaic authorship of the Pentateuch and in the other books traditionally ascribed to their authors. Now these Jews surely knew more about their own books than the modern scholar sitting in his easy-chair. If they were wrong or if our Lord were wrong, surely there would be some indication about such disagreement in the records that have come down to us. But on this point there was absolute agreement between Jesus and the Jewish leaders.

3. Disregard of the traditional dates.

a) Critical view presented. Naturally the date and authorship of a book go together. It is impossible for a man to write a book, if the book is placed a hundred or several hundred years after his death. And this is exactly what the critical school does. Did Moses write the law? No, because the Pentateuch as we know it today did not come into existence until a number of centuries after the death of Moses. Did Isaiah write the Book of Isaiah? No, because the book as we know it did not come into its present form until a couple of centuries had rolled by. Did Daniel write his apocalypse? No, because the book was not actually composed until several centuries after the historic Daniel. Thus, in this way or that, books are taken away from their traditional authors by removing the book by a century or more, depending upon the particular case involved, from the reputed author.

b) Conservative view. If it can be proved, on the grounds of unimpeachable evidence, that we have assigned books to their wrong authors, then we will be ready to admit our error. But, having examined the reasons assigned by critics for divorcing Biblical authors from the books they are reputed to have written, we do not believe that the facts in a single case support the critical assumption. To document this statement further would require a volume in itself. Such a work is at hand in E. J. Young's *Introduction to the Old Testament* (1953).

E. *The Modern View Imputes Unworthy Motives*

One of the characteristic marks of the modern approach to the Bible is found in the way scholars impute unworthy motives to the authors of Biblical books. It is affirmed that books were piously written in the name of some ancient worthy, such as Moses or Daniel. Let us note the critical view with its reasons and our refutation.

1. Critical view presented. It is affirmed quite dogmatically that it was quite the common thing in antiquity to put forth a writing in the name of some renowned hero of the past. There was, we are assured by the modern critic, no thought of immoral deceit attached to this quite common practice. In fact, we are told that the end surely justified the means used, for in every case the "pious fraud" served a moral purpose in the advancement of the kingdom of God. The two outstanding cases of such a practice in the Old Testament are found according to the critical estimate, in the D (Deuteronomy) document that was found in the Temple during the reign of Josiah (621 B.C.) and the Book of Daniel that was put forth by the pseudo-Daniel during the time of Antiochus Epiphanes or around 165 B.C. Of course, other books come in for their share in this fraudulent practice.

2. Conservative view. Such a concept as outlined above is utterly detestable from the conservative viewpoint. The following reasons must be considered simply as a summary of what could be offered against the critical view.

a) The conservative view of the Bible's origin is such that it is unthinkable that any book now in the Bible should have arisen out of deceit. Call this the *a priori* method if you will. It is entirely illogical for us to accept a book as authoritative in moral teaching and yet suppose that the author who produced the book resorted to methods of forgery that have put many a man behind the bars. Can a book, even in the Bible, rise above its author? If the book was produced by a fraud and crook, can it teach us not to steal and to tell the truth? Can the leopard change its spots?

b) It cannot be proved in any particular case that Biblical books arose in a fraudulent manner as described by the critical school. It is one thing for that school to assert such a thing, it is quite another thing for them to prove it. It cannot be proved, for example, that the D-document of the Pentateuch arose in the time of Josiah and was the concoction of some priest who put it in the Temple so that, when found and presumed to be the work of Moses, the reputed Lawgiver of Israel, it would bring about the centralization of worship in Jerusalem. Such a view is so glaringly inconsistent with historical facts, not to speak again of the moral problem involved, that it can be held only by those who reject the Bible as a trustworthy account.

c) Leading archaeologists are warning the higher critical school that the theory of literary fabrication, which that school has applied to almost every book in the Old Testament at one time or another, simply will not hold when tested against historical research in the realm of ancient literature. An authority no less than W. F. Albright, in his *From the Stone Age to Christianity* (2nd ed.; 1946), pp. 44ff, tells us that in the ancient Near East there is hardly any evidence for the documentary or literary fabrication which has been imputed to the writers of Scripture. From a scientific standpoint, irrespective of one's attitude toward the Bible, it is impossible now to defend the thesis, so popular among negative critics, that the Bible is largely the result of the same literary fabrication that they supposed was almost universal in the ancient world. This is not to deny, of course, the obvious fact that in pre-Christian Judaism, as well as in the history of the Christian Church, many fabrications have been set forth as the work of some saint of Bible times. Even the Middle Ages and the papacy could claim their notorious Pseudo-Isidorian Decretals. But all such fabrications belong to a different class from the Biblical literature. They have been rejected by the ancient Jews, by our Lord, and by the Christian Church as spurious and fraudulent in character.

F. *The Modern View Destroys the Literary Unity of the Bible*

1. The critical view presented. Very few books of the Bible have escaped the process by which critics have divided their fragments among two or more authors. This process was begun by Jean Astruc, who supposedly found two different documents (J and E) embedded in the Book of Genesis. Eventually this method was employed on the entire Pentateuch (J, E, P and D). Then it spread to

Joshua and other books. Isaiah has been especially subjected to this divisive criticism. Not much of it, even in the first thirty-nine chapters, belongs to the original Isaiah. There is hardly a book in the Bible, however, that has not suffered at the hands of critics who have presumed to detect the hands of different authors in books which, up until their arrival on the scene, were never supposed to be the product of multiple authorship.

2. Conservative view. As diversity of authorship is a characteristic mark of the critical school, so unity of authorship is equally characteristic of the conservative position. So far as we know, conservatives as a class have never accepted any of the "assured results" of negative criticism on this subject. Their reasons are such as follow in digest-form.

a) No such case of diversity of authorship can be absolutely proved. The critics lack manuscript evidence to show that originally a Biblical book existed in various fragments. There is no textual evidence supporting the diverse authorship of the Pentateuch or the Book of Isaiah or the Revelation of John. Nor is there any other evidence existing in the books themselves or in the external history of the time of their origination that would give the least support to the theory of multiple authorship.

b) The "facts" invented by the critics to prove diverse and composite authorship can be better explained on the basis of unified authorship. It would take a volume to substantiate this statement adequately. This has been done by conservative scholarship. For example, M. G. Kyle, in his *The Problem of the Pentateuch: A New Solution by Archaeological Methods* (1920), has conclusively shown how the stylistic differences in the Pentateuch (which critics have attributed to diverse authorship) are entirely consistent with Mosaic authorship. W. H. Green, in his *Unity of the Book of Genesis* (1895) has proved the same thing on a smaller scale and from a different angle. O. T. Allis has proved the unity of Isaiah.

c) Our Lord and the New Testament are absolutely on the conservative side in regard to this matter of the unity of Biblical books. For example, quotations from the first part of Isaiah are attributed to him just as well as quotations from the latter part (cf. Isa. 6:9f with Acts 28:26ff; Isa. 10:22f and 1:9 with Rom. 9:27ff; Isa. 11:10 with Rom. 15:12; Isa. 65:1f with Rom. 10:20f; Isa. 53:1 with John 12:38ff; Isa. 42:1ff with Matt. 12:17ff; Isa. 53:4 with Matt. 8:17). The New Testament appears to be entirely ignorant of any dual or triple authorship of the Book of Isaiah. Both Christ and His apostles speak of only one Isaiah.

d) Usually diversity of authorship in the critical estimate can be traced to some reason other than differences in style and language alleged to exist in a document. One cannot properly understand the critical attitude toward Isaiah, for example, until he gets the total conception that the critics present concerning this book. They believe that, because of the prediction in 44:28 and 45:1 concerning Cyrus (although this is not the only reason advanced), Isaiah must be divided into two or more segments, the earlier section (at least in parts) belonging to the historic Isaiah of the eighth century and the latter section (or parts) belonging to the man whom they speak of as the "unknown prophet" of the post-exilic era. Thus there is an ulterior reason why the critical school demands a division of the Book of Isaiah. This other reason (that is, the explicit rejection of predictive prophecy) cannot be supported by the facts and is utterly repugnant to the conservative view regarding Biblical supernaturalism. We should remind the critics that their trade had a bad beginning, for it is a well-known fact that Marcion, one of the arch-heretics of the early days of Christianity, practiced this business in his abridged edition of the Gospel of Luke. But he did this because his gnostic philosophy would not allow him to let the Gospel stand as it was written by Luke. Is it not for a similar reason or reasons that the modern critic will not allow the Biblical books to stand as unified compositions?

e) The modern critic has made one concession to the conservative side which is fatal, we believe, to his position. A generation ago it was quite the custom in critical circles to speak of the disunity of Biblical revelation and to pit one part of the Bible against another part. This usually took the form of showing the disharmony of the Old Testament with the New Testament or of matching Peter against Paul or Paul against Christ. It was fondly supposed that the viewpoint of one writer or portion of Scripture was contradictory to another and that all attempts to unify were doomed to failure. This radical position is by no means accepted today among those who pose as leaders of the modern attitude toward the Bible. Such a book as H. H. Rowley's *The Unity of the Bible* (1953), although accepting the diversity of authorship typical of the critical school, repudiates much of the older skepticism regarding the theological unity of the Bible. This change is, of course, a step in the right direction. One more step will bring them to the acceptance of the unified authorship of the individual books of the Bible, which is, we believe, the foundation upon which the theological unity must be based.

G. *The Modern View Undermines the Bible's Textual Authority*

1. Critical view presented. It is not too much to say that the critical school deals with the original text of the Bible lightly, fantastically, and sometimes contemptuously. Since the adherents of this viewpoint have, as a prior thesis, rejected the infallibly inspired character of Holy Writ, it is not at all unreasonable for them to deal with the Biblical text in an irreverent and arbitrary way. We say these words advisedly and we believe they can be substantiated by the facts. We cite here some instances of the critical attitude.

a) If one will consult a modern one-volume commentary on the Bible (such as the one edited by Bishop Gore), and if he will read the comments on Amos 2:4f; 3:13; 5:5, 25; 8:4-14; 9:5f, 8-10, 11-15, he will find that these verses are called "interpolations" of a later hand. If we ask our critic for the authority he has for such drastic statements, we find that he has none — that is, none except his own theory that demands that the verses under consideration, because of their content, be placed at a later time than the original author. In classical scholarship such a thing would be called a high-handed treatment — a method most arbitrary. But among modern liberals it appears that the Bible can be treated in any sort of way in the name of scholarship.

b) C. A. Briggs' treatment of the Psalms (in his two-volume work in the *ICC* series) is a notorious example of the way critical scholarship handles the Bible. For example, the words of Psalm 45:6f are left out entirely in his printed translation of this Psalm — as if the words did not belong to the original. This is only one of many such instances in which Briggs calls a passage a "gloss" of a later hand. If we ask again for textual authority for such deletion, we are told that such ideas could not appear at such an early date.

c) This critical reconstruction of the original text is by no means limited to the Old Testament or the erudite commentary. We find it in popular translations of the Bible. Note, for example, how often James Moffatt's translation will depart from the verse sequence in the Gospel of John. Turn to R. H. Charles' commentary in the *ICC* series and note how he changes around the text of Revelation (e.g., Rev. 20:13f). Are these changes made in the interest of better textual evidence than that which we formerly had? Not at all! They are made in the interest of some unsupported theory held by the critic involved. If the critical school had its way, we could not certainly know if any part of the Bible today is actually what it was in the original. For the method of arbitrary manipulation grows and is not easily satisfied until it has devoured the last text of Scripture. The names of Schmiedel and Bultmann will suggest to any person even remotely acquainted with the critical theories of modern times the arbitrariness that has characterized the critical movement.

2. Conservative view. That the conservative view in regard to the handling of the text of Scripture is at the opposite pole from the critical view is obvious to anyone who is at all conversant with the literature on both sides.

In general, it may be said that conservatives as a class hold to the following propositions.

a) Every text of Scripture should be tested in the light of the soundest principles of textual criticism. No conservative is interested in retaining as Scripture a passage which is not found in the best manuscripts and which is unsupported by accepted principles of textual criticism. What the conservative wants is the original Bible — not what has been added by copyists or otherwise. Therefore, the conservative will encourage all sincere and honest attempts to get at the basic and original text of Scripture.

b) However, the conservative scholar simply will not accept some of the methods employed by negative critics to get rid of certain passages of Scripture. He will reject as wholly foreign to real scholarship the effort to rid the Bible of Psalm 45:6f (alluded to above). He will absolutely repudiate the methods employed by Briggs, Charles, Moffatt, and others like them who, on subjective grounds, would take away from the basic text of Scripture many passages and who would, in other cases, arbitrarily change the verse-sequence of Scripture on the presupposition that they know exactly how (yet without manuscript evidence) the original writer wrote his document.

c) Believing that the original text of Scripture was immediately inspired by God's Spirit, the conservative will be extremely cautious in regard to his treatment of the Sacred Word. He will, of course, not regard the Bible in a superstitious manner — as some of the ancient Jews did; but he will, nevertheless, exercise constant restraint on all attempts or efforts to tamper with the original text. He will remember that he is on holy ground: he must not accept any alteration of the Sacred Text — either additions or subtractions — unless it can be demonstrated on the grounds of unimpeachable evidence, that such alterations must be made in the interest of truth. But no wild theory of a negative critic will be counted as evidence; for the theory, like the critic, will soon die and be forgotten.

H. *The Modern View Changes the Nature of Biblical Books*

1. Critical view presented. In order that we might see the modern view more in detail, we present here the following illustrations of their method.

a) We are told by the liberal side that the Book of Ruth has no other motive or reason for existence than that of telling a tale of long ago which was nothing but pure fiction. This book really originated, we are informed, in the post-exilic period as a propaganda-leaflet written as a protest against Nehemiah's prohibition of mixed marriages. Any introduction on the Old Testament from a liberal viewpoint (such as Pfeiffer's) will substantiate this statement.

b) Esther is looked upon the same way by the critical school. Some critics have the audacity to tell us that this book is mythological in its basic concept. Milder critics tell us that it really has no place in the canon because of its vindictiveness.

c) Jonah likewise is treated as unhistorical. It is, we are told, nothing but an allegory. As the fish swallowed Jonah, so Babylon is to swallow Israel. As the fish vomited Jonah, so Babylon will permit Israel to go back to her land. But any one is "gullible," we are told, if he takes the imaginary events in Jonah as real.

d) We shall not take the space to enumerate many more instances of this process. It was formerly supposed that the New Testament at least rested upon sure historical footing, but not so today. If Jonah is allegory, why not the Gospel of John also? If Esther has little historical credibility, why must we still believe the Gospel of Mark as actual history? So, to put it bluntly, the same virus that attacked the Old Testament has spread over into the New Testament. As a result, modern critics are not sure about much that Jesus actually said or did. With the advent of "form-criticism" and the "de-mythologizing" process, we are not sure whether we even have a whisper of the words and acts of Christ.

2. Conservative view. It can be truthfully said that the conservative school is united in the conviction that the Biblical books are what they purport to be. To state this more in detail, let us observe the following remarks.

a) In no case can it be proved that the Christian Church has misconstrued the true nature of a Biblical book. Those books that are historical have been recognized as historical; those that were prophetic have been categorized as such. The Church has never looked upon her canon of Scripture as containing fiction, myth or allegory. In other words, Ruth, Jonah, Esther, Mark and John have all been recognized as being historical descriptions of real events. It was not until the advent of modern criticism that this picture was altered and modified. Thus the critical view has against it the weight of centuries. To say that capable scholars in other and more conservative days of Christianity were mistaken in their conception of canonical books of Scripture is to affirm that they lacked evidence (which we presumably now have) to distinguish between fact and romance, between historical reality and imagination. We do not allow that one iota of new information has been discovered in the last century or so that would compel us to re-examine and revise the historic Church's view regarding the nature of Biblical books.

b) The instability and changeableness of the critical method is a cogent reason against its truthfulness. As we said above, the deadly virus began in the Old Testament when it was affirmed that such books as Ruth, Jonah and Esther were not historical. If such books can be called romances, myths, allegories and the like, then it is impossible to keep the deadly virus from spreading to other books of Scripture. The result is that there is hardly a book in either Old or New Testament whose true nature as history or prophecy has not been questioned or denied in whole or in part by some modern critic.

c) The conservative likes to believe that he has the Lord Jesus and the apostles on his side. And that is so, for there is not a single instance in which our Lord or His apostles ever took a different view of an Old Testament book from the view universally held by the Church down to modern times. Christ never uttered one syllable insinuating doubt in regard to the historicity of any part of the Old Testament or suggesting in a subtle way that its prophecies were not real. The ancient Jews, our Lord and His apostles, and the Christian Church all unite in the same conception regarding the canonical books of Scripture.

I. The Modern View Undermines the Scientific Accuracy of the Bible

1. Critical view presented. There are a number of aspects of the critical view regarding the scientific accuracy of the Bible. The following are among the most characteristic of this view.

a) The Bible is divided into three categories — the historical, the scientific, and the moral or religious. In the first two we find erroneous statements; in the third, we find (or usually find) truth expressed in one form or another. This simply means, as far as our present subject is concerned, that the scientific statements in the Bible are not to be accepted at their face value. Such things as the account of creation must be interpreted so as to harmonize, if such is at all possible, with the dictates of modern science.

b) The Bible actually contains scientific errors. In some cases this accusation is made without citation of examples; in other cases, as, for example, in W. W. Hyde's *From Paganism to Christianity* (1946), p. 104, specific instances are cited, such as the story of Jonah, the talking ass (Num. 22:23-30), the talking serpent (Gen. 3:1), the sun's being stopped (Josh. 10:12-14), and the size of the ark.

c) Furthermore, we are told that the writers of Scripture shared the prevalent conceptions of the universe found among their pagan contemporaries. In fact, it is claimed that the Jews were never good at science and had to borrow their account of creation from the astrologically-minded Babylonians, from whom they secured, during the Babylonian Captivity, their cosmological ideas. All this means that the Jews considered, like their neighbors, the earth to be flat and the sky to be a fixed "firmament."

d) The critical view, of course, accepts the general trustworthiness of the theory of evolution and applies it to the religion of Israel. It follows that the following features enter into their reconstruction of Israel's religion: (1) Genesis 1-11 is considered as belonging to the prehistorical period and as, thereby, possessing little value as a source of history. These early chapters are equated with that period in the early life of man when man was gradually being distinguished from lower forms of life. Naturally, we are told, we should not expect in these early chapters either true history or true science. (2) Biblical doctrines are vitally and drastically affected by the theory of development applied to the religion of the Semites. If one will read, for example, such articles as "Adam," "Creation," and "Fall" in J. Hastings' one-volume A Dictionary of the Bible (1909), he will realize what devastating effects the theory of evolution has on time-honored Biblical doctrines. (3) Furthermore, the critical view regarding the rise of monotheism is a direct result of the application of the naturalistic theory of evolution to the religion of the Old Testament, for, according to the critical view that attained ascendancy until recent times, Israel's religion began in animism, then came polytheism, then henotheism (when Israel, at the instigation of Moses, adopted "Jahweh" as her tribal deity), and finally, during the time of the great prophets of the eighth century, monotheism. (4) Some critics have been bold enough to apply evolution to our Lord and call Him "the crown of the evolutionary process." This means that He reached ahead of time what the race will eventually attain in its slow progress upward.

2. Conservative view. It is believed that the following propositions will fairly represent, with minor modifications, the view held by conservatives regarding the Bible and science.

a) The Bible contains phenomenal language in its description of the things of nature. The Bible speaks in terms that the average man can understand. It speaks of the rising and setting of the sun, but this fact must not be taken as scientific language. No inaccuracy should be imputed to the Bible because it uses the language of appearance in describing the facts of nature. To say that the Bible is in error when it uses such language would be the same as saying that a great scientist today is in error when he speaks of a beautiful sunset.

b) If a person will thoroughly study the original language of Scripture and if he will compare Scripture with Scripture, he will find that the Bible is consistent in speaking of scientific facts. It has yet to be proved that the Bible is mistaken in its account of creation or in any other description of nature. In fact, it can be shown that the Bible not only harmonizes with true science but, in addition (as one can see in S. Merson Davies' *The Bible and Modern Science* [n.d.]), anticipates some of the discoveries of modern science.

c) The conservative view toward evolution is somewhat difficult to state at the present time, for it is quite evident that not all who call themselves conservatives take the same attitude toward the theory of organic evolution. Without attempting to speak for all, we believe that most conservatives will agree to the following propositions.

(1) Evolution as a theory has not been proved to be a scientific fact as yet. In fact, there are some outstanding problems which it has not solved and, from the data available, which it seems unlikely to solve. In addition, there are some formidable arguments which have been brought against it. For substantiation of this statement, one may consult George Barry O'Toole's *The Case Against Evolution* (1925). The conservative, therefore, will reject all forms of naturalistic evolution as incompatible with the supernaturalism of the Bible.

(2) A conservative will most certainly reject the application of the theory of evolution to Biblical history and theology. To be specific (but not exhaustive) he will repudiate the following: (*a*) The idea that man was not created in the image of God. No conservative will allow that man came from some sub-human ancestor. The Bible is so plain on this subject that to reject what is said is the same as rejecting God's Word as our absolute authority. (*b*) The idea that the first stage of man on earth was that of savagery and barbarism. If there is anything clear in the Genesis account, it is that the first human beings were

intelligent and civilized. The only way to get rid of this evidence is to assign the early chapters in Genesis to folklore and myth. (c) That man grew through various stages into a belief in monotheism. The idea here is that monotheism was not the original belief of mankind but a much later development. Man's first worship was animistic, then came polytheism, then henotheism, and finally monotheism. This sounds fine to a humanistic naturalist, but it is repugnant to a conservative. (d) The idea that Jesus Christ was the product of the evolutionary process. This idea, according to the conservative view, is not only lacking in proof but is also, from the very nature of the case, incapable of being proved. Jesus Christ is the climax of supernaturalism; but the theory of evolution is naturalistic.

(3) A conservative will have little patience with those who try to wed the naturalism of evolution to the supernaturalism of the Bible by some idea such as theistic evolution. The Bible gives no room at all for such a theory, and its acceptance in the interest of trying to harmonize the Bible with modern science can but harm those who make the attempt. There is no middle position between the absolute supernaturalism of the Bible and its account of direct creation and the absolute naturalism of evolutionism and its dogma of gradual development by resident forces within the substance evolved until man is reached.

(4) The conservative will remind those who call him obscurantist that his position does not rest upon an *a priori* acceptance of the Bible as his final authority. There are facts outside of the sciences of biology and zoology which considerably reduce any weight that one may attach to the theory of evolution. We speak of the facts discovered by the science of archaeology. We can but mention two such facts here. (a) The first fact concerns monotheism. Modern archaeologists are telling us that the earliest religion of mankind was monotheistic — not animistic. It has been discovered that the religion of a people is purer the closer we get to their origin. (b) The second fact concerns the earliest civilization of mankind. It is practically

certain, from an archaeological standpoint, that the original home of the race was somewhere in the Tigris-Euphrates sector. And the earliest people were the Sumerians. These people had a flourishing civilization long before Egypt rose to power. It is positive that these Sumerians had a written language in which are recorded all the things of a people's life — their religion, customs, trade, etc. Thus it would appear that man appeared on the pages of human history as full-grown, intelligent and as a worshiper.

d) A final word should be said regarding the conservative's attitude toward the Bible and science. It is this: the freedom of the Bible from those inaccuracies that characterize all human writings. The Bible is not in need of constant revision to keep up with the latest scientific theory. Many things have been put forth in the name of science which are now repudiated. Can we forget the fact that Galileo was condemned by the Inquisition because he adopted (but abjured later) the Copernican or heliocentric system of the universe? But the heliocentric system was proved conclusively within fifty years of Galileo's death by Newton. Did the Bible's science need to be revised because the Copernican system was proved to be true? Not at all, for the Bible had never taught the opposite system, which men had wrongly imputed to it for generations. Even in the best of the Church Fathers there are unscientific statements which one will look for in vain in the Bible. God so guided the Biblical writers that they were kept free of those scientific errors that characterize the writings of other men not so inspired.

J. *The Modern View Undermines the Moral Teaching of the Bible*

1. Critical view presented. This view can be briefly put under the following heads with appropriate illustrations.

a) Accepting the theory of evolution as their yardstick by which to determine the date of a document on the basis of its content, critics tell us that a book which contains high spiritual conceptions cannot come early. Jonah, for instance, with its universalistic outlook, simply cannot

M

be pre-exilic, for such a concept in the earlier period had not yet arisen in the slow development of religious ideas. The Psalms, we are told, could not have been written by David, for in his time the age was too crude and barbaric to produce such wonderful concepts.

b) As a corollary, the critical view maintains that there is much in the morality of the Old Testament that we cannot justify. It is asserted, for instance, that the command to exterminate the Canaanites cannot be attributed to the God of love depicted in the New Testament. Thus we have our expurgated or "short" Bibles that presumably leave out certain moral ideas repugnant and offensive to the modern mind.

c) Strange and inconsistent as it may appear, the modern critic still holds on to the basic morality of the Bible. As we have previously seen, he rejects the absolute accuracy of the Bible in matters of science and history but will not include all the moral teachings in this rejection. Though the Biblical writers may clothe their thought in unscientific language and may make historical blunders, yet still we find some moral or spiritual truth that will help us today.

2. Conservative view. It will not be necessary for us to go into minute details here, for it should be obvious by this time what the conservative view is on the Bible's moral teaching. Let it be counted as sufficient that we include the following items.

a) The conservative, of course, rejects the underlying assumption that evolution is true and is applicable to the morality of the Bible. There is not, he believes, a constant upward tendency of the human race toward more spiritual ideas. The Bible teaches that there has been a definite deterioration and devolution of the human race from a superior knowledge to an inferior one in the matter of morals (cf. Rom. 1:18-32; 3:10-18).

b) The conservative thus denies that any Biblical book can be dated on the basis of the evolutionary development of ideas. God can reveal Himself to man in any way and at any time that is pleasing to Him. If this is so, as the conservative most emphatically insists it is, then Jonah, for example, can come in the eighth century just as well as in the second or third centuries. The conservative, of course, does not allow that the latter date is a possible one (in view of all the facts); but he does insist that God could reveal His love for a heathen city in the time of the historical Jonah as well as in the pseudo-Jonah who presumably lived centuries later. God never waits for man to catch up with Him before He reveals Himself further to the human race. If this had been so, the greatest of all revelations, that is, the coming of Jesus Christ into the world, would never have taken place at the time when the pagan and Jewish world was at the very bottom spiritually and morally.

c) The conservative reminds us that we should distinguish between the absolute moral and spiritual teaching of the Bible and that crude and erroneous morality often found among the people of Israel to whom the Sacred Oracles had been committed. In Elijah's time, for example, Baalism was the popular religion. Was that the religion of the Bible? To ask such a question is to answer it. Baalism, as everyone must know, was a corruption of the pure religion that centered in the worship of the true God and which was taught by the true prophets of the Lord. In the time of Jeremiah the popular religion had fallen to such a low level that the Jews were worshiping the queen of heaven (7:18; 44:17). Will even the most radical critic affirm that this was the true worship of God? Did not God through Jeremiah pronounce the severest kind of punishment upon the Jews for their perversion of the truth and their turning to the idolatry of paganism? In fairness and justice one simply cannot call the religion that the people often practiced the true religion of the Bible. Will one affirm, to cite another case, that all the rites, ceremonies and traditions that the Catholic Church added during the Middle Ages represent the pure faith of the New Testament?

d) The conservative will, of course, admit that there is a true progress of doctrine in the Scriptures. He denies that this progress is from error to truth; it is rather from one truth to a greater revelation of the same truth. The seed must grow and develop. But the seed is of the same nature as the fully developed tree. The morality of Genesis is not outdated by subsequent revelations. Abel, Enoch, Noah, Abraham, and the rest of God's saints in the Old Testament had as high a conception of the difference between right and wrong, or what was acceptable or unacceptable to God, as men of a later time. This does not mean that they always followed the right, but their failure was not due to a lack of knowledge but rather to a lack in their wills. God has given to every generation from the beginning, an adequate knowledge of Himself and of what was acceptable as praiseworthy conduct in His sight.

CHAPTER SIX

THE TEXT AND CANON OF THE OLD TESTAMENT IN THE LIGHT OF CRITICISM

The subject of the present chapter bristles with problems. Some of these problems are due to the nature of the subject and some are due to the modern view of the Bible. Thus it can be truthfully said that conservatives, as well as liberals, have some common problems here. This does not mean, however, that they share the same viewpoint or reach the same conclusion. Nor does it mean that they solve their problems in exactly the same way.

I. THE LANGUAGES OF THE OLD TESTAMENT

First of all, then, we must consider the languages of the Old Testament. Since there are only two languages in which this portion of the Bible was written, this means that we are to consider here the Hebrew and the Aramaic languages.

A. *The Hebrew Language*

Our discussion will take in such matters as the significance of the name "Hebrew," the origin and history of the language that bears this name, some characteristics of Hebrew and its place in the Semitic family, and the importance of the language.

1. The name "Hebrew." Some things are still in a nebulous state in regard to the significance of the term "Hebrew." Some scholars take this term to be the name of those people who descended from Eber (Gen. 10:21, 25; 11:14ff), who was the great grandson of Shem. In this sense the name is a patronymic attached to those who were descendants of Eber. Others derive the name more specifically from the Hebrew word 'abhar, which means "to

cross over." In this sense it would designate those descendants of Abraham (and also of Eber, since he was a progenitor of Abraham) who came from the other side of the
(Euphrates) river (Josh. 24:2f, 14f).

The exact relationship of the Biblical Hebrews to the
people known in the inscriptions as the Habiru has not
yet been fully determined, but conservative scholars are
inclined to equate these people, especially in the Tell el-
Amarna correspondence, with the Hebrew nation. Aside
from the Biblical data, there is very little monumental evidence regarding the origin of these people. A statement
in Ezekiel (16:3) makes Canaan their birthplace and attributes their paternity to the Amorites and their maternity
to the Hittites.

One thing is now absolutely certain regarding the Hebrew people. They have had a long history and have continued down from ancient times to the present day. No
reputable scholar today holds the view of nineteenth century skepticism that the Patriarchs represent either Canaanite deities whom the Israelites came to revere as their an-
cestors or eponyms of tribal movements. Archaeology has
confirmed the historical trustworthiness of the Biblical narrative.

2. The origin of the Hebrew language. Here again we
touch a problem about which little is known. It is true,
however, that, thanks to modern archaeology, we know
much more today than a century or so ago. The following
question will help to state some of the problems and their
possible solution.

a) When and how was Genesis composed? This book
records the earliest history we have of Bible times. Critics
of the negative school have, of course, denied its Mosaic
origin and have scattered its supposed documents or sources
(J, E, P) from 850 B.C. down to about 550 B.C. On this
view, Genesis is contemporary with the time of the great
prophets of the pre-exilic period and, therefore, tells us
little about the origin of the language. On the other side,
conservatives agree that Genesis is one of the earliest documents in the Bible. There is not absolute agreement in

regard to the time of its origin. One group holds that it is a contemporary account of history from Adam down to Joseph and was written by members of the line of faith (such as Abel, Enoch, Noah, Abraham, etc.) and transmitted in this same line as a sacred deposit until Moses came on the scene and constituted it as the first volume of a history of mankind and of the chosen seed. There can be no question today that writing was in use at the time required by the Biblical history. Since Babylonian cuneiform was the prevailing language in the time contemporary with Genesis, it is supposed that this book was written in such a language and later (by Moses?) translated into Biblical Hebrew. In the present state of our knowledge of early Hebrew, this assumption cannot be denied nor affirmed dogmatically. The next question will afford further light on this subject.

b) Did Moses write in Hebrew? Up until 1868 little was known about the existence of Hebrew writing, for the simple reason that there was no monumental evidence of the use of Hebrew. But in the year just mentioned the famous Moabite Stone was discovered (see S. H. Gehman [ed.], *The Westminster Dictionary of the Bible* [1944], p. 403f). Written in a language akin to Hebrew, this stone was placed around 850 B.C. The Siloam inscription comes from about the same period (700 B.C.). More recent discoveries (the Lachish letters and the Ras Shamra alphabetic letters) push back our knowledge of Hebrew to the period of the conquest. A discovery in 1904-1905 near Mt. Sinai indicates the probable existence of a proto-Semitic script that dates from about the time of Abraham. The evidence, therefore, clearly points in the direction of the early use of the Hebrew language. It is reasonable to suppose that Moses wrote in the Hebrew language. This language has remained fairly fixed down through the centuries. At the present stage of our knowledge, it seems possible to infer that Hebrew is one of the earliest of the languages and that it (or something similar to it) was used in the composition of Genesis. There are evidences of an ancient age in Genesis but there are no real evidences that lead us to believe that that book is a translation from some other language.

3. History of Biblical Hebrew. Here there are primarily two things that need to be discussed. One of these concerns the actual period of time covered by the writings of the Old Testament. The other matter concerns the transmission of the Biblical text from the close of the Old Testament canon down to the present time. Each will be dealt with briefly.

a) The history of Biblical Hebrew. Our subject here naturally divides itself into two questions — on each of which there is a radical difference between the conservative and liberal views.

(1) When did Hebrew writings begin? In the conservative view, the Book of Genesis and the Book of Job are probably the earliest written documents in Hebrew. The modern, critical view violently objects, of course, to this viewpoint, and would place both books centuries later (even putting Job in the post-exilic period). The modern school places very little of the Old Testament prior to 1000 B.C. See Julius A. Bewer, *The Literature of the Old Testament* (1933), pp. xii-xiv. The following reasons are more or less advanced for this late dating of the beginning of Hebrew literature: (a) The nineteenth century view of the primitive condition of Israel still largely dominates much of the modern view of Old Testament literature. It is still thought improbable, on the critical assumptions, that Israel could have had such a vast literature at such an early date (that is, around the time of Moses). (b) The same nineteenth century also spawned the idea of evolution and its application to Biblical history and religion. This meant that certain books with lofty concepts about God could not be placed early; necessarily they were brought down to a much later date to make them conform to the development-hypothesis. (c) Finally, a parallel was unconsciously drawn between Hebrew and Greek literature. It was considered unthinkable that the primitive Hebrews could have developed a literature far superior to the best of Greek literature centuries before the Greeks. It is a well-known fact that the

golden age of Greek literature did not take place until after 500 B.C. By that time, on the traditional dating of Hebrew literature, the Old Testament writing was drawing to a close. But the modern school of criticism puts a considerable portion of the Old Testament in this post-exilic period, thus making it contemporary with the Greek literature of Plato and Aristotle.

There are, however, some cogent arguments supporting the traditional view of the antiquity of Hebrew literature. Let us carefully note the following: 1) Modern archaeological research has completely shattered the earlier notion that writing is late. We have writings now that go back to a date as early as any date one has claimed for Biblical literature. In view of the discovery of the Code of Hammurabi, no one today could possibly claim that the Hebrews could not have had a similar code in the time of Moses (who came several centuries after Hammurabi). 2) Tradition is not necessarily false because it is tradition. The view among the Jews that Moses wrote the Law and that other books were written where tradition has placed them ought to be given some weight — unless it can be proved that these traditional views are wrong. Up to the present time the proof (especially from archaeology) has been in support of the traditions. 3) Finally, since every book more or less betrays the date of its origin by internal evidence, it can be asserted that there are sufficient data of an internal nature supporting the antiquity of Hebrew literature. It can be conclusively proved that the foreign words found in the Old Testament books constitute an absolute argument that such books arose as contemporary documents, depicting the actual history of the time to which they belong. The same kind of evidence is found in the study of Hebrew diction in the Old Testament books. For evidence for these statements, the reader may profitably consult R. D. Wilson's article on "Foreign Words in the Old Testament as an Evidence of Historicity" in *The Princeton Theological Review*, XXVI (April, 1928), pp. 177-247.

(2) When did Hebrew writings stop? We mean here,

of course, the writings which are now incorporated in our Old Testament. On this subject there is, as in the former topic, a considerable difference between the conservative and the liberal views. Since this matter has already been partly discussed under our previous heading and since it will come up again in the discussion concerning the canon, we omit further treatment of it here.

b) The transmission of the Hebrew text of the Old Testament. It is impossible to give exact dates for the periods we are about to discuss; but it is, nevertheless, pretty definite that the Hebrew text has come down to us in three stages or periods. The following outline will make this point clear.

(1) The scribal period. This began when the Old Testament was completed and continued down to the time of the Massoretic Text. On conservative grounds, this period began at about the time of Ezra but, on grounds held by the critical school, it did not begin until about a century or two before Christ. Most adherents of this modern view place the completion of the Old Testament canon about 100 B.C.

During the scribal period the Old Testament was copied with meticulous care. Interpretations and paraphrases were made upon the text. It was during this period that the Jews began using Aramaic in preference to Biblical Hebrew. It was also during this time that the first major translation of the Hebrew was made into another language (the Greek Septuagint). The scribes also made divisions in the Hebrew text for use in reading in the synagogue. The change to the square form of Hebrew writing took place sometime during this period. The recently discovered Dead Sea Scrolls (1947), containing the Book of Isaiah, show that there is practically no evidence supporting the idea that the Hebrew text changed materially during this period.

(2) The Massoretic period. The word "massora" means the body of traditions which the Jews had preserved for the correct pronunciation and interpretation of their text. It is now admitted on all sides that the Hebrew of the original documents consisted of a consonantal text without vowel pointings. While the language was alive and used, it was

not necessary to indicate the vowel points; but when the use of Hebrew was beginning to die out, especially after the devastating Jewish wars in the first and second Christian centuries (since Jerusalem was now destroyed and the Jewish people scattered and unorganized), it became essential that a system of vocalization be applied to the consonantal Hebrew text so that the correct pronunciation and interpretation might be preserved for posterity. The scholars who performed this necessary task are known as the Massoretes and their resultant text is called the Massoretic Text (MT).

It is not certainly known when the unpointed text was pointed by the Massoretes. But that there were no vowel points as such in the original text is evident from the fact that such a scholar as Jerome (340? - 420), who became a student of Hebrew before he translated the Hebrew into the Latin (known now as the Vulgate), knew nothing of the pointed text. Another proof is found in the fact (as we shall see later) that many of the variations between the Hebrew and the Septuagint can be explained on the basis of a different reading of the consonantal text.

It is not necessary, therefore, to maintain the view once strongly propounded by some of the Puritans of the seventeenth century that the Hebrew vowel-system was a part of the original text. The evidence appears to point to the fact that, by around A.D. 700, the Massoretic Text was established.

(3) The post-Massoretic and modern period. This covers the time from about the eleventh century to the present date. During this period the Hebrew Bible was printed and many subsequent editions, with revisions, published. The Psalms came from the press in 1477 and the whole Hebrew Bible received printed form in 1517. Much study has been devoted to the Hebrew text in modern times and standard texts have been printed with critical apparatus. See Lefferts A. Loetscher (ed.), *Twentieth Century Encyclopaedia of Religious Knowledge* (1955), Vol. 1, pp. 133f.

4. The place of Hebrew in the Semitic family. Hebrew and Aramaic belong to the same family of languages which

is now called Semitic (after Shem, the progenitor of the Hebrew race, cf. Gen. 10:21-31). The Semitic languages have many features in common and are perhaps more closely related than French, Spanish, and Italian among modern languages. The members of this family and their geographical location are usually designated as follows:

a) Northern group. This includes the Aramaic and its numerous dialects (including Syriac).

b) Eastern group. Here is put Accadian, which is the modern designation for Assyrian and Babylonian.

c) Southern group. This includes Arabic and Ethiopic.

d) Western group. Here we find Hebrew, Canaanite, Moabite and Phoenician.

Some members of this family are now dead languages (such as the Assyrian and the Babylonian). Arabic is now spoken by a larger number of people than any other Semitic language. And it should be remembered that the Koran is in this language. Hebrew, dead for many centuries, is being revived in the modern Israeli nation.

5. Characteristics of Hebrew. Only a first-hand knowledge of Hebrew can acquaint the student with the many characteristics of the Hebrew language. What we give here must be looked upon merely as the briefest kind of digest.

a) Hebrew is written from right to left. To us in the modern world this may appear quite odd, but it is purely a matter of what one is accustomed to. A beginner can be as readily taught to read from right to left as from left to right.

b) Hebrew (like the Semitic languages in general) is tri-consonantal. By this is meant that there are three consonants in the root of a word. The lexicon-form of a Hebrew word usually has three consonants. To this basic root are added performatives (at the beginning) and suffixes (at the end) to indicate such things as person, place, kind of action (whether completed or continuing), etc.

c) Hebrew has a small vocabulary. There are about 5,000 words (not including proper names) in the Old Testament. Only about one-tenth of this number is of frequent occurrence. However, because of the flexibility of the verb-system, ideas can be represented by the same root which require different English words in translation.

d) Scarcity of compound words. A person passing from Greek to Hebrew will notice the striking contrast between the two languages. Greek, as is well known, is fond of compound words (such as a preposition prefixed to a verb). Compare our English (derived from Latin): provoke, revoke, invoke, convoke. It is only in proper names that Hebrew uses compound forms: Immanuel ("God with us"); Daniel ("God is my judge"); Joel ("Jehovah is God"); Jehoshaphat ("Jehovah has judged"); Zechariah ("Jehovah has remembered"); etc. It should be noted that the "el" in a Hebrew word (at the beginning or close) usually designates God ("Elohim"); whereas the "je" (or "jeho") and "ah" (at the beginning or end) commonly designates Jehovah (Lord).

e) Large variety of synonyms. Due largely, perhaps, to the literary device called "parallelism" (found most frequently in Proverbs and Psalms), the Hebrew Old Testament has a significant number of synonymous words and expressions of like meaning. One can readily see the frequency of similar words for the law of God in Psalm 119 and the various terms used by Daniel in confessing his nation's sins (Dan. 9). An excellent book for the study of this subject is R. L. Girdlestone's *Synonyms of the Old Testament*.

f) The use of the construct state. This feature corresponds roughly to our genitive case in English. Hebrew is quite deficient in adjectives and compensates for this lack by the construct state. The English uses "his holy throne" where the Hebrew reads "throne of His holiness" (Ps. 47:8). "The seed royal" is in Hebrew "the seed of the kingdom" (II Kings 11:1). The Hebrew has no comparative or superlative degree, but the comparative is often indicated by using the adjective with the preposition *min* ("from") and the superlative is often made by using a noun in construct relationship with itself — "holy of holies" (that is, "the holiest"); "servant of servants" (that is, "the lowest servant").

g) The Hebrew tense-system. It is impossible to explain

this system in the space at our command here. Essentially, Hebrew has a perfect tense and an imperfect tense. Time, however, is not the fundamental idea in these designations. The perfect rather indicates that the action is considered as completed; the imperfect is used when the action is looked at as still going on or incomplete. Since the future tense usually designates actions not complete as yet, that tense in English most frequently is used for the Hebrew imperfect. Since ideas that belong to the subjunctive (including what is conditional, potential or general) are usually future to the speaker, the Hebrew imperfect is used where we (or the Greek or Latin) use the subjunctive. The perfect tense in Hebrew is often used in prophecy. In Isaiah 5:13 we are told that "my people are gone into captivity" — the Hebrew using the perfect to describe an event in the future which is considered so real and certain, from the divine standpoint, that it can already be spoken of as past. A special feature of the verb-system is the process (known as "waw consecutive") whereby a series of events in the past is described by the initial verb in the perfect, but the succeeding verbs, describing other events in the series, are put in the imperfect with a connecting "waw" ("and"). The same process is used when the initial verb is in the imperfect; the succeeding verbs use the perfect with "waw."

6. The importance of Hebrew. It is rather difficult, in the present theological situation, to make Hebrew seem important to the average young student of theology, who is preparing for the Christian ministry. Too many more practical subjects engage his time and his attention; and he hears repeated stories telling how older ministers never use their Hebrew after they leave seminary. However, a case can still be made for the place that Hebrew has in the theological discipline. Here are some of the points that can be offered in its behalf.

a) The greater part of the Bible is in Hebrew. This Old Testament part is considered by the Christian Church to be an integral component of the sacred canon. If it is necessary to study the New Testament in Greek in order to know that part better, so it can be reasoned logically that it is necessary to study the Hebrew also. In no sense can it be said that the Christian Church is ready to discard the Old Testament; in no sense, therefore, should the Church give up the study of Hebrew.

b) The New Testament Greek cannot be adequately understood apart from the Old Testament Hebrew. About the turn of the present century it was the fashion to de-emphasize "semitisms" in the New Testament. The papyri discoveries made scholars look to the koiné Greek as the background of the New Testament. This was, of course, partly so; but the New Testament has its greater background in the Old Testament. Today it is properly recognized that there is a strong semitic influence in the New Testament. The expression "kingdom of heaven" is probably equivalent to the Hebrew idiom known as the construct state (already discussed) and undoubtedly means "the heavenly kingdom." The modern notion that Christ was proclaiming an "earthly" kingdom when He used this expression, is thus dissipated entirely.

c) One can test the newer translations only if he knows the original. There was perhaps never a time more urgent than the present when the minister needs to examine carefully the newer versions (RSV, Moffatt, Goodspeed, etc.) against the original. Some ministers slavishly take what the translation says — even when it departs widely from an older translation. Many of them are quite unprepared, because of their neglect of Hebrew or because they never kept up their studies after they left seminary, to make any critical judgment as to whether the newer translation is nearer to the original than those formerly made. Any minister, by a few minutes daily on the subject, can, in the space of a few years, become an authority on Hebrew and can pass judgment on all translation. Nothing less than this should satisfy the real messenger of the eternal Word of God.

d) The richer meanings of the Old Testament can never be discovered apart from a knowledge of the Hebrew. Nothing else will suffice or take the place of an intimate knowledge of the original. Even commentaries, as useful as they are at times, are no substitutes for the Hebrew itself. One

can make syntax an interesting and profitable study; and
the more one studies it, the more one's sermonic material
will increase.

e) Finally, there are ways of studying Hebrew that greatly
increase its value and importance. One may, as suggested,
study its syntax without ever expecting to finish the subject
in this life — so inexhaustible is the field. One may make
word-studies that will enrich one's knowledge of theology
immeasurably. Begin with words that occur only a few
times and then go on to some of the major words in the
Old Testament (such as "righteousness," "truth," "mercy,"
etc.). See, for example, N. H. Snaith, *The Distinctive Ideas
of the Old Testament* (1946). This same writer has authored
a series of volumes on various segments of the Old Testament called *Notes on the Hebrew Texts* and designed to
help the beginner in his exegesis of the text. The Abingdon
Press distributes this series.

B. *The Aramaic Language*

Aramaic is, of course, the other language used in the
writing of the Old Testament. Although the part actually
written in Aramaic is, as we shall soon see, small, yet this
language has assumed a major place in modern criticism
because of certain theories that have been advanced concerning it. These will be touched upon rather briefly in the
ensuing remarks.

1. The scope of Biblical Aramaic. There are three sections in the Old Testament written in Aramaic: Daniel 2:4-
7:28; Ezra 4:8 - 6:18 and Ezra 7:12-26. At the time when
these books were written (that is, at the time of the Babylonian Captivity) Aramaic was becoming more and more
the language of the Hebrew people. The word "Syrian" in
Ezra 4:7 should more properly read "Aramaic." Possibly
the statement in Nehemiah 8:7f refers to the difficulty that
some of the people had, now that they had adopted Aramaic,
in understanding the Law of Moses (the Pentateuch) as it
was read by Ezra (Neh. 8:2f) and the Levites (Neh. 8:7f).

2. The use of Aramaic in modern criticism. Much use has
been made of the Aramaic in the matter of criticism of Bib-

lical document. Part of the discussion has centered in the Old Testament and part in the New Testament, as the following remarks will manifest.

a) The use of Aramaic in the criticism of Old Testament literature. Here we must first of all present the view of critics before we prove how inadequate their view is.

(1) The critical thesis. Put briefly, it is affirmed that the presence of an "Aramaism" (that is, an Aramaic word borrowed and embodied in the Hebrew text) in a document is a sure sign of the lateness in date of the book in which the "Aramaism" occurs. This argument, as we shall see later, is used in dating the Book of Daniel late. It is also used in a number of other cases. The idea back of it is that an Aramaic word in an Old Testament book is positive proof of the post-exilic date of the document.

(2) Refutation of the critical assumption. In order to show the invalidity of this view it will be necessary to give a few details about the use of Aramaic as a language and its connection with the Hebrew.

(a) The Arameans were an ancient people and go back in Biblical history at least to the time of the Patriarchs. Rebecca, Leah and Rachel were from the country of Aram Naharaim, the land of Laban.

(b) These people had contacts with the people of Israel a number of times during their history. The account about Job, for example, is probably laid in their country. According to Judges 3:8, one of their kings conquered the Israelites. Both David and Solomon ruled over their territory. The kings of Judah and Israel had contacts with them at various times. In the time of Isaiah Aramaic ("Syrian"—Heb., *Aramean*) was so well known by the Jewish leaders that they requested Rabshakeh to speak in that language rather than Hebrew (Isa. 36:11). By the end of the Exile, the Jews generally knew Aramaic seemingly better than their Hebrew (cf. Neh. 8:2f, 7f, and the remarks above). Thus the largest sections of the Bible in Aramaic (see above) are found in this period.

(c) At any time during this long period of contact, Aramaic words could have been adopted and naturalized into

N

the Hebrew language. No one can dogmatically assert, in view of the evidence just presented, that an Aramaic word in a document is an absolute proof of lateness of date. There are too many unknown factors involved here to make such a conclusion valid.

(d) Furthermore, it can be proved that most of the words claimed as "Aramaisms" are not Aramaic words at all but rather good Hebrew words. The proof of this is too complex and intricate to be given here, but is ably presented in an article on "Aramaisms in the Old Testament" in *The Princeton Theological Review* (April, 1925), pp. 234-266. In that article Dr. R. D. Wilson examines all of the alleged "Aramaisms" (some three hundred or more words) and shows that only fifty have an apparent ground for such a claim.

(e) Finally, in line with what we have seen, the true "Aramaisms" embedded in the Old Testament text come at those places and times when the Israelites were in contact with the Arameans; and the greatest contact produced the greatest influx of Aramaic. By this we see that the Book of Daniel and the Book of Ezra (in which books are found practically all the Aramaic in the Old Testament) show very plainly that they originated when Aramaic had become the language of the Jews. If the so-called P-document of the Pentateuch had actually originated in the Exile (where the critical school puts it), it would undoubtedly, like Daniel and Ezra, have contained sections in Aramaic. As a matter of fact, "Aramaisms" in the P-document are practically zero!

Thus it can be positively stated that the critical use of "Aramaisms" is unjustified. Furthermore, it is pure arbitrariness when critics charge that some late redactor has inserted an Aramaic word (in the place of its Hebrew original) in a pre-exilic document. There is no evidence that in the scribal period of the transmission of the Old Testament text insertions or changes were made in the original text. The recently discovered Isaiah scroll (1947) shows how tenaciously the Jews transmitted their manuscripts down to us.

b) The use of Aramaic in New Testament criticism. It is a well-known fact that in the time of Christ Aramaic had become the common language of the Jewish people. Out of this historic fact has arisen a theory of literary criticism involving the use of Aramaic in the New Testament. It will be in order to present the theory and then to offer our refutation.

(1) The critical theory. C. C. Torrey has advanced the idea that the Gospels were originally written in Aramaic and that our present Greek Gospels represent a translation from the Aramaic original. Burney declared that the Gospel of John was written in Aramaic in Syrian Antioch about A.D. 75. Other portions of the New Testament have been added to the list. The evidences for such a view are so weak and the arguments against it so strong that it has been repudiated even by liberal scholars. Briefly put, the evidence is like this:

(a) The strongest evidence is found in the fact that there are no extant manuscripts of the New Testament in Aramaic. If the Gospels were originally in this language, it is historically unaccountable why no such manuscripts have survived. A statement· in Papias and a passing reference in Jerome (who knew of a Gospel in the language of the Jews) cannot be properly used as supports for this nebulous theory.

(b) Even before the Gospels were written, the Jews had abandoned Aramaic as a literary language. Both Philo and Josephus wrote in Greek. It is unthinkable that the early Christians would record the life and words of their Lord in a language which the Jews had already rejected as a literary device. When we add the further fact that the Christian movement was rejected at an early date (Acts 7) by the Jews, it approaches the impossible to suppose that the Early Church would use a language (Aramaic) which the Gentile world did not understand.

(c) Furthermore, the Gospels present practically no evidence of their being translation-Greek. Since all the New Testament writers (except possibly Luke) were native Jews, it is natural that they would think in terms of their Hebrew background. There are undoubted "semitisms" in the New Testament. We must also understand that the New Testament Greek is far more like the koiné than it is like classical Greek. Scholars who hold to an original Aramaic translate our Gospels back into Aramaic and then re-translate their fictitious Aramaic original into English. The process requires a great deal of ingenuity — and its results are quite unconvincing!

(d) Finally, the conservative scholar has a serious objection to this whole theory. If the critical theory be true, which is not the case, then we do not have the original words of a great part of the New Testament. According to this theory, we are without the autographs (which we all admit) and are also without the original language. We can very well do without the autographs since we have evidence that supplies that lack; but we cannot get along without the original Aramaic (if that was indeed the original language used), for we have nothing by which to test our Greek Gospels to determine whether they correspond to the (non-existent) Aramaic original. Thus we can never determine, if this theory be true, whether we have the very words of our Lord; perchance the translator may have failed to convey to us the exact sense of the original (just as Jerome failed in some of his translations from the Greek).

With all these points against it, it is unlikely that the theory of an Aramaic original can long survive among true scholars. For a much fuller refutation than we have here given, see Oswald T. Allis' article on "The Alleged Aramaic Origin of the Fourth Gospel" in *The Princeton Theological Review* (Oct., 1928), pp. 531-572.

II. The Textual Criticism of the Old Testament

The evangelical Christian, believing in the inspiration and infallibility of the original text of the Bible, is naturally much concerned about the original words of Scripture. He is well aware of the fact that, during the centuries of its transmission, various changes have taken place in the original text. It is the effort and aim of textual criticism to ascertain the nature and the extent of such variations. In the present section we shall show how we can be reliably assured that our Old Testament as represented in the Textus Receptus

has been transmitted to us essentially unchanged and un-
corrupted.

A. *The Need of Textual Criticism*

Perhaps the need of textual criticism will be best illustrated
by citing the changes that have taken place in some of the
best-known hymns used today in various churches. In some
cases whole verses of the original hymn have been deleted
in the modern hymnbook. In other cases, either for doctrinal or literary reasons, words have been omitted or
changed. As illustration, "From Thy wounded side which
flowed" was also sung as "From Thy riven side which flowed"
or also as "From Thy side a healing flood." "Could my zeal
no respite know" was also sung as "Should my zeal no lan-
guor know." "See Thee on Thy judgment-throne" appeared
as "And behold Thee on Thy throne" in other hymnbooks.
Dr. Edwards A. Parks found, for example, that in a hymnbook used by the New School Presbyterians there were
1,336 variations in 774 of their most used hymns (see Louis
F. Benson, *The Hymnody of the Christian Church* [1927],
pp. 189-224). It is thus quite evident that almost anything
that is sung or written is subject to variations as it is transmitted from generation to generation.

B. *Some Differences Between Old and New Testament*
Textual Criticism

It will be of interest at this point to note some of the
differences between textual criticism in the Old and New
Testaments. Among the more important we note the following:

1. The two differ considerably in the matter of manuscripts. In the Old Testament field, our earliest manuscripts
(not including the recently discovered Isaiah scroll), go
back to about A.D. 900. In the case of the New Testament,
the manuscripts date from a much earlier time. It was the
custom among the Jews, however, to destroy all manuscripts
when new ones were made. In the New Testament field
we hear much more about the authority of important manuscripts (such as Aleph and B) than we do in the Old Testament criticism.

2. The two differ in the value attached to ancient versions. In the Old Testament field the authority of the Septuagint stands high in the matter of ascertaining the correct text. Although ancient versions are used in New Testament textual criticism, there is no version (not even the Latin Vulgate) that commands the place of the Septuagint.

3. The two differ in the value attached to quotations. In the Old Testament realm the quotations found in the New Testament are naturally considered valuable (since the New Testament is an inspired authority). On the other hand, the quotations of the New Testament in the Church Fathers cannot receive the same esteem.

4. They differ also in the scholars interested in the two texts. Jews as well as Christians are both equally concerned in arriving at a correct text of the Old Testament; whereas in the New Testament only Christian scholars are concerned, since the Jews have never recognized the New Testament as a part of the sacred canon.

C. *The Integrity and Trustworthiness of the Hebrew Text*

We have every reason to believe that the Hebrew text which we have in modern editions of the Hebrew Bible is substantially the same — word for word — as that which was originally written by the ancient seers. The reasons for this well-grounded conclusion are not hard to find. Let us note, in particular, the following:

1. Textual purity proved by manuscript evidence. It is now possible to trace the Hebrew text back to the close of the Hebrew canon. The steps in our backward journey are the following:

a) Our earliest manuscripts, as we have already seen, allow us to go back to about A.D. 900. These manuscripts are based upon the Massoretes. The variations among them are almost altogether found in the defective writing of the pure long vowels. Such insignificant variations (about the same difference as between "-ize" and "-ise" in English) amount to about 1,200 or about one per page for the Hebrew Bible.

b) The ancient versions of Scripture (such as the Syriac

Peshitto and the Latin Vulgate) agree substantially with our Massoretic Text.

c) The quotations from the Old Testament in Philo, Josephus and the New Testament (which will be considered more fully later) agree likewise with the Massoretic Text. Thus we are now back to the first century for our evidence for the purity of the Hebrew text.

d) The recently discovered Isaiah scroll (1947) must now be included as another and earlier evidence for the Hebrew text. Although this matter has not been fully settled by scholars, it seems now clearly evident that this scroll goes back to pre-Christian times (somewhere around 100 B.C.). Too little is known about its origin to evaluate it as an independent witness for the Hebrew text. It may have been a copy used by some sect; it appears to have been poorly copied. It cannot be said to be superior to the Massoretic Text in those places where it differs.

e) The Septuagint carries us back to around 280 B.C. as an evidence for the Hebrew text. We shall attempt to explain most of its variations later. It suffices for the present to say that it is an excellent witness for the purity of the Hebrew text.

f) The Samaritan Pentateuch carries back evidence for the Pentateuch to about 400 B.C. It substantially agrees with the Hebrew.

It will be seen, from the six steps outlined above, that we can trace the essential purity of the Hebrew text right back to the time when the Old Testament canon was completed. So much, then, for our manuscript evidence.

2. Textual purity proved by monumental evidence. The Lachish ostraca, bearing Hebrew inscriptions which are dated around 589 B.C., constitute a valuable aid in the textual criticism of the Old Testament, inasmuch as the Hebrew of these ostraca bears a striking similarity to the Hebrew of a book like Jeremiah. See, further, H. H. Rowley (ed.), *The Old Testament and Modern Study* (1951), pp. 239f.

Furthermore, and even more important, there are twenty-six or more foreign kings mentioned in the Old Testament whose names have been discovered on contemporary documents. These kings represent such nations as Egypt, Assyria, Babylonia, Moab, and Persia. Their reigns cover the period from about 2000 B.C. to 400 B.C. Two striking things emerge here: On the one hand, these kings are placed at the exact time in history where archaeological research now puts them (thus confirming Biblical history); and, on the other hand, the transliteration of their names in the Massoretic Text agrees meticulously with the evidence on the ancient monument (thus confirming the remarkable purity of the Hebrew text as it has come down to us over the centuries). Much of the material given above is based on an excellent article by Dr. R. D. Wilson entitled "Scientific Biblical Criticism" in *The Princeton Theological Review* (April, 1919), pp. 190-240. The assumption is that, if the names were transmitted with such careful accuracy, surely the accounts in which the names are found were transmitted with the same fidelity.

3. Textual purity proved by parallel evidence. It appears quite evident now, due to archaeological research, that all nations in antiquity kept records of their national history. Writing, as we now know, goes back to the very beginning of man's life in this world. Some of the ancient records were made on stone (like the Annals of Thutmose III on the walls of the great temple at Karnak) and have thus survived down to the present time. Others, made on more perishable material, have long since perished. However, even records made on papyri have come down to us intact.

Now it is perfectly true that the Israelites, as far as we know, did not put their laws and records on stone for public display (like the Code of Hammurabi). We do not, therefore, have an ancient monumental record parallel to something in the Bible by which we can test the verbal accuracy of the Biblical records. However, we can apply another test.

The Hebrew documents were transmitted by making additional copies of the older copy before it was discarded or destroyed. That the scribes of Israel were as meticulously careful in copying their books as the priests of other nations (Egypt or Babylon) we have every reason to believe.

And when we turn to some of the copies made by priests or scribes of Egypt or Babylon, we find that their records were transmitted with careful accuracy. The variations that do occur are usually minor and insignificant and are similar in nature to those found in Biblical manuscripts. For evidence, see "The Textual Criticism of the Old Testament" by R. D. Wilson in *The Princeton Theological Review* (January, 1929), pp. 36-59.

4. Textual purity proved by the failure to prove corruption. This subject we list here as one of the evidences supporting the purity of the Hebrew text as we have it today, but our discussion must await a subsequent heading.

D. *Variations in the Hebrew Text*

There are, as is well-known, variations in the Hebrew manuscripts and there are variations between the manuscripts and the versions (particularly the Septuagint). There are also variations in duplicate accounts found in the Bible itself. These variations, as we shall soon see, do not affect the thesis already established above, namely, the integrity and trustworthiness of the Massoretic Text. We shall, however, address ourselves to the problem concerning these variations.

1. Sources of variations. It will be well for us at this point to find out exactly where variations occur. Such sources may be classified as internal and external.

a) Internal variations. About one-fifth of the Old Testament is what might be called duplicate or parallel (cf. the Synoptics in the New Testament). Most of these "deuterographs" are found in the parallel accounts in Samuel-Kings on the one side and Chronicles on the other side. Admittedly there are numerous variations in the two accounts of the Israelitish history during the period covered (from Saul's time down to the Exile). It is also admitted that the account in Chronicles is the later in time of the two (cf. II Chron. 36:22f). Both Kings and Chronicles mention other sources where the records of particular kings are to be found (e.g., I Kings 11:41; I Chron. 9:1). In regard to the variations in these duplicate accounts, let us note the following:

(1) There is no absolute proof that the author of Chronicles copied from Samuel-Kings. There are too many variations, even minute ones, to obstruct such a theory. Just as we cannot prove that any one of the Gospel writers copied from his predecessors, so we cannot prove that Chronicles copied from Samuel-Kings.

(2) These parallel accounts obviously do not require absolute verbal agreement. If they were exactly the same, there is no reason that can be given why they should be retained as separate documents in the canon. Their variations (just as we have four accounts of the life of our Lord) justify their existence in the canon of Scripture. So, if we are to have two separate and independent accounts of the history of Israel, we are to expect that there will be minor variations.

(3) Many of the variations in the two accounts are either stylistic (due to the individuality of the writers) or due to a later date (when certain words and idioms had changed) or due to other material included by the later source. The identical variations meet us when we compare the Synoptics with one another or compare them with the Gospel of John.

(4) Up to the present time no real problem regarding the transmission of the Hebrew text has arisen in our study of the parallel accounts in Samuel-Kings and Chronicles. There is one problem for which no completely satisfactory solution has been offered. It is found in the variations in numbers between the two accounts. For example, in I Kings 9:28 we find the number 420; whereas in the parallel account (II Chron. 8:18) we have 450. The explanation usually given is that numbers are extremely difficult to transmit and that some scribal error may be involved in the copying. These variations may test our faith but they by no means undermine our conviction that we have in our present Hebrew Bible the essential text as it came from the pen of the inspired writer. For an interesting study of

the parallel accounts in the Old Testament, one may consult Robert B. Girdlestone's *Deuterographs* (1894).

b) External variations. Here we compare the Massoretic Text of the Hebrew Bible with external sources such as ancient versions and the quotations in other parts of the Bible.

(1) The Hebrew text and the Samaritan Pentateuch. It is probably true that the Samaritan Pentateuch is our earliest witness to a part of the Hebrew Bible. We need not here detail the probable origin of this document. There are about 6,000 places where it differs from the Massoretic Text. In about 1,900 places it agrees with the Septuagint against the Hebrew text. Its major differences are either deliberate (as in the substitution of Gerizim for Ebal in Deut. 27:4, 13) or due to some other purpose not readily ascertainable. Since the time of Gesenius scholars have rejected the idea that the Samaritan Pentateuch is superior as a source of textual purity to our Massoretic Text. Most of its differences with the Hebrew text are trivial. See H. S. Gehman (ed.), *Westminster Bible Dictionary*, s. vv., "Samaritan Pentateuch" and "Chronology."

(2) The Hebrew text and the Septuagint. Here is our most complex and baffling source of variations. It is an intricate study and we must put our information in summary fashion. However, it is important enough to justify an adequate treatment.

(*a*) The value of the Septuagint. This ancient version has undisputed value in Biblical criticism. Let us note some of its values.

First, its general value. Here we must note the fact that this is the most ancient translation of the Bible. It was made undoubtedly in Egypt and was begun during the reign of Ptolemy Philadelphus (285-245 B.C.), being concluded probably as late as 150 B.C., although this later date is quite uncertain. This translation, furthermore, introduced the religion of the Jews into the Gentile world and was, in a real sense, a *preparatio evangelica*. Undoubtedly, according to early testimony, pagan writers began to borrow some of their best ideas from this translation.

Second, its textual value. From the standpoint of the Greek language, we have in the Septuagint the largest and most ancient deposit of what scholars called koiné or common Greek. This is the same kind of Greek (in contrast to the classical) that forms the foundation of New Testament Greek. Furthermore, the Septuagint gives us the most ancient witness whereby we may test the integrity and purity of the entire Hebrew Bible. There is no other authority that rates as high as it does in the matter of the textual criticism of the Old Testament text. Finally, by its general usage in the New Testament, the Septuagint has assumed a place given to no other version of the Bible. This version has been used by Christ and His apostles to convey to us the meaning of the Hebrew itself. It has, in a certain sense, been sanctioned by the New Testament.

(b) The variations of the Septuagint. There can be no doubt regarding the fact that this ancient version differs in many places and ways from the Massoretic Text. In order that we may grasp the full extent of this problem, let us note the following factors that are involved.

First, general variations. Under this description we place three features of this translation. In the first place, we note the fact that our manuscripts of the Septuagint contain books which Protestants consider as uncanonical (e.g., I and II Esdras, Tobit, Judith, etc.). This matter will be dealt with when we take up the canon. Suffice for the present to state that that fact does not prove there was a "larger" canon at Alexandria than that which the Jews held at Jerusalem. The Jews and the New Testament agree that there was but one Old Testament canon and that it is the one held by Protestants (in contrast to Roman Catholics). In the second place, there are some large differences between the Septuagint and the Hebrew text, especially in the Book of Jeremiah. In this book the text in the Septuagint is about one-eighth shorter than the Hebrew. There are subtractions and alterations in the order also. It is not felt generally, however, that the Septuagint here is to be preferred to the longer Hebrew text. In the third place, there is quite a bit of unevenness in the Septuagint — some parts are done well (e.g., the Pentateuch), others were slavishly translated (Ecclesiastes), and others were poorly rendered (Isaiah and Jeremiah). No single theory can account entirely for the variations in the quality of this translation.

Second, specific variations. There are, as we have intimated, a large number of variations between the Hebrew Massoretic Text and the Septuagint. It will be our purpose now to consider these variations and ascertain in what ways they have a bearing on the purity of the Hebrew text.

It should be noted, first of all, that there is a time-element that possibly helps to explain some variations. If the Hebrew canon was completed around 400 B.C. (as is held by most conservatives), then there is an interval of over one hundred years between the latest book in the Old Testament and the time when the Septuagint was begun. This time-interval is greatly increased if we take into account the earlier books of the Old Testament and the latest limit (about 150 B.C.) for the completion of the Septuagint. It should be remembered that the Jews had in the intertestamental period adopted both Aramaic and Greek as their languages. It is possible that, in some cases, the Septuagint translators did not know the exact meaning of some of their Hebrew words.

But a far greater cause of differences between the Septuagint and the Hebrew text is to be traced to the fact that the translators of the Septuagint were using the unpointed (pre-Massoretic) text. Since this is such an extensive subject, we cite here a few of the many possibilities of variations that could arise.

Variations due to different vowels applied to the unpointed text. In Amos 1:11 the Massoretes read "ever"; whereas the Septuagint has "witness." The unpointed Hebrew text has two consonants which may, by the use of different vowels, be read either way. Many more examples of this sort of variation could be cited. It is evident that these variations are not due to any impurity in the Hebrew text, but are rather due to the possible ways in which the same consonants can be read with different vowels.

Variations due to syntax and the difference in vocabulary

of the two languages. Sometimes two words are used to translate one in the Hebrew. This device is quite frequent with modern translators of the Bible.

Variations due to a difference in the division of words, clauses, and verses. Thus the Septuagint read "hidden" in Exodus 17:16, where the Massoretes have "throne of Jehovah." In Psalm 48:14 the Septuagint has "ages" where the Massoretes have "unto death."

Variations due to an attempt to modify certain expressions and make them more palatable to the Greek mind. It seems that in some cases, though the principle was not carried out consistently, anthropomorphic expressions were softened down somewhat.

Variations due possibly to a different text. This is, of course, purely hypothetical. If the translators of the Septuagint had a different text from our Massoretic Text, it cannot be proved that their text was superior to the Massoretic.

It will be seen, therefore, that differences between the Massoretic Text and the Septuagint are due primarily, if not exclusively, to the fact that the Jews, who translated the Septuagint, read the consonantal (unpointed) Hebrew text in a way different from the Massoretes. Since a period of more than five hundred years separates the Septuagint translators from the Massoretes, it is not improbable to suppose that the same text could have been read differently at different periods. None of this, however, seriously affects the fundamental purity of the Hebrew text as it has been transmitted to us.

E. Some Questions About the Hebrew Text

In this section we intend to answer some of the most important questions regarding the Hebrew text as given to us by the Massoretes. The answers to these questions will further enhance the value of our Hebrew Bible.

1. Why does the New Testament use the Septuagint when it differs from the Hebrew? Of the three hundred or more quotations in the New Testament the vast majority agree with the Septuagint. At the time Christ came on earth the Greek Bible had become the Bible of the Jewish people. It later became the Bible of the Christian Church. It was

quite natural, therefore, that the quotations found in the New Testament should be taken largely from the Septuagint rather than the original Hebrew. There are, of course, some quotations that agree with the Hebrew where it differs from the Septuagint. Our present concern, however, is to consider those places where the New Testament quotes from the Septuagint in which it differs from the Hebrew text.

a) Illustrations. We cite here two of the most striking examples. One is found in Acts 15:16ff (based upon the Septuagint of Amos 9:11f). The other is found in Hebrews 10:5ff (based upon the Septuagint of Ps. 40:6ff). In each case there is a striking difference between the Hebrew original and the Septuagint.

b) Explanation of these differences. Without attempting to deal with this subject exhaustively, let us set forth the following propositions: (1) Undoubtedly in each of the two cases cited there was a good reason why the Septuagint was followed. Providentially, we may believe, the Septuagint hit upon the basic meaning in each place and brought out its evangelic reference. If James had used the Hebrew in his quotation at the Council of Jerusalem, it is hardly likely that it would have supported his thesis about the present inclusion of the Gentiles in the Christian Church. (2) Furthermore, James does not specifically cite Amos. He affirms that "all the prophets" here agree. So it may be supposed that James is freely citing Amos (in the Septuagint) because it agrees with what other prophets (like Isaiah) say about the Gentiles. In the passage in Hebrews 10:5ff the word "body" (Septuagint) rather than "ears" (Hebrew) suits the Messianic interpretation although it does not contradict the original Hebrew. (3) Because the apostolic writers used these quotations from the Septuagint, even when it disagreed with the (literal) Hebrew, it does not warrant the conclusion that the New Testament gives its sanction to all variations from the original Hebrew found in the Septuagint. (4) Finally, we must suggest the thought that the New Testament writers were divinely led in their selection of Old Testament quotations and we can, therefore, believe that in the cases cited above they gave the intended meaning of the original.

2. Has the Hebrew text been corrupted intentionally? It has been asserted that our Hebrew text does not represent what was originally given but that it has been intentionally changed by the Jews. Let us look briefly at the argument and its refutation.

a) The argument stated. Here we present the three main lines of "evidence" that are said to support this thesis: (1) Certain statements found among some of the early Christians tell us that the Jews, in order to evade the force of the prophecies that Christians said were fulfilled in the Messiah, tampered with their sacred books and thus changed the meaning of the prophets. (2) It is said (and this is true) that certain revisions of the Septuagint made by Jews or renegade Christians (and now known as the versions of Aquila, Theodotion, and Symmachus) altered certain passages. For example, the Greek word *parthenos* ("virgin") in Isaiah 7:14 was changed to *neanis* ("young woman"). (3) It is maintained that evidence for this corruption is seen in the New Testament itself. Here are cited the two passages (Acts 15:16ff and Heb. 10:5ff) which we have already had under observation. It is maintained that the Septuagint retains the original meaning which the Jews had corrupted in their effort to evade the Messianic interpretation.

b) The argument refuted. It is quite easy to refute the charge that the Old Testament text was corrupted intentionally by the Jews. (1) The integrity of the Hebrew text can be tested by evidence that goes back before any controversy arose between Jews and Christians and this evidence shows that there was no designed corruption of the Hebrew text to refute claims made by Christians. For example, the recently discovered (1947) Isaiah scroll agrees substantially with the Massoretic Text. Thus from 100 B.C. (the date generally assigned to the scroll) to about A.D. 900 (the date of our earliest Hebrew manuscripts) the text of Isaiah (one of the most Messianic of the prophets) remained substantially the same without any evident attempt at alteration. (2) The references to the corruption of the text of Scripture by Jews undoubtedly have in mind the one-man revisions of the Septuagint (the Old Testament of the early Christians) made by Aquila, Theodotion and Symmachus. These were the "modernists" of their time and they attempted in some places (as Isa. 7:14) to tone down the Messianic reference (just as some modern versions have tried to do). (3) If the Jews had really tried to corrupt their Hebrew text to evade Messianic interpretations, they surely did a poor job, for some of the best Messianic passages (such as Isa. 7:14 and Isa. 53) remain unaffected, that is, they are quoted Messianically in the New Testament.

Thus the argument cannot be sustained that maintains that the Jews intentionally corrupted their Hebrew Bible in order to undermine or rule out any application of its prophecies to Christ.

3. Is the Septuagint superior to the Hebrew text? It has been held by some scholars that the Septuagint gives us a text superior to that which is found in the Massoretic Text. We shall state the basic facts on both sides.

a) The argument presented. There are three factors that appear to give the precedence to the Septuagint: (1) There is, first of all, the obvious fact that the New Testament quotes from this version most often and even in some places (as we have seen) where it differs from the Hebrew text. (2) Furthermore, the Septuagint readings are based upon manuscript evidence that carries us back over five hundred years closer to the original. (3) Finally, it is claimed that there are some places where the Septuagint undoubtedly gives the better reading.

b) The argument refuted. Very few reputable scholars at the present stage of textual criticism are willing to defend the thesis that the Septuagint text represents a closer approximation to the original than the Massoretic Text. To fully state this position, let us note the following factors: (1) The preference in the New Testament for the Septuagint does not rest on any supposed superiority of its translation over the Hebrew text. The Greek translation is used for quotations simply because it was the Bible with which people were familiar (just as we quote today from the Authorized Bible). Therefore, it is a *non sequitur* to argue for the Septuagint's superiority on this basis. (2) The earlier manuscript evidence for the Septuagint does not, in this case, prove a necessary superiority. Other factors must be taken into consideration. It is undoubtedly true that the Jews, even in their unbelief, preserved their Hebrew Bible better than the Christian Church preserved its Greek Old Testament (which was the only Old Testament that most of them knew until about the time of the Protestant Reformation and the revival of learning). The Septuagint manuscripts themselves have suffered some corruptions during the centuries of their transmission. (3) Finally, there are very few places where it can be claimed that the Septuagint gives a better reading than the Hebrew text (see a list in Sir Frederic Kenyon, *Our Bible and the Ancient Manuscripts* [1941], p. 91). There are, on the other hand, many places where the Hebrew text is manifestly superior.

4. Is there a place for conjectural emendations? It is claimed that our present Hebrew text does not make sense in some places and must be emended by other sources. Where other sources do not help, we are told that some plausible conjecture must be used. This, it seems to us, has two aspects:

a) In the Hebrew text of I Samuel 13:1 we read "Saul was —— years old when he began to reign, and he reigned —— and two years over Israel." The numbers here are omitted in the Hebrew; the Septuagint lacks the verse entirely. ASV supplies "forty" in brackets here and in a marginal note informs us that the number is added conjecturally. See also J. Patterson Smyth, *The Ancient Documents and the Modern Bible* (n.d.), pp. 189ff, for further information and other illustrations. It appears that it was quite legitimate in this case for the translators to supply the missing words and to call attention to it in a footnote. Such cases are rare indeed.

b) There are cases where scholars, dominated by some theory, make conjectural readings at their pleasure. Dr. Charles A. Briggs, for example, in his *Commentary on*

Psalms (1906) in the ICC series, very frequently resorts to conjecture in his emendation of the text of the Psalms in line with his theory of their literary composition. One of the most notorious cases of conjecture is found in Psalm 45:6. Contrast the difference here between RSV and ASV. That the RSV translation here is based upon pure conjecture is evidenced by the following considerations: (1) The Hebrew text as it stands has no ambiguity about it and should be translated as in ASV and AV. (2) Both the Septuagint and the Latin Vulgate agree here with the Hebrew text and should be translated as in ASV and AV. (3) The verse is cited in Hebrews 1:8 (apparently from the Septuagint) and is rendered there in ASV and AV just as in the Psalms. Thus it would appear that the evidence for the ASV rendering is unimpeachable. And so it is. But in spite of the overwhelming evidence RSV inserts here a conjectural rendering which was concocted in the brains of two German professors in the last century. For full details and refutation of this abominable rendering, see Oswald T. Allis' article entitled " 'Thy Throne, O God, is for ever and ever' " in *The Princeton Theological Review* (April, 1923), pp. 236-266.

F. *Certain Conclusions About the Hebrew Text*

On the basis of the data presented in this chapter it appears that we must accept certain conclusions about the Massoretic Text of the Old Testament. The first such conclusion is that there is no authority that stands higher than the Massoretic Text. It must be accepted unless there is indubitable evidence against it. The second such conclusion is that any kind of reading based on the sole authority of the ancient versions must be accepted only in extreme cases (such as I Sam. 13:1). The third conclusion is that no reading is to be accepted that runs contrary to the Massoretic Text as supported by the ancient versions and by the New Testament. Therefore, the rendering in Psalm 45:6 in RSV must be utterly rejected as due to theological bias against the deity of Christ. It stands on not one single thread of evidence!

III. THE CANON OF THE OLD TESTAMENT

The questions about the Old Testament canon are just about as complex as those questions which we have just considered about its text. However, our study of this part of our subject will be somewhat more brief.

A. *The Divisions of the Old Testament Canon*

Here we must note the threefold division and its recognition among the Jews and in the New Testament and the explanations that have been given for such a division.

1. The threefold divisions of the canon. We have ancient testimony to a threefold division of the books of the Old Testament. The three divisions are:

a) The *Torah*, or Law. This section included the books that we call the Pentateuch (Genesis, Exodus, Levitius, Numbers, Deuteronomy).

b) The *Nebhiim*, or Prophets. This section was further divided into two parts: (1) The Former Prophets (Joshua, Judges, Samuel, Kings). I and II Samuel were counted as one book; so also were I and II Kings. (2) The Latter Prophets (Isaiah, Jeremiah, Ezekiel, and the Twelve Minor Prophets, which were counted as one book). Thus there were four Former Prophets and four Latter Prophets, or a total of eight.

c) The *Kethubhim*, or Writings. This division included eleven books that were divided into three groups: (1) Psalms, Proverbs and Job. (2) The five Megilloth, or Rolls (Canticles, Ruth, Lamentations, Ecclesiastes, Esther). (3) Daniel, Ezra-Nehemiah (counted as one book), and I and II Chronicles (also counted as one book).

2. Recognition of this tripartite division. It is not certainly known when the Jews began to catalog their sacred books according to this threefold division. Our English Bible divides the Old Testament into four groups according to their contents. This division was derived from the Latin Vulgate, which, in turn, took it from the Septuagint. There are three witnesses to the threefold division:

a) In the prologue of The Wisdom of Jesus ben Sirach (Ecclesiasticus), written by the writer's grandson (about

132 B.C.) we have a reference to "the Law and the Prophets and the other books of our fathers." This shows that by at least 132 B.C., if not much earlier, there was the general recognition of the tripartite division of the Old Testament. Although the books are not mentioned as such, the presumption is that this list contains the same as given above.

b) The New Testament itself seems to bear witness to the threefold division of the Old Testament. The reference to the Law, Prophets, and Psalms in Luke 24:44 (cf. 24:27) appears to give confirmatory support to this division of the Old Testament held by the Jews.

c) Josephus (writing about A.D. 100) enumerates twenty-two books and divides them into three groups. His list, of course, is identical with the list given above.

3. Explanations of the tripartite division. Divergent views have been held regarding the reason why the Old Testament books were classified under three headings. It will serve our purpose to present concisely what can be said for, or against, each of these views.

a) Degrees of inspiration. This view was held by Jewish theologians. It maintains that Moses represents the highest form of inspiration. The prophets shared a lower inspiration. At the bottom stood the authors of the Writings or Kethubhim. This view is objectionable since it implies different levels of inspired writings. Naturally it follows that the authority of the prophets is less than that of Moses and the authority of the Writings is still less than either the Law or the prophets. Such a view has no justification from the New Testament, which treats all of the Old Testament as equally inspired and authoritative.

b) Three stages of canonization. This is the almost universal view held by those who take the modern view of the Bible. Briefly put, this school holds the Law was canonized around 444 B.C.; the Prophets about 200 B.C.; and the Writings somewhere around 100 B.C. (cf. S. H. Gehman [ed.], *The Westminster Bible Dictionary* [1944], p. 92). Many arguments are advanced in favor of this viewpoint, the chief of which are the following:

(1) It is maintained that certain books of the Old Testa-

ment did not originate until after the time of Ezra. Such books as Ecclesiastes, Esther, Daniel, Chronicles and some of the Psalms are dated by the critics down into Persian and Greek times. It naturally follows, if this be so, that the canon could not have been completed at the time of Ezra. In fact, according to this school, it was just begun at that time.

The answer to this argument is found in the fact that it cannot be proved, on objective grounds, that the books mentioned above came into existence at the times indicated by the critical school of higher criticism. This matter, of course, belongs to the special introduction of the books involved.

(2) It is claimed that the Samaritans, who split from the Jews at the time of Ezra and Nehemiah, accepted the Pentateuch alone as authoritative. Ezra read the Law (the Pentateuch) to the assembled people in 444 B.C. Manasseh, expelled by Nehemiah in 432 B.C. because he had married a non-Jew, took with him the Pentateuch. The reason why other books were not taken, according to this view, is due to the fact that the other books were not yet considered canonical.

The answer to this assertion is readily found in the fact that the critics do not give the real reason why the Samaritans hold the Pentateuch alone as authoritative. It is well known that they established a rival worship on Mt. Gerizim and changed the Pentateuch accordingly (putting Gerizim for Ebal in Deut. 27:4, 13). Since Zion or Jerusalem is generally recognized throughout the prophets and especially in the Psalms as the center of true worship, it would have been impossible for them to have acknowledged these books as authoritative. That the prophets were looked upon in the time of Ezra as authoritative can be readily deduced from the statements made about them by prophets who were contemporary with Ezra (cf. Neh. 9:30; Dan. 9:2; Zech. 7:7, 12).

(3) It is affirmed that the Jews were indefinite about their canonical books down to the time of the Council of Jamnia (A.D. 90). Such books as Ezekiel, Proverbs, Can-

ticles, Ecclesiastes and Esther were objected to by certain Jews. This would prove, so liberals maintain, that the Old Testament canon was not completed in the time of Ezra.

The answer to this supposed proof is easily seen. On the one hand, disputes by certain Jews about certain books cannot be taken as disproving the early origin of the books disputed. The contention was about the canonicity of the disputed books — not about their age or about a threefold division of the canon. Furthermore, the critical claim here really goes too far; for, if their view is correct, then they can no longer claim a completion of the canon around 100 B.C. Some critics have at least been consistent and have maintained that it was not really completed until around A.D. 90 (cf. Robert H. Pfeiffer, *Introduction to the Old Testament* [1948], p. 64). This would carry with it the implication that when the New Testament was written (during the first century) it had not yet been authoritatively determined which Old Testament books were properly canonical. However, it is positively certain that no New Testament writer ever questioned his right to quote authoritatively and indiscriminately, as the occasion demanded, from any one of the thirty-nine books of the Old Testament (or twenty-two according to Josephus' listing of the same books). If the New Testament writers did not quote from Esther, Canticles or Ecclesiastes, neither did they quote from Obadiah or Nahum. Furthermore, Ezekiel and Proverbs (both under dispute by the Jews) were quoted authoritatively by the New Testament. In fact, Revelation borrows heavily from the language and symbolism of Ezekiel (cf. G. T. Manley [ed.], *The New Bible Handbook* [1947], p. 231). It can be readily understood, without any reference to their canonicity, why the New Testament writers did not quote from the books mentioned above.

c) The position of the writer. Conservatives generally maintain that the tripartite division of the Old Testament rests fundamentally on the difference in status of the writers. This will be explained and defended in the following propositional statements:

(1) There was a recognition of the inspired character

and canonical authority of the Old Testament books from the very time of their origin. See the many references in John H. Raven, *Old Testament Introduction* [1910], p. 18). Joshua (1:8) as well as Malachi (4:4) considered the Law of Moses authoritative. The prophets were looked upon as authoritative (Zech. 7:12). All were equally inspired — whether Moses or Isaiah or Job — from their inception and considered likewise authoritative.

(2) There is no place in Biblical history where the writings of any man were officially canonized. When the Book of the Law was found in the temple during the reign of Josiah (II Kings 22f), there was an immediate recognition of its divine authority. No canonization is conceivable in such a situation. The Jews instinctively recognized its canonical authority. The reading of the Law by Ezra (Neh. 8:1-8) in the post-captivity era did not, as critical scholars maintain, constitute the Law as canonical. The Law of Moses was already recognized and accepted by the people and the leaders as inspired and authoritative. Thus it is pure fiction when the liberal school designates 444 B.C. as the time when the Law was officially canonized and 200 B.C. as the time when the Prophets were canonized and 100 B.C. as the time when the remaining books received canonical authority. There is not a line in Biblical or Jewish history that gives the least credance to such an arbitrary theory. It has been invented out of imagination to back up an unprovable theory.

(3) The conservative view explains best why certain books are in each of the three divisions. According to this view (as explained by W. H. Green, *General Introduction to the Old Testament: The Canon* [1898], pp. 80ff), Moses stands, so to speak, in a class by himself (although his inspiration is not higher than those who followed). The difference between the other two groups — Prophets and Writings — is determined by the status of the writer. The second group included only those who were prophets in the technical or official sense of the term. Thus Joshua, Judges, Samuel and Kings are included along with Isaiah, Jeremiah, Ezekiel and The Twelve, since they all wrote (his-

tory or exhortation and prophecy) from the standpoint of official prophets. The third group contains men who were inspired but were not official prophets. They may have had, of course, the gift of prophecy even without the official status. This explains why Daniel is in the third group rather than the second group. There is much of prediction in Daniel, for he had the gift of prophecy (cf. Matt. 24:15), although there is barely any exhortation in his book similar to what is found so fully in Jeremiah and other official prophets.

(4) The conservative view thus explains a fact for which the critical view cannot give an adequate reason, namely, why Chronicles is in the same division with Daniel. Chronicles, it would appear, ought to have been in the same division with Kings, for it covers the same general period as Kings and presumably was not written much later than Kings. A date generally given for Chronicles is around 400 B.C. (cf. S. H. Gehman [ed.], *The Westminster Bible Dictionary* [1944], p. 101). But this date would put Chronicles at approximately the same time when the Law (444 B.C.) was canonized, according to the liberal view. It would put it right in the period when the Prophets were canonized (200 B.C.), according to the same view. Thus it is extremely difficult to explain why Chronicles is in the third division if it had been in existence long before even the second division was closed. On conservative grounds this is not a difficulty at all, for the writer of Chronicles presumably did not have the same status as the writers of Joshua, Judges, Samuel. If Ezra was the writer of Chronicles (and a strong case can be made for such an assumption), then he wrote as a man inspired but not possessing the status of an official prophet.

B. *The Completion of the Old Testament Canon*

This subject is naturally closely related to the one just discussed. For the sake of definiteness it will be necessary to repeat here part of the material already presented above. There is a radical conflict between the conservative and modern views on this issue, as will soon appear.

1. The modern view. We need not here elaborate in detail the critical view of the completion of the Old Testament canon. As indicated above, its basic principle (accepted generally as one of the "assured results" of modern criticism) rests upon the premise that the tripartite division of the Old Testament proves that there were three chonological stages in the completion of the canon. To illustrate, Daniel is in the third division (according to the liberal school) because when Daniel was written (about 165 B.C. according to their dating) the second division (the Prophets) had already been closed (around 200 B.C.). Thus it was impossible for Daniel to be included with the Prophets. The fallacies of the modern view are almost too self-evident to require exposure. Note the following:

a) This view, as we have formerly intimated, is based upon pure theory for which no solid facts can be advanced. No one can prove, on the basis of facts that would stand in any court, that the canon of the Old Testament was developed in three historical stages. Let the critics bring forth evidence — not conjecture — supporting the thesis that Daniel was excluded from the Prophets because the canon of the prophetic books had been closed before he wrote — and then we will believe their view! But it is impossible for them to present such evidence, for nothing of that sort exists except in the critical fancy.

b) This theory is really the daughter of desperation. It is required by the whole reconstruction of the Old Testament which the critical school has invented during the past century. Let us note some of the points in this complex story. (1) The Graf-Wellhausen theory advanced as one of its fundamentals the thesis that the Pentateuch could not have been finished until the Babylonian Captivity. So, as the theory goes, when Ezra read the Law to the returnees (Neh. 8:1-8) that act officially canonized the Law! It sounds plausible until you ask for evidence for such an official act. (2) Therefore, assuming the previous proposition to be true, the critical school jumps to the conclusion (for which there is not a syllable of evidence) that all the other books were not recognized as canonical until someone (whose existence is unknown) declared them to be canonical. In the case of the Prophets this official canonization took place about 200 B.C.; but in the case of the other books it did not happen until around 100 B.C. Thus the critical school is compelled by its theory to date either the origin or the canonization of all the Old Testament books (except the Law or Pentateuch) in the post-exilic period. This explains why it is imperative that this school dump a large part of the Old Testament into the period after the Exile.

c) This theory cannot be sustained on the basis of facts. In order to present these facts adequately it would be necessary to write a book on Old Testament Introduction, in which it could be proved that very little of the Old Testament was written in the post-captivity period. It could also be shown how the books written in the pre-exilic period were recognized as canonical, along with the Law, from the time of their origin. Thus the theory of three successive stages of canonization invented by the critical school breaks down on the basis of the proper dating of the Old Testament books.

2. The conservative view. So much of this view has already been presented indirectly in refutation of the modern view that we need not go into it in extensive detail. It will be needful to present only a brief summary of this position.

a) It can be proved, on the basis of internal and external evidence, that no book in the Old Testament requires a date for its origin later than about 400 B.C. Esther, Ezra-Nehemiah, and Chronicles record the last events in Old Testament history and not one of these events can be proved to come much after 400 B.C. The same is true of the post-exilic prophets (Haggai, Zechariah and Malachi).

b) Linguistic evidence, which we cannot present here, confirms the fact that the books just mentioned were written in the early post-exilic period. The same kind of evidence confirms the dating of Old Testament books in the places in history where they have been traditionally located. The facts involved have been ably set forth by R. D. Wilson in an article entitled "Evidence in Hebrew Diction for the Date of Documents" in *The Princeton Theological Review* (July, 1927), pp. 353-388.

c) There is evidence from the post-exilic books (especially Zech. 13:2-5 and Mal. 4:5) that the prophets of that period sensed the soon departure of the Spirit of prophecy from them. Two confirmatory sources support this thesis. On the one hand, it is well known that some of the apocryphal books written in the intertestamental period acknowledge their non-inspiration (e.g., II Macc. 2:23; 15:38). On the other hand, Josephus informs us that the Old Testament canon was completed in the time of Ezra during the reign of Artaxerxes Longimanus (465-424 B.C.). Although Josephus lived in the first century A.D., he must have had some substantial tradition upon which to base his assertion.

C. *The Test of Canonicity*

What feature, quality or characteristic of an Old Testament book gave it a right to be in the list of canonical books? This is a question which has been answered in a large variety of ways. We shall now address ourselves to this problem and its solution.

1. False tests of canonicity. There is, as we have already shown, no actual place in the Old Testament where any book or set of books was officially declared to be canonical. Neither the finding of the Law (II Kings 22f) nor the reading of the Law (Neh. 8:1-8) is to be understood as a canonization. In both cases the peoples and the authorities recognized the Law as already authoritative. Modern scholars, however, have tried to find some tests guaranteeing the canonicity of individual books. The following are among such attempts:

a) The age of a book. This cannot apply because some books obviously as old as our canonical books (such as "the Book of Jashar") are not now in the canon.

b) Some have supposed the use of the Hebrew language was the test of canonicity. But some of the intertestamental books (such as Ecclesiasticus, Tobit and I Maccabees) were written in Hebrew originally and yet they were not included in the canon. This view would also exclude those portions of the Old Testament that were written in Aramaic.

c) Agreement with the Law has been considered to be an absolute test. But this test is invalid because it gives no test for the Law itself. What makes the Law canonical? Is it without any test except its right to test later documents? This view would automatically place the Law in a superior position as if it could test but could not be tested. Thus we get degrees of inspiration as a result of this view. It is perfectly true, however, since the Word of God is self-consistent, that all revelation after the Law must agree with the Law. The reference in Isaiah 8:20 (cf. verse 16) "to the law (or, teaching) and to the testimony" is not necessarily to the Mosaic Law.

d) Others suppose that books went through a period of public testing to determine their edifying characteristic before they were admitted to the list of canonical books. This theory overlooks some patent facts: (1) No Biblical book is ever submitted to the religious public to test its authority or inspiration. This would make the people the judge as to which books were canonical. (2) This theory mistakes the effect for the cause. Biblical books are universally uplifting and edifying, in spite of what infidels may say to the contrary. But this effect is not the cause of a book's right to canonicity. The cause lies deeper than the effect, as will be seen under the following heading.

2. True test of canonicity. According to the historic Church and according to the conservative position, there is a quality resident in every canonical book which manifests its intrinsic right to be numbered in the sacred canon. Since the Holy Spirit is the real Author behind all Biblical books (II Tim. 3:16), it is logical for us to believe that He will leave on every book He inspires the impress of its divine nature. That men do not readily or always recognize this divine quality in every God-breathed book of Scripture is due more to the blindness of man's spiritual perception than to any defect in the book itself. It will be quite natural, therefore, for the unregenerate man, ignorant or learned,

to fail to see any peculiar difference between the canonical books of Scripture and those which are not canonical. Since the Spirit of God is not in such an individual (cf. Jude 19), there is no testimony in that person to the supernatural character of the Word of God. But when a man is regenerate, the Holy Spirit bears witness with the human spirit of the regenerate that the books of the Bible were authored by the Spirit. That some Christians have not always recognized the canonical right of some of the books of Scripture is due more to the remnants of spiritual blindness still abiding in their renewed nature than to any failure in the books themselves to manifest their divine origin.

D. *Two Remaining Questions*

In any discussion of the Old Testament canon, two questions of paramount importance must be dealt with before the discussion can be said to be complete. In the light of what has already been advanced, it should not take us too much time to decide these questions rightly.

1. Are there any books which should be excluded? If this question were answered affirmatively, it would imply that certain books had crept into our sacred canon surreptitiously and that, due to our more recent discovery of their fraudulent character, they ought now to be excluded. This would also imply that we had additional knowledge today to base our judgment upon, which was not available to those in previous generations. There are, we believe, only four reasons that have been, or could be, advanced for the exclusion of any of the thirty-nine canonical books of the Old Testament. We present each very briefly with its refutation.

a) Because of its fraudulent character. This would apply, on the modern view of the Bible, to such books as Deuteronomy and Daniel, both of which are spoken of as "pious frauds" by the critical schools. Of course, if their view is correct, and if the Bible is designed to teach truth and not falsehood, then it is impossible to justify the inclusion of such books in the sacred canon. But conservative Christianity has never (and we hope will never) accept the critical view of these two books. To the Bible-believing Christian they are just as much the Word of God as any other portion.

b) Because of inferior morals. This charge is especially made against Esther and Canticles. It is affirmed of the first book that it teaches national pride and vindictiveness and of the second book that it is a sensual description of an oriental harem. These accusations are made especially by those who take the modern view of the Bible. It is almost self-evident that neither charge is true. The history of Esther undoubtedly shows the guiding hand of God in Israel's history (although God is never mentioned once in the book) and shows also how God can make the wrath of men to work out His purposes. The book itself is a wonderful illustration of providence. The true Church has never understood Canticles as a sensual description of a harem. The real meaning of the book is found in its rich symbolism. The Puritans found in it a realistic description of the mystical relationship of Christ to His bride, the Church (cf. Eph. 5:22-33).

c) Because of fictitious history. On this ground the Book of Esther, for example, would be excluded, for it is, so some modern critics claim, little more than a transformed pagan myth containing numerous historical discrepancies and improbabilities, thus making it difficult, if not impossible, to claim for it canonical authority. But conservative scholars have never regarded the story in Esther as mythical and have defended its historicity on the objective grounds of archaeological research. It has as high a rank in history as any other Biblical book — in so far as it has been or can be tested.

d) Because of bad theology. This accusation is particularly hurled against Ecclesiastes. It is affirmed that its pessimism is more after the order of Greek Stoicism than prophetic truth. But this estimate completely misunderstands its nature. If it was written by Solomon, as conservatives believe is the case, then it (especially if written in his old age) represents what a man comes to when he searches for wisdom and turns away from God (as Solomon did in his later years). The Bible is the most realistic book of all books written. It pictures life graphically in all of its moods and tenses. If Ecclesiastes is understood as part of the total picture given to us in the Bible of God and man, then it has a place in the sacred canon. If II and III John have a right in the canon, even though they are short, personal letters, who will deny that Solomon, under divine influence, cannot tell us his spiritual autobiography?

2. Are there any books which should be included? Practically all Protestants will give a universal negative to this queston, affirming that in the thirty-nine canonical books of the Old Testament we have the only sacred deposit of the older revelation. On the othei hand, the Roman Catholic Church argues vehemently that certain apocryphal books should be added to the thirty-nine. We are persuaded that the Roman Church has greatly erred on this point. We give here but a summary of the valid arguments against the inclusion of apocryphal books:

a) These books belong to the intertestamental period when, as we have already seen, the Spirit of prophecy had departed from Israel. Some of them even disclaim inspiration (II Macc. 2:23; 15:38).

b) Their content generally shows that they are inferior to the canonical books in their historical accuracy and moral teaching.

c) They inculcate some things (such as praying for the dead) which are considered to be obnoxious to the teaching of the Bible.

d) It cannot be proved that they were ever considered by the Jews as a part of their official canon. The fact that they are included in manuscripts of the Septuagint cannot be used to prove that a "larger" canon existed among the Jews of Alexandria.

e) These books are never quoted in the New Testament nor considered in any wise as inspired or canonical. The supposed references to the apocryphal books can all be explained otherwise.

f) The inclusion of these books in the canon by the Council of Trent (1546) cannot but be regarded as a sad departure from Christian truth. That Council went against her best teachers and the best evidence. For a fuller presentation of the Protestant case against the Apocrypha, see George L. Robinson, *Where Did We Get Our Bible?* (1928), pp. 64-74.

CHAPTER SEVEN

ARCHAEOLOGY AND CRITICISM

A book written on Biblical criticism must inevitably take into account the contribution made by modern discoveries to critical questions and problems. In the present chapter, therefore, we intend to present briefly the main points in the field of Biblical archaeology as they throw light on literary problems raised by modern criticism.

I. WHAT IS ARCHAEOLOGY?

As the name indicates in its etymology, archaeology is the science of ancient things. It is the attempt, as far as possible and by whatever means are available (writings, objects, pictures, etc.), to reconstruct the history of man from the very beginning. Archaeology is a science with its own canons of research and investigation. It does not limit itself to Biblical lands but goes wherever any remnant of man's ancient life is found on the globe. Our study limits our investigation primarily to the lands connected with Biblical history. Archaeology is a comparatively recent science (as we shall soon see) but stands today tall and upright with a dignity all its own. It speaks with an authority which seriously affects some of the theories held before, and even after, its advent on the scene of action.

II. THE CHANGED SITUATION CREATED BY ARCHAEOLOGY

One cannot doubt the fact that the study of modern archaeology has produced quite a change in the views formerly held by some critics about the Bible. In order to show the extent of this changed situation, let us compare the situation today with that which existed at the beginning of the nineteenth century.

A. The Situation at the Beginning of the Nineteenth Century

When the nineteenth century began, scholars had little evidence outside the Bible itself for the things which the Bible records as historical events. The situation then could be described as about like the following.

1. Biblical sites and geography not well-known. Of course, some of the most outstanding places mentioned in the Bible were known and correctly identified, but there were others about which very little was actually known. Because of various factors, contact with the Holy Land was at a minimum.

2. Inscriptions in ancient languages utterly unknown. The traveler in the ancient East could have seen in Egypt and elsewhere inscriptions which meant nothing to him. They could be seen on public monuments, but their meaning could not be known.

3. Extant literature outside the Bible was late and scanty. Writings of Homer, Herodotus, Xenophon and other Greek and Roman authors were known, but these contained little bearing, either directly or indirectly, on the Biblical story. The ancient world was largely shrouded in mystery and there was no general outline in the remains then known by which to test the history of the Bible.

4. In view of the situation just described, it was inevitable that when the spirit of rationalism arose in Europe, the Bible would become one of the chief targets of that movement. Such outstanding scholars as Wolf and Grote (cf. O. T. Allis, *The Five Books of Moses* [1943], pp. 206f) believed that real history began in Greece about 776 B.C. It was considered quite improbable that Moses could have written the Pentateuch centuries before Greek civilization began to flourish. Around 1800 it was easy to make statements about the Bible that could neither be defended nor refuted by outside sources. It was a time, therefore, that easily gave birth to many conjectural theories that flourished brilliantly for a while until archaeology arose and stunted their growth.

B. *The Situation Today*

In the middle of the twentieth century we find ourselves in happy contrast with the situation that prevailed just a little over a century ago. This contrast may be detailed in the following manner.

1. Flood of new light on Bible geography, sites and customs. Any map of the early part of the last century is completely antiquated today. Many of the places that were simply names in the Bible have been identified and excavated.

2. Unknown languages of antiquity have been deciphered. About one hundred years ago nothing could be read which was written in Egyptian hieroglyphic or Babylonian cuneiform. Today, due to the discovery of the Rosetta stone (1822) and its decipherment by J. F. Champollion, the hieroglyphic has opened up its vast treasure. In a similar way, the Babylonian cuneiform can now be read, through the discovery and deciphering of H. Rawlinson (in 1851) of the famous Behistun inscription of Darius I (521-486 B.C.). Some other ancient languages await deciphering.

3. Many new manuscripts now known. Some of these manuscripts are parts of the Bible; others belong to the secular world. The discovery of the papyri revolutionized our concept of the language of the New Testament. The full impact of the *Dead Sea Scrolls* (containing a very early manuscript of Isaiah) has not yet been completely felt in critical circles.

4. Bible history now understood better than ever before. The older skepticism, that found in Homer a myth and in the fall of Troy a glorified legend, is no longer acceptable in the scholarly world. Applied to the Bible, this means that the critical theories connected with the Graf-Wellhausen hypothesis have had to undergo radical revision with a definite slant toward more conservative conclusions.

III. THE METHOD OF ARCHAEOLOGY

The science of archaeology has a definite method by which it reaches its results. Every step in this method is absolutely necessary. The steps are so related that, if there is a misinterpretation at one point, it will seriously affect the result. There are three definite steps about which we must speak a word.

A. Discovery and Identification

Using the Bible or any other ancient source as his guide, the archaeologist identifies some mound as a definite site of an ancient city. Only by actual excavation of a part or all of the mound can it be determined whether the identification was right. Although much work has been done along this line, there are still many places that await identification.

B. Excavation

The excavation of an ancient mound is an intricate task that must be performed with great care so that every possible "find" might be discovered in the remains. Each article as discovered is carefully marked and identified as far as possible.

It should be remembered that by wars and the ravages of natural forces ancient cities were often destroyed and were also often rebuilt on the same site. This means that in some cases the excavator will find a number of successive layers, each one of which contains remains (pottery, tools, etc.) belonging to its period. A most remarkable illustration of this is found in the excavation of ancient Troy by Heinrich Schliemann. He found nine ancient settlements, one on top of the other, down to Roman times. Schliemann identified the Troy of which Homer sang as being the second from the bottom; more recent excavations identify it with the seventh city. A good illustration of this same method is seen in the excavation of Jericho.

C. Evaluation and Interpretation

It is a simple truism to state that the "finds" of an archaeological expedition mean nothing unless they are rightly evaluated. As we have said above, everything of any significance is kept and tabulated. Pictures are taken, maps and diagrams are drawn, and all facts concerning the discovery are carefully recorded. There are at least two things that enter into a proper evaluation of any "find."

1. Translation. If the object found is written (as clay tablets or papyri), it must be translated. This is now possible, as we have already seen, in the case of some of the more important ancient languages. We have now translations of the famous Code of Hammurabi and many other outstanding inscriptions and documents.

2. Time. From what period does the discovered object come? Here the archaeologist has discovered various clues that give him a fairly good yardstick by which to date his "finds." One of the most widely used clues is found in the pottery remains discovered at the various sites (cf. *The International Standard Bible Encyclopaedia* [1930], *s. v.,* "Pottery"). If his discovery be an ancient manuscript (as, for example, the *Dead Sea Scrolls*), then he will examine the material used, the type of handwriting, and other such features to determine the age of the document.

The result of the prolonged and painstaking task of excavation is made known to the world in scholarly as well as popular publications. For want of funds, as well as for lack of competent scholars, much of what is excavated often is stored away in some museum or university. It is possible that some of the most important discoveries of modern times are already within reach of the archaeologist.

IV. THE NATURE OF ARCHAEOLOGICAL EVIDENCE

It will be well worth our time to put down some of the characteristics of archaeological discoveries. It will be seen at a glance that we are dealing here with something of extraordinary value to the Biblical student.

A. *Archaeological Evidence Is Ancient*

The first characteristic is the most obvious: archaeology deals with ancient things. It seeks to uncover all that remains of ancient peoples or civilizations. It wants to know man's original home and his succeeding history as far as it can be traced. It wants to know how man lived at each stage of his history. This includes man's religion, his customs, his laws, his business; in fact, everything that can be found out about ancient man.

B. *Archaeological Evidence Is Often Contemporary*

By this we mean that the objects found in an ancient mound were usually left there at the time when they were used by the people of that time. There are many "finds" that are undoubtedly contemporary with some known event in Biblical history. The famous Amarna Letters are undoubtedly contemporary with the time of Joshua. The Elephantine papyri are contemporary with the early post-exilic period. The epic literature of Ras Shamra is undoubtedly contemporary with early Israelitish history. The Code of Hammurabi is doubtlessly of the same age as Genesis 14. We could go on and multiply instances. The fact that so much of archaeological evidence is of the same date as some Biblical event adds greatly to its worth as evidence. We have, so to speak, another voice speaking to us from the time of Abraham or Moses or Isaiah.

C. *Archaeological Evidence Can Be Dated*

It is probably true that most of the "finds" of archaeology can be successfully dated within a century of the time to which they belong. An ancient scroll or papyrus can, as we have seen, be dated by the material used or the script employed or by internal or external facts. Pottery and scarabs, which are often dated in a king's reign, give us good clues as to the time of a particular site. In some cases archaeologists are agreed as to specific date of an event; in other cases, where the excavation is incomplete or where the "finds" are differently interpreted, specific dates are not yet agreed on. Two striking illustrations of what we are here referring to are found in the debate about the fall of Jericho and about the identification of Amraphel (Gen. 14) with Hammurabi. Further excavation and study will undoubtedly clear up some of the problems that exist today.

D. *Archaeological Evidence Is Undersigned*

By this we mean, to put it bluntly, that no object or inscription was ever put away in the ground or written in ancient times by some Egyptian, Babylonian or Israelite to confirm or refute something in the Bible in modern times. The ancient man never anticipated such debates about the historicity of Jonah or the accuracy of Daniel or the exilic origin of the P-document, as characterize much of modern criticism. An Israelite back in Isaiah's time did not know that after twenty-five hundred years there would be a debate about the unified authorship of Isaiah's prophecy. And we can say that no contemporary of Luke ever thought of writing something on a papyrus or inscribing it on a monument so that two millenniums afterwards it would confirm, against hostile attacks, the historicity of Luke's account of the census taken during the governorship of Quirinius. Such things were no more in the ancient mind than they are in our mind today to confirm some statement about history that is perfectly obvious to us but which may be under attack a thousand years from now.

E. *Archaeological Evidence Is Not Infallible*

Somehow the opinion exists that the Bible must always harmonize with what the archaeologist finds. This is based on the assumption that the records discovered by the excavator are always right and the Bible always wrong if it relates a different situation. For example, the Egyptian monuments are practically silent on the Israelitish bondage which looms so large in Biblical history. This great disparity is used by some to show that the account in the Bible is either fictional or legendary.

But it can be proved on objective grounds that the events recorded in the Bible are just as reliably reported as an event that may be found in an ancient clay tablet, inscription or papyrus. If there is any disparity between the Bible and the archaeological material, the weight of probability, even on naturalistic grounds, would surely be in favor of the Bible. So many of the "finds" of the archaeologist are detached, fragmentary, and unrelated to other documents or things that it is quite often impossible to reconstruct the exact historical context out of which they arose.

F. *Archaeological Evidence Often Bears on Critical Questions*

Though archaeological evidence is not infallible, yet it does go far in the settlement of critical disputes about the Bible. There are still some, however, who deny that the "assured results" have been materially affected by modern discoveries. This denial is by no means universal even among liberals. There can be no doubt that liberals are still trying to live in the period before the advent of modern archaeology when it was easy to make a theory reconstructing Bible history out of the critic's imagination. That day is gone forever. One who ignores the contribution of archaeology to critical problems jeopardizes thereby his right to be called scholarly. When such a scholar as William Foxwell Albright, although by no means a conservative, calls in question some of the skepticism about early Israelitish history and religion, it is time for his disciples and lesser lights to take heed. See his *From the Stone Age to Christianity* (1942), *Archaeology and the Religion of the Hebrews* (1942), "Old Testament and Archaeology" in *Old Testament Commentary* (1948), and "The Old Testament World" in *The Interpreter's Bible* (1952), vol. 1.

To affirm, therefore, that the critical theories of the nineteenth century, modeled after the evolutionary pattern, are unaffected by the modern science of archaeology is simply to date one's self as an obscurantist or to hide one's head in an intellectual fog. This statement, strong as it may appear, is justified by what we shall present in the ensuing discussion.

V. THE BEARING OF ARCHAEOLOGY ON CRITICAL QUESTIONS

We shall not attempt an exhaustive analysis of critical questions in the light of modern discoveries. Such a task would be quite impossible in our limited space. We shall, however, indicate briefly some of the ways in which archaeology has a bearing on critical questions. Since archaeology's contribution is manifold, we must look at our subject from different perspectives. In a word, we shall see how archaeology completely refutes some critical theories and how, in general, it confirms the traditional view held down through the centuries and now equated largely with the conservative view.

A. *Critical Theories Discredited by Archaeology*

When we speak of "critical theories" we have in mind those views of the Bible that largely originated in the nineteenth century under the influence of German rationalism. Such names as Graf, Wellhausen and Cheyne would represent this position, although they had numerous disciples who advocated their theories with equal brilliance. That these men and their disciples advocated theories which can no longer be considered valid no one today can deny. Swallowing the naturalistic theory of evolution and making it a part of their mental outlook, they, under the spell of that theory, completely revised Israelitish history and religion so as to make it conform to their preconceived theory. As a result, many books of the Old Testament and many events therein described were put at different times than where they had been placed for centuries. And so drastic was this revision by the yardstick of evolution that some statements in the Bible were categorically denied as true. They became merely the invention of a later age without any historical foundation in fact. That these assertions regarding the critical viewpoint are true will appear more evident as we cite particulars.

1. The ignorance of the Patriarchal age. Critics of the liberal school have imputed ignorance and a very low state of civilization to the age of the Patriarchs. Such a scholar as Dillmann denied the Mosaic authorship of the Pentateuch on the ground that such an extensive literary production would be unbelievable at that time (cf. quotation in M. G. Kyle, *The Deciding Voice of the Monuments in Biblical Criticism* [1924], pp. 83f). This grew out of the idea, prevalent in the last century before the advent of archaeology, that written history hardly began before the first Olympiad (776 B.C.). Thus it would be quite unthinkable that Moses could have written the Pentateuch hundreds of years before the earliest Greek writers. That this position is no longer tenable will become quite evident from the following:

a) Modern archaeology has discovered a vast literature that is contemporary with Moses and the Patriarchs. The famous Code of Hammurabi, to cite only one example, is admittedly contemporary with Abraham, showing that, in that time, there was a high degree of civilization.

b) Archaeology has also proved the antiquity of writing. It is now known that man was in possession of the knowhow of writing as far back as 4000 B.C., or even earlier. Documents are now dated back to the time just indicated.

c) Finally, since the discovery of the Ras Shamra alphabet texts (1929-1937), it is probable that alphabetic writing was known as early as the time of Moses or earlier. In fact, since the discovery of some inscriptions on the Sinai peninsula in 1904-1905, it is probable that a Semitic language in alphabetic form, midway between the Egyptian hieroglyphs and the Phoenician, existed as far back as the nineteenth century B.C. Cf. Henry Snyder Gehman (ed.), *The Westminster Dictionary of the Bible* (1944), p. 22.

All the evidence thus confirms the traditional view that Moses was the author of the Pentateuch. It is highly unlikely that a man of his background (trained in all the learning of the Egyptians) would have been incapable of composing the books attributed to him.

2. The late origin of monotheism. One of the results of the application of evolution to the religion of the Old Testament is found in the supposition that Israel's monotheism is the climax of a long period during which the Hebrews went through such stages as animism, polytheism, henotheism, and monotheism. In books by liberals on Old Testament religion this development was almost taken for granted. It was considered practically inconceivable that Moses was a monotheist — not to mention the patriarchs. It was also considered highly probable by some liberals that Israel may have borrowed her monotheism from other nations. That this position is no longer tenable in the light of archaeology will be evident from the following particulars:

a) There is archaeological evidence that monotheism preceded polytheism in the ancient Sumerian religion at around 4000 B.C. This is the conclusion of Dr. S. H. Langdon, pro-

fessor of Assyriology at Oxford (cf. his article on this subject in *The Evangelical Quarterly* [April, 1937], pp. 136-146).

b) There is also archaeological evidence that the primitive monotheism was early corrupted into polytheism and
animism. Dr. Langdon tells us that the early god of the
Sumerians was considered personal and had the name *An*
(Heaven or Sky). By about 3000 B.C. the Sumerian pantheon contained around 750 deities. Eventually there were
5,000 gods in this pantheon.

c) There is no evidence that Israel borrowed her monotheism from any surrounding source. How could she borrow monotheism from peoples that had already sunk into
polytheism and animism? If anything, she borrowed her
polytheism from other nations, as the Bible so plainly shows.
Baalism, for example, corrupted the people of Israel during
a considerable part of their history; but this corrupt Canaanite cult was never considered by the true prophets as
representative of the true religion.

d) Since the earliest narrative in the Bible (Gen. 1-11)
is located in the Tigris-Euphrates valley, it is strikingly
significant how the Biblical account agrees with the earliest
description of the religion of Sumer. There is not the slightest suggestion of polytheism in the Genesis account (1-11).
And, as we have seen above, the early religion of the Sumerians was undoubtedly monotheistic. The corruption of
the Sumerian religion at a later date was probably one of
the causes why God commanded Abraham to leave Ur.

e) The primitive monotheism of the race, a direct result
of supernatural revelation at the very beginning of human
history (cf. Rom. 1:19ff), has been retained in the further
revelation given to Israel in the Old Testament and consummated in the New Testament revelation. It is also retained in the "Sky-God" concept found among primitive
peoples scattered throughout the world today (cf. Samuel
M. Zwemer, *The Origin of Religion* [1945]).

Thus the evangelical view of Israel's religion and supernatural revelation is on a firmer basis today than ever before — thanks to discoveries made in the Near East in recent
years. The reconstruction-theories of the nineteenth century

must be reconstructed again in the light of modern archaeology.

3. The mythical content of Genesis 1 to 11. The liberal school has characteristically described these chapters as myths. They are put in the category of the prehistorical. The remaining chapters in Genesis (12-50) are called legends. The difference is this: myth designates something that never actually took place; whereas legend identifies that which may have taken place regarding a person or thing (cf. B. Davie Napier, *From Faith to Faith* [1955], pp. 74ff). That the mythical character of Genesis 1-11 can no longer be maintained will appear from the following:

a) There are parallels to the events described in Genesis 1-11 among other ancient peoples. The Babylonians had their traditions of creation, the flood and other such events. They are also found among many other peoples even down to the present day. That these uniform traditions grew up spontaneously without any foundation in fact is simply unbelievable. It is a known fact that traditions, even among uncivilized tribes, persist with a fixed uniformity from generation to generation as transmitted from father to son.

b) It is more than probable that the accounts in Genesis 1-11 are the originals. This is proved by the following circumstances: (1) The lack of any evidence regarding the existence of polytheism points, as we have shown above, to the early origin of these chapters. The later Babylonian accounts are permeated throughout with polytheism. (2) There are certain features about these chapters that make it appear probable that they are contemporary with the events described and were handed down in the line of faith (Abel, Enoch, Noah, Abraham, etc.) from the very beginning. We cannot here detail these features (cf. P. J. Wiseman, *New Discoveries in Babylonia About Genesis* [n.d.]).

c) Some of the events described in Genesis 1-11 have been confirmed by archaeology and have been found to be within historical times. We cite a few examples here: (1) The earliest home of the race in the Tigris-Euphrates valley appears now to be an established fact. Nowhere else has a more ancient home been found (cf. William Foxwell Al-

bright, *From the Stone Age to Christianity* [2nd ed.; 1946],
p. 6). (2) There is increasing evidence that a flood com-
mensurable to the one described in the Bible took place
within historic times. This evidence comes from ancient Ur
(cf. C. Leonard Woolley, *Ur of the Chaldees* [1930], pp.
26ff), which has been somewhat debated by archaeologists;
but it comes more strongly from some geologists (cf. George
McCready Price, *The Modern Flood Theory of Geology*
[1935]; *The New Geology* [1923]; Alfred M. Rehwinkel, *The
Flood in the Light of the Bible, Geology and Archaeology*
[1951]). (3) The high degree of civilization in ancient
Sumer. It has been shown that the land around Ur had a
flourishing society centuries before Egypt became a world-
power (cf. C. Leonard Woolley, *The Sumerians* [1928], pp.
183ff). (4) The change in man's life-span caused by the
Flood. Sir Leonard Woolley, in his discoveries in the land
of Sumer and Akkad, has uncovered king-lists that differ
radically in their ages before the Flood and after the Flood
(op. cit., pp. 21ff).

d) One word here will help to explain the paucity of
evidences coming down to us from before the Flood. If
that great catastrophe was as devastating as the Bible describes (cf. also Matt. 24:37ff; II Pet. 3:4ff), then it is highly
unlikely that we will ever discover much material or documents that can be definitely dated before the Flood. By
its very nature it was a destruction of man and his society;
very little could have survived. But the memory of that
catastrophic upheaval was put indelibly in man's mind in
succeeding generations. Such an event could not rest, as
claimed by negative critics, on fiction or myth.

4. The unhistorical character of the Patriarchs. Those who
followed Julius Wellhausen in the last century believed and
taught that it was impossible to find real history in the
narratives in Genesis (12-50) concerning the Patriarchs (cf.
quotation in William Foxwell Albright, *The Archaeology
of Palestine and the Bible* [1932], p. 129). It was believed,
and is still believed by some, that the narratives concerning
the Patriarchs were legendary in character. Three types of
legends are found in these chapters of Genesis — the eth-

nological, the etymological, and the cult legend (cf. B. Davie Napier, *op. cit.*, pp. 78ff). These chapters, written according to the critical view in the ninth and eighth centuries B.C., reflect the beliefs and customs of the time when they were actually written — and thus, glamorized as they are and embellished by the later prestige of the Hebrew people, they possess little historical value. That this view is now completely discredited by archaeology will be evidenced by the following facts:

a) Genesis 11-50 fits in well with the known facts discovered through archaeology. The whole social, economic and religious situation delineated in these chapters harmonizes with information obtained by the modern excavator. Details confirming this statement may be found in almost any book on archaeology (cf., for example, J. Garrow Duncan, *The Accuracy of the Old Testament* [1930], pp. 34-76).

We should here call attention to the fact that liberal critics inform us that their reconstruction-theories have not been disproved by the general accuracy which archaeologists attribute to these chapters. For, they remind us, the archaeologist has not yet uncovered any specific evidence showing us that these ancient leaders of Israel lived and did the things described in the Bible. Against such a claim, we make the following statements: (1) The critical attitude here is unreasonable and arbitrary. Must we actually find the cave in which Sarah was buried and must we have the bones of Abraham before our eyes before we believe the Genesis narrative? Must we have a contemporary account outside the Bible telling about Abraham's migration to Canaan before we believe the account in Genesis? Such confirmatory evidence is not required in other realms of research. (2) It is unthinkable that a writer of the eighth or ninth century B. C. could have described so minutely and accurately the historical situation existing a millennium before his time. Is it not far more reasonable to believe that the actual account of the Patriarchs goes back to the time when they lived and is based on contemporary records now embodied in Genesis? Such must now be accepted as the view that squares itself with the facts.

b) Genesis 12-50 has embedded in it documents whose historicity can now be determined with a great degree of accuracy. We refer here to Genesis 14 — a chapter which will not fit into any critical theory regarding Genesis and has, therefore, been called "a literary and historical enigma." In order that we might see more clearly the contribution of archaeology to the proper understanding of this chapter (Gen. 14), let us state the usual critical view and see what can be said against it.

(1) The critical view. This chapter is not assigned to any of the major documents that make up the Pentateuch, according to the liberal view of the composition of Genesis. Presumably, it is claimed, the chapter was written during the Exile to elevate Abraham as the father of the Hebrew people and to glorify Jerusalem as the holy city of the Jews. When the Book of Genesis was finally composed, this chapter was inserted by some late redactor.

(2) Conservative view. Those who hold that Genesis is real history acknowledge, of course, that Genesis 14 is real history. And if Genesis is a contemporary document based on original accounts, then it is more than likely that this chapter embodies an ancient episode of history. That this is the true view is substantiated by the following factors:

(a) There are linguistic features in this chapter that point to an early date. Albright tells us that there are some words found in this chapter that do not occur elsewhere in the Bible; but these words are known to belong to the second millennium B.C. (cf. his article in *Old Testament Commentary* [1938]).

(b) Some conservatives believe that the Amraphel of Genesis 14 is none other than the great Hammurabi. Let us look at this argument more in detail. On the one side, we must take into account the objections that are made against this identification. They are mainly the following: First, it is affirmed that there is no record of such an expedition in the monuments of Hammurabi's reign. But T. B. Pinches, *The Old Testament in the Light of the Historical Records of Assyria and Babylonia* (1908), pp. 214f, gives three explanations of this silence. On the one hand, the records of Hammurabi's reign are admittedly incomplete. Then, it is hardly likely that Hammurabi, in line with other oriental monarchs, would record a defeat. And, moreover, why should he chronicle something which was in the interest of Chedorlaomer, for whom he had no fondness?

Another objection against the identification of Hammurabi with Amraphel is found in the uncertainty regarding the dates of Hammurabi's reign. If Hammurabi is a contemporary with Abraham, then it is not too difficult to make an identification. Scholars are by no means agreed as yet regarding Hammurabi's time (cf. *Westminster Bible Dictionary*, s.v., "Hammurabi"). Until his date is definitely fixed and until that date proves that he is not a contemporary of Abraham, then it cannot be dogmatically asserted that no identification is possible.

A third objection against identifying Hammurabi with Amraphel is found in the difference of the two names. On the surface this looks like an insurmountable problem. However, W. T. Pilter, whose *The Pentateuch: A Historical Record* (1928), devotes over 350 pages to the defense of the historicity of Genesis 14, shows that it is linguistically possible to equate the two names (pp. 17-31).

The conservative position says it is possible, in the light of present knowledge of the Near East, to identify Amraphel with Hammurabi. If further investigation and discovery should show that this identification is in error, then we must admit that we misinterpreted the evidence. Such an admission will not affect our belief in the absolute historical trustworthiness of Genesis 14.

(c) Our final reason for believing that this chapter is reliable history is based upon our total view of the Bible. We do not believe that the Melchizedek-episode (recorded in this chapter) is a legend, because this incident is the basis of Christ as the Great High Priest, as depicted prophetically in Psalm 110 and as fulfilled in Hebrews 7. It is unthinkable that a legend could be the foundation of the glorious high priestly ministry of our blessed Lord.

We have thus shown how four critical theories of modern times (namely, 1) the ignorance of the patriarchal age,

Q

2) the late origin of monotheism, 3) the mythical content of Genesis 1-11, and 4) the unhistorical character of the Patriarchs) have been completely discredited in the light of modern archaeology. We now present another use to which archaeology has been put.

B. *How Archaeology Helps Solve Historical Problems*

It is undoubtedly true that light from modern research in Biblical lands has contributed to the solution of some vexing historical problems. In the remainder of the present chapter we shall devote our attention to two such problems and show how archaeology lends a helping hand. One of these problems comes from the Old Testament; the other is found in the New Testament.

1. The date of the Exodus. Today few critics — even the most radical — would categorically deny the historical reality of Israel's sojourn in Egypt and her Exodus therefrom. Such critics will have their doubt about this detail or that in the Biblical account, but hardly any would deny the historical foundation upon which the account is based. The main difference between critics today concerns the date of the Exodus from Egypt. On this subject we find a variety of opinions; however, it can be truthfully said that basically there are but two main views.

a) Views regarding the date of the Exodus. Here we find an odd situation — that the traditional date for the exodus, which makes Rameses II the Pharaoh of the oppression and Merenptah the Pharaoh of the Exodus, and which places the Exodus around 1220 B.C., is the one generally held today by those who take the "higher critical" approach toward the Bible. Among those who advocate this date are such names as Kuenen, Driver, Sayce, Petrie, Breasted, and most of those who take the modern view of the Bible. Albright places the Exodus at 1290 B.C. and H. H. Rowley at 1225 B.C. (cf. Merrill F. Unger, *Archaeology and the Old Testament* [1954], p. 141).

Long before the advent of modern archaeology Ussher, on the basis of the Biblical data, had placed the Exodus at 1491 B.C. Now it so happens that, on the basis of archaeology, this date appears to be relatively confirmed. Today a date around 1445-1441 B.C. is the one held by most conservatives (Orr, Conder, Aalders, Unger) and even by some liberals (J. W. Jack, J. Garstang).

b) The evidence for the early date of the Exodus. Without attempting to state the evidence exhaustively, it will be well for us to list here the main facts that appear to support the early date.

(1) The testimony of I Kings 6:1. This passage explicitly informs us that 480 years elapsed between the Exodus and the building of Solomon's Temple. Scholars are not absolutely agreed as to the exact time of the latter event, but a date between 967 B.C. and 961 B.C. would satisfy most of them. Adding 480 years to the dates just mentioned placed back to the time around 1447-1441 B.C. In Exodus 12:40f we are told that the sojourn in Egypt lasted 430 years. This would take us back to around 1877-1871 B.C. as the time of Israel's entrance into Egypt.

Now it is highly probable that the time given in I Kings 6:1 is correct. There is no question about the text. Furthermore, it is probable that the Israelites remembered the date of the Exodus. It was the "big date" in their national history. It was just as unlikely that they would forget that date, as it is now unlikely that people in the United States will forget 1776 — the Declaration of Independence!

Believing that the Bible is infallible in its statements of facts, we accept with the greatest assurance the statement in I Kings 6:1. And if this statement is accepted as historically reliable, it surely follows that the early date of the Exodus is the true one.

(2) The historical situation in Egypt. We follow here the outline suggested by Thorwald C. Thorson in his *The Oppression and Exodus* (1930). According to this view, the "new king" who knew not Joseph (Ex. 1:8) becomes Aahmes, the one who created the rebellion that brought into being the famous eighteenth dynasty. The princess who took the child Moses from the Nile and tried to make him her royal son and successor is considered to be the famous Hatshepsut. The Pharaoh of the oppression naturally becomes the ruth-

less Thutmose III, who ruled Egypt and Canaan with an iron hand. It is likely that this man would further enslave the Israelites and increase their burdens. Amenhotep II becomes the Pharaoh before whom Moses appeared with his request for Israel's release.

If the question be asked why none of these characters is called by his proper name in the Exodus narrative, our reply is that when Moses wrote the account it was not proper socially for a non-Israelite to call a Pharaoh by his name. Either he was called "the king of Egypt" or "Pharaoh" (a title meaning "great house"). This is, in fact, a strong proof that the Exodus account is the product of such a contemporary as Moses, who knew Egyptian life and customs intimately.

Dates for the Pharaohs mentioned above (Aahmes, Hatshepsut, Thutmose III, and Amenhotep II) agree essentially with the Biblical date for the Exodus on the basis of I Kings 6:1. If we did not have the statement in I Kings 6:1 as our guide at all, it would still be more than probable that scholars would find in Thutmose III's reign the best location for the oppression. There is no other time in Egyptian history where so many facts point to one conclusion.

(3) The fall of Jericho. If, on the basis of the evidence already presented, the Exodus took place around 1447-1441 B.C., then, by subtracting the forty years in the wilderness, we have 1407-1401 B.C. as the date when the conquest of Canaan began. Ernst Sellin and John Garstang have been the chief excavators of this ancient city. The latter scholar places the destruction of Jericho (City D—the symbol designating the city of Joshua's time) about 1400 B.C. This date is arrived at on the basis of dated scarabs and pottery found in the city and in the cemetery. These are dated by the names of Egyptian Pharaohs going down to the reign of Amenhotep III, whose reign was from 1411-1375 B. C. (Breasted). This fact surely seems to indicate that Jericho was destroyed at some time during the reign of Amenhotep III. This approximate date, therefore, would agree with the date already arrived at on the basis of the Biblical statement (I Kings 6:1) and on the basis of the historical situa-

tion in Egypt. Thus three lines of evidence seem to con-
verge on 1447-1441 B.C. as the time of the Exodus.

(4) The testimony of the Tel el Amarna letters. These
clay tablets, constituting one of the major discoveries of
modern archaeology, come from the time of Amenhotep III
and Amenhotep IV, whose reigns cover the period from
about 1410 B.C. to 1360 B.C. (cf. Sir Frederic Kenyon, *The
Bible and Archaeology* [1940], p. 72). These tablets contain correspondence between Canaanite chiefs and the
Egyptian Pharaohs and they frequently refer to a people
called *Habiru*. There is still some question as to nationality
of the *Habiru*, but a number of scholars (e.g., Toffteen, Zem-
mern, Conder, Winckler, Clay, Thorson) believe that they
are the Hebrews under Joshua attacking the cities of Canaan. Several factors confirm this conclusion. In the first
place, it is possible, from the etymological standpoint, to
identify the Hebrews of the Bible with the *Habiru* of the
Tel el Amarna letters (cf. Jack Finegan, *Light from the
Ancient Past* [1946], pp 56f). As another circumstantial
evidence, we note the fact that these clay tablets mention
a number of the same cities described as under attack in
the Book of Joshua. Furthermore, it is evident from these
letters that Egypt did not send the requested help. If Thutmose III had been on the throne of Egypt, there is little
doubt but that he would have sent troops immediately to
Canaan to drive out the invading *Habiru*. But if our chronology is right, as arrived at by the converging lines of evidence indicated above, we are now in the reign of Amenhotep IV (otherwise called Akhenaten, the heretic king).
This king, weak and frail in body and erratic in mind, was
far more interested in Atenism, his newly discovered faith
(which some have characterized as a near approach to
monotheism), than in any military expedition to Palestine
(cf. James Baikie, *The Amarna Age* [1926], pp. 231-262).
It is also likely that Egypt had not yet fully recovered from
the devastating defeat at the Red Sea, when the flower of
her army and generals perished. It is quite likely that this
defeat, known to be a supernatural act visited upon Egypt
by Jehovah, the God of the Hebrews, made an indelible

impression upon the Egyptian mind and made them think twice before sending another army against a people whose God had so thoroughly defeated them before.

(5) The testimony of the Merenptah stele at Thebes. This inscription speaks of Israel as destroyed — "its seed is not; Palestine has become a widow for Egypt." Israel is here called by her race name. At the time of this inscription Israel was inhabiting Palestine (about 1228 B.C.) and a defeat over her was considered noteworthy enough to be memoralized on a public monument. This evidence conflicts with the theory that Rameses II was the Pharaoh of the oppression and Merenptah the Pharaoh of the Exodus for, in Merenptah's fifth year of reign, Israel was already in Palestine.

We have now outlined five lines of evidence that all seem to point in one direction. One of these lines is in the Bible (I Kings 6:1); the other four are outside of it, although directly related to it. We do not mean to put the Biblical reference on the same level with the external witness of archaeology. We would believe the statement in I Kings 6:1 if it stood alone. But we are happy over the fact that, in this case, our faith in the Bible's trustworthiness in a historical reference can be tested objectively by archaeology and that, after the testing, it remains unshaken. Surely God will stand by His Word and cause truth to spring out of the ground (Ps. 85:11).

2. The census of Quirinius. The question regarding the trustworthiness of Luke's account of the census of Quirinius is fully commensurate in importance and in intricacy of solution with the Old Testament problem regarding the date of the Exodus. But just as archaeology offered a helping hand in attempting to solve the Old Testament difficulty, so it offers the same kind of help in the New Testament problem. To that matter we now address ourselves.

a) The problems. Negative critics have claimed that there are things about Luke's account which do not coincide with known facts of history, such as the following: (1) It is stated that Augustus never issued such a decree as implied here by Luke. At least it is affirmed that we have no record coming from Augustus' time. (2) It is claimed that the wife's presence with her husband was not necessary (as indicated in Luke's narrative about the holy family's visit to Bethlehem). (3) It is denied that Quirinius was governor of Syria at the time stated by Luke. (4) And it is further claimed that Luke erred in putting back at the time of Christ's birth another and later census (mentioned in Acts 5:37 as well as by Josephus) which was actually taken. These are some of the major problems which liberal scholars at one time or another have charged against Luke's historical accuracy.

b) The assumptions. Back of the problems just mentioned are certain assumptions which critics of Luke's accuracy have used to support their position. (1) It was assumed, for example, that Luke, in searching around for historical background for the nativity stories, actually took a later census (the one of A.D. 6-7 mentioned in Acts 5:37 and by Josephus) and pushed it back ten years earlier so as to make it synchronize with the birth of Christ. This would then give historical support to the actuality of Christ's birth. (2) It was assumed, furthermore, that Luke took the local census of A.D. 6-7 (Acts 5:37 and Josephus) and turned it into a universal affair. (3) Carrying on his literary and historical fabrications, Luke is now supposed, according to the assumptions we are now investigating, to have made the census, which he audaciously transposed back to the nativity, one of a series of census-takings in the Roman Empire. (4) To climax it all, it is supposed Luke conceived the fictitious idea that it was necessary for the father and mother (or husband and wife) to return to their native city. This was done, so the theory runs, to get the holy family at Bethlehem so that the prophecy of Micah (5:2) might be fulfilled.

c) The solutions. We have just mentioned some of the assumptions upon which the older rationalism based its attacks on Luke's accuracy as a historian. For a time, as is true of so many other Biblical problems, Luke stood alone and had practically nothing from external sources to sustain his statements. The situation is somewhat different today. Time in this case, as in other similar cases, has been on the Biblical author's side. We shall now see how this is so.

(1) Attempted linguistic solutions. Many attempts have been made to change Luke's text or alter his syntax. But there is practically no evidence supporting any change in Luke's text in 2:1ff, and there can be even less justification for tampering with his syntax. The student who desires evidence for this assertion may consult P. J. Gloag's *Introduction to the Synoptic Gospels* (1895), pp. 269-284, or Alfred Plummer's *Commentary on Luke* (1896), pp. 50f. The conservative Bible scholar will, of course, resist all efforts toward conjectural emendations of a text of Scripture. In this case there is no need to resort to such risky business, for a better way out of our difficulties is afforded by modern archaeology.

(2) The archaeological solution. The method of the archaeologist is to let the Biblical text stand as it is on the assumption that it is right. Then, with the Bible in his hand as an authoritative guide, he searches into the records of the past to see if there is any external evidence that supports the Biblical passage. Having learned by similar experiences how the Bible has been sustained by careful research, the archaeologist is ready to trust it in a believing manner. Perhaps the best illustration of this is found in the work of Sir William Ramsay, whose life was largely spent in an elucidation and confirmation of New Testament history, especially that part connected with Luke and Paul. And one of the chief problems that Sir William Ramsay was able to solve concerns the statement of Luke (2:1ff) with reference to the census of Quirinius. In his *The Bearing of Recent Discovery on the Trustworthiness of the New Testament* (1914), Chapters 18-21, one will find a full treatment of this problem. The following statements largely summarize his conclusions.

(*a*) There is no question that such a man as Quirinius actually lived and was governor of Syria. This fact is confirmed by such ancient writers as Josephus, Tacitus and Justin Martyr.

(*b*) Inscriptions and papyri have been discovered in recent years showing that Luke was right in all the cases cited above where radical critics supposed him to be in error. It has been proved, for example, that Quirinius was twice governor of Syria and that the first governorship was during the time when Christ was born as indicated by Luke. It has also been found that there was a regular census-taking in the Roman Empire and that it was necessary for husband and wife to go together to their native city. One will see a papyrus to this effect in C. M. Cobern's *The New Archaeological Discoveries* (1921), p. 47.

(*c*) The only thing that has not been fully confirmed is the idea that Augustus instituted such a census-taking. Such, of course, is an appeal to silence. But Luke breaks this silence; and if Luke has been confirmed as a competent historian in other parts of his record, he surely ought to be entitled to stand in his own right here. Ramsay's scholarship and historical research have proved to the modern world that Luke must be heard and believed even when he stands alone. If there are still some unsolved difficulties about Luke 2:1ff, it cannot be asserted that Luke made any mistake in what he recorded. The problems that remain are due to our ignorance — not to Luke's accuracy. And it can be expected, in the light of what has already happened, that the remaining problems will be completely solved by further research. For confirmation of Luke's general accuracy one may profitably consult A. T. Robertson's *Luke the Historian in the Light of Research* (1920).

VI. CONCLUSIONS

From our brief survey of the vast field concerning criticism and archaeology, it is now in order for us to set down some conclusions which our investigation makes abundantly evident. It is not to be expected, however, that the evidence now presented will make the same impression or be evaluated in the same manner by all; nevertheless, we believe that the following conclusions will be generally accepted.

A. *Confirmation of the Bible*

When competent scholars write books on "the accuracy of the Old Testament" or "the trustworthiness of the New Testament," it is time for all to acknowledge that, thanks to modern archaeology, the Bible has been wonderfully confirmed in its historical statements in the last century. This corroboration of the Bible has sometimes extended to minute details; in other cases, it has extended more generally to the historical and social background of the peoples and times of Bible history. Although there are still some unsolved problems in regard to archaeology's relation to Biblical criticism, it can be stated that there is no case where one can dogmatically assert that a Biblical statement has been disproven by modern archaeology. The whole trend of archaeology has been on the side of faith. The spade has made more than one archaeologist a stronger believer in the historical trustworthiness of Holy Scripture.

B. *The Old Skepticism Refuted*

As a natural corollary, it follows that the skepticism of the nineteenth century, that spawned the Graf-Wellhausen hypothesis, has been completely repudiated. It has been found that the Bible was right and the critic wrong in the evaluation of Biblical history. The spade has produced a general retreat from the older criticism. This does not mean, of course, that the critics who held to the wrong view have, as a group, become conservatives. Many of them have become more conservative than they formerly were as a result of the vindication of the Bible's historicity; but this is not to be interpreted to mean that there are no liberal critics in the world. As a matter of fact, in spite of archaeology's wonderful contribution, negative scholarship still insists that there are many errors in the Bible and that the doctrine of an infallible Book cannot be held. It is plainly evident that something more than confirmation is needed to change a man's attitude toward the Word of God. There must be, after all, a change in his heart, causing him to exclaim: "Oh how love I thy law! It is my meditation all the day" (Ps. 119:97).

C. *What Does the Future Hold?*

No one, of course, can prophesy regarding the nature or extent of discoveries in Biblical lands or how such discoveries will affect the Bible. In the light of the past, however, it is not presumptuous to affirm that the Bible will be increasingly confirmed and illuminated by the excavator in the days and years that may still lie ahead of us. Surely there is still more confirmatory truth to spring out of the earth (Ps. 85:11) to establish the believer and confound the unbelieving critic. Past discoveries plainly show that we have no need to fear what further research may yet uncover. It is the critic who needs to fear, for so many of his conjectures and hypotheses have been overthrown that he should be extremely hesitant about making new conjectures or concocting additional theories. It is within the range of probability that the Bible will be so completely vindicated in the next generation that skepticism, even of the most moderate sort, will have nothing upon which to stand. It is surely true today that the believer has more reasons for believing the Bible as the Word of God than the unbeliever has for disbelieving it. The Bible has never stood on a surer foundation, so far as external and independent testimony is concerned.

CHAPTER EIGHT

THE BOOK OF DANIEL IN THE LIGHT OF CRITICISM

In a book on Biblical Criticism it is quite appropriate that we include a chapter on the Book of Daniel in the light of criticism. There is hardly any book in the Bible that has become more of a test-case for the truthfulness of what is called higher criticism. And there is hardly any book about which negative critics are more certain of their "assured results" in regard to the date, authorship and historical character. It becomes imperative, therefore, that we examine carefully what can be said for the modern, critical view of Daniel. Having done so, we then shall just as carefully present in detail a summary of the evidence that can still be presented for the conservative view.

I. THE MODERN, CRITICAL VIEW OF DANIEL

If one should turn to almost any book or article written about the Book of Daniel from the modern, liberal viewpoint, he will find that there are four things about Daniel that are either assumed as true or taken for granted. In some cases the critic will attempt to present proofs for his contentions, but most such "proofs" are simply repetitions of what a Driver or a Farrar said in the *ipse dixit* style of the Wellhausen school of criticism of the past century. We shall here present briefly the four things which the critical school affirms dogmatically about the Book of Daniel. The "proofs" for such statements we will deal with under the presentation of the conservative position so as to avoid as much repetition as possible.

A. Daniel Is a Pseudonym

This statement carries with it the assertion that the historic Daniel of the Babylonian Exile is not the author of the book that bears his name. The book, according to the critics, does not come from the Exile at all. It is to be dated somewhere in the Maccabean Age or more particularly in the time of Antiochus Epiphanes, especially in the time between 167 and 165 B.C. Most liberal critics are fairly certain that the Book of Daniel came into existence in 165 B.C. Some unknown writer at that time used the name of the historic Daniel of the Exile to foist upon the Jews an "apocalypse" that would encourage them to stand firm during the awful persecutions visited upon them by Antiochus—with the hope and promise that God's kingdom would soon appear.

B. Daniel Is Unhistorical

Since the Book of Daniel comes centuries after the time when its main events are supposed to have taken place, it naturally follows, according to the critical scheme, that we shall find in the book statements about the Exile and the subsequent periods that cannot harmonize with historical data as found in non-Biblical sources. This means that the author, who wrote this book in the name of Daniel and who used Daniel as his main character, made a number of historical blunders that considerably weaken the book as a source of real history. Of course, even the most extreme critics will admit that there are one or two factual statements in the book that harmonize with history obtained from other sources. It is certain, for example, that the writer was correct when he affirmed that Nebuchadnezzar built Babylon. It is also certain that Belshazzar was functioning as king when Cyrus conquered Babylon in 538. Certain other events closer to the author's time (that is, events concerning Antiochus Epiphanes) are also said to be true. Thus the critics allow a minimum of historical trustworthiness to the Book of Daniel.

C. *Daniel Is Not Predictive*

It is sometimes said by the modern interpreter of Daniel that, living centuries after the assumed standpoint, the author really gives the reader the intended impression that there are real prophecies in the book. More bluntly, it is affirmed that the "visions" are simply history masquerading as prophecy. The author, we are confidently told, employed the device, characteristic of "apocalypses," whereby the hero of the book (the historic Daniel of the Exile) receives visions and revelations outlining minutely the course of human history from the Exile down to the time when the author actually lived. This practice, we are informed, was typical of the age when the book was written. It served to give authority to the promises of relief from persecutions which the Jews were suffering for their faith under Antiochus. But having discovered the "key" to the book, that is, having discovered that the predictions are fictitious, we know now, so the modern scholar assures himself, that we cannot use such "predictions" as proofs for the supernatural origin of the Bible.

D. *Daniel Is Not Messianic*

This is the ultimate in the modern remodeling of the Book of Daniel. It is also the logical consequence of the negative assertions already mentioned. According to the modern view, we do not find the Messiah as such in the Book of Daniel. We are categorically informed that the reference in Daniel 9:24-27 is not to the Messiah but rather to a martyred priest during the time of Antiochus. Thus our Lord, as the Christian Church has consistently held down through the centuries, is not the object of this great prophecy. In fact, according to the critical reconstruction, nothing in the Book of Daniel goes beyond the lifetime of its author, that is, nothing goes beyond the time of Antiochus. 165 B.C. stands as the *terminus ad quem* of the history and the visions of the book. Some critics allow that the author did make an attempt to predict certain things beyond his date but he was considerably mistaken in his "predictions."

Having briefly reviewed these four main elements in the critical view of Daniel, we note here the following facts. In the first place, it is rather significant that each of these statements is negative. This attitude of mind is characteristic of the critical school. It reaches its climax in the Book of Daniel. In the second place, we call attention to the fact that each of these four statements more or less depends upon its predecessor and, in turn, prepares the way logically for its successor. When once the historical and supernatural character of the Word of God is challenged by unbelief, there is no limit to which that unbelief will go in undermining the credibility of the Scriptures. Thirdly, we are facing here a system of unbelief, often posing as "reverent criticism" and "devout scholarship," which is nothing less, when the false cloak is removed, than the unbelief of an ancient Porphyry. The acceptance of the critical reconstruction of the Book of Daniel is not an insignificant matter in one's faith. It is rather the acceptance of a system that, if allowed to work out logically in one's soul, will eventually destroy all that we hold sacred about the Bible and the Christian life. Unbelief meets us in the criticism of Daniel in one of its most subtle forms. We must resist it or die spiritually.

II. THE CONSERVATIVE VIEW OF DANIEL STATED

It will not take us long to state the main points in the conservative view of the Book of Daniel. This is the view that is known also as the historic, orthodox view, since it has been held down through the Christian centuries by those expositors of Scripture who have been known for their defense of the historical credibility of the Bible. This view can be succinctly stated as follows.

A. *Positive Affirmations*

Stating their position in a positive manner, conservatives believe: 1, that the Book of Daniel was written by the historic Daniel who lived during the Babylonian Captivity; 2, that the book is true and accurate history; 3, that the book is predictive of events from the time of the writer (Daniel) to the time of the Messiah; and 4, that in particular the main purpose of the book was to point to and date the coming of the Messiah "in the fulness of time" (Gal. 4:4). These are affirmations to which practically all who call themselves conservatives or who believe in the supernatural origin of the Bible will give their assent.

B. *Questions*

Within the rank of conservatives there are some questions about the Book of Daniel. Aside from the historical problem regarding the identity of "Darius the Mede" (5:31; 9:1; 11:1), conservatives as a whole have no doubt about the historical character of this book. Their main problem is in regard to the interpretation of the prophecies in the book. All conservatives would agree, we believe, that the book's main purpose was to point to the coming of the Messiah into the world. We might summarize the difficulties of conservatives in the following manner.

1. Is the fourth empire (chapters 2 and 7) the Roman and is it yet to be restored before the second advent of Christ? Practically all conservatives believe that the fourth empire was the Roman Empire and that Christ came during the Roman reign in accordance with Daniel's prophecies. However, there are some, especially among dispensationalists, who teach that the prophecy in Daniel has not been completely fulfilled and cannot be until the Roman Empire is restored in its ten parts at, or before, the second advent of Christ. This is a problem of interpretation that does not affect the supernatural character of the book. It is not our purpose to attempt a solution of it here.

2. Is Antiochus Epiphanes the predicted "little horn" of chapter 8 (also chapter 11) or does this prophecy refer to the future Antichrist (cf. II Thess. 2:1-12; Rev. 13)? This, again, is a question of interpretation that does not affect the supernatural origin of the book.

3. Was the prophecy of "the seventy weeks" (Dan. 9:24-27) fulfilled at the first advent (Christ being the "he" of verse 27) or does the seventieth week of that prophecy still await fulfillment in a period of seven years which is called by some "the great tribulation?" This, too, is a problem

of interpretation that does not in itself affect the supernatural character of the prophecy, since all sides here have the highest regard for the prophecy as a real prediction of coming events.

4. What is the relationship, if any, of the Book of Daniel to the Book of Revelation? This is a question about which different views are held among those who call themselves conservatives. Whatever the view may be, there is among all conservatives the highest regard for each of these books as a real prophecy of things to come. It is not our purpose, as we said before, to enter further into the solution of these problems existing among those who hold that the Bible is the Word of God and that Daniel, in particular, is an important part of that Word.

III. THE CONSERVATIVE VIEW OF DANIEL DEFENDED

In some circles of scholarship it is assumed that no competent scholar would defend the view outlined above as the conservative view. In fact, so cocksure are the liberals of their position in regard to Daniel that they practically ignore, as beneath their notice, any attempt to prove the falsity of their position. Good and able books have been written by conservative scholars against the critical view concerning Daniel, but these books (written by such men as R. D. Wilson, Charles Boutflower, H. C. Leupold, E. B. Pusey, E. J. Young, and others) are largely ignored by the critical wing. Most of the recent one-volume commentaries (Dummelow, Peake, Abingdon, Gore, etc.) take the position outlined above as the modern, critical. It would be difficult to get an article, in defense of the traditional view concerning Daniel, published in most theological quarterlies. They simply do not consider such defenses as characteristic of scholarship. One must take the negative, critical view to be counted among scholars!

In spite of the big names against us in the modern world of scholarship, we still believe that the old, traditional view regarding the Book of Daniel is the right one and that this view can be defended with more facts than the critical

R

view can ever find. We shall attempt, therefore, to defend this view against the higher critical position.

A. *The Book of Daniel Is Genuine*

By "genuine" here we mean that it was written by the historic Daniel of the Exile and that it comes from his time. This opposes the critical view that the author used a pseudonym and that the book was written by some unknown person of the time of Antiochus Epiphanes. If it can be proved that a pseudo-Daniel wrote this book in the time of Antiochus Epiphanes, then everything else falls in place in the critical scheme. If the opposite, however, is proved, namely, that the historic Daniel wrote this book, then the conservative view is true throughout. It is of paramount importance, therefore, that we be able to defend the genuineness of this book as written by the historic Daniel. Here we shall give and refute the main contentions set forth in critical works for the late date and pseudonymous nature of the Book of Daniel.

1. **The linguistic argument.** Much has been made of certain linguistic features regarding the Book of Daniel. These features have been used to argue a late date. Let us here note them in turn and their refutation.

a) **The critical claim.** S. R. Driver cogently stated the critical view by affirming that the Persian words in Daniel presuppose a date after the Persian Empire had become well established; the Greek words demand a date after Alexander the Great's conquests (332 B.C.); and the Hebrew and Aramaic confirm such a late date. This is, in essence, the critical claim.

b) **The conservative claim.** We must here take up separately each class of words found in the Book of Daniel and show how their use in this book is entirely consistent with the date of the book in the time of the Exile. We shall deal with the facts as impartially as possible.

(1) It is a well-known fact that there are in Daniel 3:5 three musical instruments called by their Greek names. Such words, as we have indicated, are used by the critics as if they were conclusive proof for the date of Daniel

after the conquests of Alexander the Great (332 B.C.). Against this critical assumption the following can be fairly set forth.

(a) The Greeks, as we now well know, had long before Alexander's time gone up and down the Mediterranean world as traders and merchants. Between 750 and 650 B.C. there was a great expansion of the Greeks as colonizers (cf. J. H. Breasted, *Ancient Times* [1935], pp. 346ff). The Asiatic Greeks had contacts with the Assyrians from as early as 515 B.C. (the time of Sargon) down to the Exile (cf. C. Boutflower, *In and About the Book of Daniel* [1923], Table No. 3). These contacts, prior to the Babylonian Captivity, show that it was easily possible for Greek musical instruments to find their way to the court of Babylon by the time of the historic Daniel. Support for this view is found in the fact that soldiers and travelers have always carried around with them musical instruments. No one knows enough of ancient times to make the statement that the names of Greek musical instruments in Daniel 3:5 betray a date after Alexander's conquests. But we do know enough to affirm that these Greek names in Daniel 3:5 are not at all out of place in a book originating in the Exile. The critic simply cannot prove his point; the conservative, on the other hand, has much to confirm him in his view that this book arose during the Exile. The ancients were not tied down to one land alone but had many contacts with other nations. This fact is one of the by-products of the modern discoveries of archaeology.

(b) The critical argument that these Greek words (Dan. 3:5) are not found in Greek literature before the time of Plato (429-347 B.C.) loses much of its force when we recall the following facts. First, our knowledge of Greek literature prior to Plato is rather scanty and sketchy. We do not have the facts from the existent Greek literature prior to Plato to prove or disprove the existence of such names in Greek. But, secondly, the critics resort here to an argument from silence. Because our scanty knowledge of Greek literature prior to Plato gives us no definite information, the conclusion is drawn that these instruments did not exist in the Greek language. Have the critics forgotten what some

of them said at one time about the existence of Sargon?
Was not the Bible called in question because it mentioned
in one verse (Isa. 20:1) his name, even though other ancient historians passed him by in silence. Does anyone
today deny Sargon a place in history? If so, he has not
kept up with archaeology. Can we, therefore, say that
Daniel was wrong in naming certain Greek musical instruments as in Babylon in his time?

(c) Let us turn this argument against our critics. Will
they explain for us why only three Greek words are in this
book if it was actually written, as they insist it was, at the
very height of Greek influence in Palestine and in Babylon?
If the Maccabean date of this book is true, according to
the critics, why should Greek words be so few at a time
when Greek culture and influence were much higher than
it was in the Exile? Even the critics will admit that the
Old Testament, in part or whole, had been translated into
Greek by the time of Antiochus Epiphanes. It is rather
strange, to say the least, that so few Greek words should
be found in a document dating from around 165 B.C. The
paucity of such words in a document coming from the
latter part of the sixth century B.C. is far more explicable.

(2) The Persian words. There are, according to the
critics, about fifteen Persian words in the Book of Daniel.
It is maintained that it is hardly probable that such a number of foreign words would appear in a book written during
the Exile. Thus the Persian words, like the Greek words,
are presented as evidence to support the late date of this
book. On the other side, the conservative can make the
following answer.

(a) It is not always an easy thing to ascertain the national
identity of a word, especially where people are closely related and have much intercourse with one another. But
let us grant that there are Persian words in the Book of
Daniel. This is not at all out of place nor is it unexpected.
Long before the conquest of Babylon by the Medo-Persian
forces in the time of Cyrus (529 B.C.), the Medes, Persians
and Babylonians had had frequent contacts. It is not at
all unlikely, therefore, that Persian words would appear in

a book written at the very beginning of the Medo-Persian Empire.

(b) The supposition just referred to is considerably reinforced when it is remembered that the Persian words appearing in Daniel are mostly of a political nature. It was quite natural that the officials of the new empire under Cyrus should be called by their Persian titles. It would be highly unlikely that, after a new power and nation had arisen, Daniel would still (even though living after the time of the new Medo-Persian monarchy's advent) give the titles after the manner of the conquered (Babylonian) nation. In this case the Jews would have every reason to use the Persian titles and names since it was the Medo-Persians under Cyrus who allowed them to go back to their native land. Cyrus was indeed their emancipator (cf. Isa. 44:28; 45:1ff).

(c) If Daniel had been written around 165 B.C., as claimed by the critics, we should expect to find fifteen Greek words and only three Persian words. The greater proportion of Persian words actually points to the origin of this book in the time of the historic Daniel. In the time of the pseudo-Daniel of 165 B.C. Persia was nothing more than a historic memory. Its national existence had been blotted out by the world-wide conquests of Alexander the Great. And since the pseudo-Daniel was anything but a good antiquarian, it is hardly likely that he could have used the Persian names as appropriately as he did. But if we assume the historical Daniel of the Exile as the real author, we have an excellent reason why these Persian words are found in the book. The Persian words, therefore, cannot be considered as arguments for a late date for this book.

(3) Aramaic words. Critics have for some time laid great stress on "Aramaisms" in Old Testament books as indicative of their late date. On this subject we shall confine our remarks to the minimum.

(a) There is hardly any scholar who has given more attention to the so-called "Aramaisms" of the Old Testament literature than Dr. R. D. Wilson. It is his sober and mature conclusion that the use of an Aramaic word to date a document as late is precarious. It is possible, our authority maintains, that an Aramaic loan-word could have come into the Hebrew literature at almost any time from David downward.

(b) A comparison of the Aramaic of Daniel with the famous Elephantine papyri, discovered in the Upper Nile and dated by all modern critics in the early post-exilic period (circa 408 B.C.), shows conclusively that the two documents come from the same general period. The proof for this is given in Boutflower's In and About the Book of Daniel (ch. 21). The Ras Shamra discoveries in 1929 showed how the peculiar relative pronoun found in Daniel (d for z), which the critics call a sign of late date, is found as far back as 1500-1200 B.C. Thus the critical school has no justification for using the Aramaic of Daniel as a proof for its supposedly Maccabean date. No entirely satisfactory reason has yet been given why so large a part of this book should be in Aramaic. But the Aramaic of Daniel is more appropriate for the time of the historic Daniel than for the time of the pseudo-Daniel of 165 B.C.

(4) The Hebrew of Daniel. Since all the other languages used by the author of Daniel have been used to prove a late date, it is hardly likely that the Hebrew of this book would escape the critic's microscopic eye. It is maintained that the Hebrew also affords an evidence for the book's Maccabean date. On this let us note the following.

(a) It is extremely difficult to date a Hebrew document simply on the basis of the language alone. Good, classical Hebrew is found in Old Testament books covering a vast extent of time. Even late, apocryphal books (as Ecclesiasticus) were written in classical Hebrew. One cannot dogmatically assert, on the basis of the knowledge we have, that the Hebrew of Daniel is out of line with the contemporary Hebrew of the exilic or early post-exilic periods.

(b) A strong protest must be made against the method employed by the critics here. They tell us that Daniel's Hebrew is similar to that of other late books of the Old Testament which they date as follows: Chronicles (300-250 B.C.), Ecclesiastes (250-200 B.C.), and Esther (250-200 B.C.).

Here we must accept their dates for these books before we accept their conclusion. We grant that the Hebrew of Daniel is like the Hebrew of the books mentioned, but we believe it can be proved, on the basis of objective evidence, that these books, and Daniel also, come from the period right after the Exile (down to possibly 400 B.C.).

Our review of the linguistic argument for the late date of Daniel has been quite extensive. It has led us to the conclusion that no absolute evidence can be gotten from such a source for a Maccabean date. The linguistic data of this book make a stronger case for a date in the time of the historic Daniel than in the pseudo-Daniel's time.

2. The religious ideas of Daniel. The ideas contained in this book have been used by the critics to back up their Maccabean date for its origin. Let us hear what can be said on their side and what can be said against their claims.

a) The critical claim. Here the critics maintain that the ideas in the Book of Daniel concerning angels, the resurrection and judgment, and the Messiah could not have arisen until such ideas had come into vogue after the rise of the apocalyptic literature (200 B.C. and later). This simply means that Daniel, being itself an apocalyptic book, reflects the theological and religious ideas characteristic of the non-canonical and late apocalyptic literature of pre-Christian Judaism. The critical school relies heavily upon the similarity of religious ideas in Daniel and in the apocalyptic literature for the lateness of Daniel.

b) The conservative claim. One need not be an expert in criticism to sense that the critical view here is lacking in proof sufficient to persuade any group of competent judges. The conservative here has a strong counterclaim. Let us hear it.

(1) Let it be brought forth, first of all, that the underlying assumption of the critics here is that the theory of development (that is, evolution) determines the origin of religious ideas and that in this development Israel is not ahead of other nations. These ideas have a long, slow growth back of them before they reach maturity. It is impossible, so the theory runs, for Israel to have these

ideas before the law of development allows them to come into her history and, more often than not, these ideas will come to Israel from some other nation which has preceded Israel in the discovery of them. Thus, if the theory of naturalism is granted, the critics can have their way; but we by no means grant that such a theory is proven or can be proved.

(2) The critics are somewhat inconsistent in their line of reasoning when they place Esther around 250-150 B.C. This book, though written in the period of apocalyptic literature, contains no reference at all to angelology or eschatology. Of course, the critics will reply that this is using the argument from silence and can, therefore, carry little weight. So let it be, but the obverse is also true; namely, that Daniel cannot be placed late because it does have an angelology and eschatology. It is just as logical to place Esther at a much earlier date because it has no angelology or eschatology as it is to place Daniel late because it contains such thoughts. But the conservative is not compelled, as we shall soon see, to use such a yardstick in determining dates.

(3) In line with the modern concept that Israel borrowed much of its religious thought from other nations, the liberal school maintains that the Jews got their ideas about angelology and eschatology from the Zoroastrian religion. It is not necessary for us here to deal with this again, having dealt with it under a previous heading. On historical grounds we reject as unprovable the claim that Israel borrowed the main concepts of her religion from other nations. It can be historically demonstrated that the pagan nations did the borrowing of their best ideas from the revelation committed to Israel.

(4) Critics affirm that the ideas in Daniel correspond to those prevailing in the second century before Christ. As a matter of fact, many books coming from that period make no reference at all to the ideas contained in the Book of Daniel.

(5) Unless we have accepted the philosophy of naturalism, we must grant that it is possible for God to reveal

supernatural truths about angels, the resurrection and judgment, and the Messiah at any time He so wills to make such truths known. No one can arbitrarily say, apart from a preconceived philosophy that rules out the supernatural, when such truths must be revealed. As a matter of fact, ideas about these things had long been known in the ancient world. The Egyptians, Assyrians and Babylonians had long had an angelology and eschatology of their own. To say that Israel did not have these ideas in her religion until late is simply to put Israel in a vacuum in the ancient world. Such could not have been the case. By her location at the crossroads of ancient civilization, Israel had access to all that was the common portion of her neighbors. Thus from a purely historical standpoint, it is impossible to maintain the isolation of Israel from her contemporaries. The Ras Shamra discoveries show what was the thinking of the ancient world along these lines as early as the fifteenth century B.C.

(6) Finally, the Bible clearly shows that Israel had a distinct angelology and eschatology, including the Messianic hope, long before the time of the historic Daniel. And the pseudo-Daniel of the critical theory could not possibly be considered to be the originator or the borrower of such ideas. On the conservative dating of Old Testament books, it is easily possible to support our thesis here with abundant testimony from the law of Moses, the Psalms and the prophets. But even the critics, unless they arbitrarily call certain passages later interpolations (such as Isaiah's "little apocalypse," chapters 24-27), are not able to rid the Old Testament of such ideas until the time of the pseudo-Daniel of the time of Antiochus Epiphanes.

Thus our review here of the evidence affords no comfort to the critics in their use of the religious ideas in Daniel as indicative of its lateness. Rather the evidence points in the other direction and thus confirms the traditional view that the historic Daniel wrote the book that bears his name.

3. Daniel's visions. The visions and symbols of the Book of Daniel enter into the question regarding the date and authorship of this book. We must, therefore, state what

the critics say on their side and then present the conservative viewpoint.

a) The critical claim. All liberal books written on Daniel assume that the writer is describing, in the language of prophecy, the history from the Exile down to his time (around 165 B.C.). The book is simply history (and rather poor at that), masquerading as prophecy. It has taken critical insight, of course, to discover the true nature of the "prophecies" of this book. It is now dogmatically asserted that these "prophecies" all terminate during the time of Antiochus Epiphanes.

b) The conservative claim. Those who hold that the Book of Daniel was written by the historic Daniel will not, of course, allow the claim of the critics here to go unchallenged. The following can be said briefly against their critical reconstruction.

(1) Critics here are guilty of reasoning in a circle. They arbitrarily (against the strongest kind of counter-evidence, which we shall present later) argue that Daniel's visions go down only to the time of Antiochus Epiphanes on the basis that the fourth empire mentioned in the visions is the Greek. Using this grand assumption, they turn around and argue that this proves that the book was written late. Contrary to all historical evidence, they will not allow that the Medo-Persian is considered as one empire in Daniel. Thus they arbitrarily have Daniel with a vision of the Babylonian, Median, Persian, and Greek Empires.

(2) Even conservatives believe that Antiochus is at least the object of prophecies in Daniel 8 and 11. But this does not mean that we must admit that the author of these prophecies lived after the events which he predicted. Such a position might agree with naturalism but not with supernaturalism. And the conservative sees no adequate reason why he should abandon his position of supernaturalism on the basis of some difficulties encountered in the visions of Daniel. But this must receive a fuller treatment later.

4. Historical blunders. The "blunders" in his historical data, that the writer of Daniel is supposed to have made, enter into the question of the date and authorship of the

book. Here again we let the critics make their claim before we answer them.

a) The critical claim. This claim we shall present more fully under a later head and need not go into details here. It is asserted, however, that if the writer of Daniel had actually lived during the time of the historical Daniel (that is, during the Exile), he would never have made the egregious mistakes in history with which his writing abounds. But if we assume that the real author lived in the time of Antiochus Epiphanes, as the critics claim, then we have a good explanation for the mistakes in the book. The author was simply too far away from the time and the facts to make his book accurate.

b) The conservative claim. Here again we must reserve our full reply to a subsequent heading. Suffice it to say for the present that we do not believe the critics have made a case for the "blunders" of this book. Even they admit that there are some bits of real history here; and the points which they still hold up as exhibitions of historical inaccuracies cannot be absolutely proved to be such.

5. Daniel's place in the canon. It is quite natural that the critics will resort to every bit of information that they can muster to support their view of the late date of Daniel. Here again we must present, before we briefly refute, the critical view.

a) The critical claim. As is known by all, Daniel is found in the third division of the Hebrew canon. It is not among the prophets. This fact is used to prove that Daniel had not been written when the second division of the canon was completed. This book, therefore, was put in the third division.

b) The conservative claim. It is not necessary for us to go into any elaborate refutation of this point. The following remarks will briefly summarize our position.

(1) The threefold division of the Hebrew canon cannot be used to prove the specific time when a book originated, since there are other factors than time that determined a book's right to one or another of these divisions. Until it can be proved that the time-element is the only factor that

determined a book's entrance to a division of the canon, this argument cannot carry the weight that the critics give to it.

(2) The use of this argument by the critics rests upon their total concept of the late canonization of the Old Testament. It is simply a segment of their complete reconstruction and re-dating of Old Testament documents on the basis of the Graf-Wellhausen-Driver-Pfeiffer school of rationalistic criticism — a criticism that will not allow a book to originate until the naturalistic theory of development of religious ideas gives it the green light.

(3) Conservatives have an adequate solution as to why Daniel is in the third division of the canon. Though a prophet in reality (as his book plainly shows), the historic Daniel was not an official prophet as Ezekiel and Jeremiah were. Daniel possessed the gift of prophecy but not the office of a prophet. This explains why in Daniel there is practically nothing of the hortatory addresses to the people that we find in Amos and other official prophets. Look at it this way: Saul was surely "God's anointed" as king of Israel; he had the office of a king. But Saul was not internally anointed — he was not like David, for David was a man after God's own heart. Saul possessed the outward, official anointing; David the outward and the internal anointing. We use this analogy not to de-emphasize the prophets as a class, for it could be proved that the prophets of the Lord were called internally and externally. But in Daniel's case we find an exception. He had the gift of a prophet but not the office; and this accounts adequately for his being placed in the third division of the canon.

6. The contents of Daniel. Naturally we would suppose that the critical view would include the contents of the Book of Daniel as another evidence for its Maccabean date. We shall, therefore, consider briefly both sides of the question before us.

a) The critical claim. It is argued that Daniel must have originated in the time of Antiochus Epiphanes because the content and outlook of the book suit that time better than any other known time. It is maintained, of course, that the primary purpose of the pseudo-Daniel was to encourage the people during their time of severe persecutions under Antiochus and to promise them a speedy deliverance in the soon coming of God's kingdom. All this avowedly gives strong support, it is claimed, for the placing of Daniel around 165 B.C.

b) The conservative claim. The critical claim just presented has its plausibility and that is the reason why it is so attractive to those who have adopted a view of the Book of Daniel that wholly unfits it for a place in the sacred canon. Call it what you will, we can never understand why a "pious fraud" that was composed by the pseudo-Daniel of the critics ever got into the canon of Holy Writ. But let us note further the following facts.

(1) Undoubtedly there are prophecies in Daniel (especially chapters 8 and 11) that relate to the time of Antiochus; but, granting this much, we do not believe that it necessarily follows that the other prophecies of this book must find their fulfillment in Antiochus and his persecutions. It is conceivable, even on naturalistic grounds, that a prophet might speak of more than one event or have different persons and times in mind. Thus we see no good reason why Daniel's prophecies must be confined to the time of Antiochus.

(2) Though there are some books of Scripture whose exact place in history is sometimes hard to determine (such as, for example, Joel), we believe that there are sufficient indications in Daniel that point to a date in the time of the historic Daniel. Unless we adopt the hypothesis of a "pious fraud," which is morally reprehensible, we cannot allow that the canon of Scripture contains a book written to deceive the Jewish people in regard to its true origin.

(3) That the critical contention here is purely arbitrary is seen in the fact that in order to locate a book at a time that fits their preconceived theory of its origin, critics are willing to reverse their dating when their theory demands such. As an example of such a method, let us remind ourselves that the same school of criticism, that puts the Book of Daniel late because it fits (so they say) the time of

Antiochus, is willing to put the Book of Revelation earlier than the best data allow because it fits (so they affirm) the time of Nero and the time of the Jewish wars leading up to the fall of Jerusalem (A.D. 70). External evidence for the traditional date is passed over in each case in the interest of a theory that demands a certain location on the basis of the supposed purpose of the author.

7. The character of the Book of Daniel as an apocalypse. It is quite natural that the apocalyptic character of the Book of Daniel would enter into the debate regarding its origin and its author. That debate will be presented briefly in what follows.

a) The critical claim. It is claimed here that the type of literature to which Daniel belongs did not originate in Judaism until 200 B.C. and afterwards. It is customary for the critics to cite the leading characteristics of this apocalyptic literature and then to affirm such to Daniel. We shall, for the sake of brevity, present these characteristics under the heading that follows.

b) The conservative claim. Rightly understood, Daniel is a true apocalypse just as the Apocalypse of John (Rev. 1:1) is in the New Testament. However, the characteristics that the critics apply to the apocalyptic literature of pre-Christian Judaism do not fit when they try them on Daniel. Let us note these characteristics in turn. (1) It is affirmed that apocalyptic literature is pseudepigraphical. Such a statement is true when applied to the apocryphal literature; but it is emphatically not true when ascribed to Biblical books. Ezekiel, Zechariah, Daniel, and Revelation are Biblical apocalypses and every one of them is as definitely related to its true author as could be thought possible. Shall we deny the plain facts that these men wrote their books and authored their visions simply because, in the counterfeit literature of Judaism, the real authors were ashamed to put forth their writings (as every forger is) under their true names?

(2) It is affirmed by the critical school that apocalyptic literature is artificial in structure. So it was with reference to the literature of pre-Christian Judaism, but such cannot be

claimed, unless one misses the real key that unlocks their meaning, with reference to Biblical apocalypses. There is, to be sure, the use of parallelism in Daniel and in Revelation. There is recapitulation in these books also. Daniel 2, 7 and 9, for example, follow parallel lines and go from the time of the historic Daniel down to Christ. But this is no more artificial than we can say that the Gospels are artificial just because they repeat and follow much the same order of events in the life of our Lord.

(3) It is said that the apocalyptic literature resorts to the profuse use of symbols. But this fact does not mean and cannot mean that Ezekiel, Daniel, Zechariah, and Revelation belong to the same type of literature that developed in the intertestamental period. The Biblical books use and explain symbols, either directly or indirectly. By the application of sane and sound principles of hermeneutics, one can understand what Daniel is writing about in his book. But in the apocalyptic books of Judaism, the meaning of the symbols is obscure and almost, in some cases, impossible to ascertain.

(4) It is claimed by critics that the apocalyptic literature of Judaism is non-historical. That is, of course, absolutely true. So vague and indefinite are the historical allusions in the apocalyptic books of pre-Christian Judaism, that these books float over the pages of history like clouds, unattached to any place or time. But this is emphatically not true of the Biblical apocalypses. Shall we say, unless we reject the most obvious evidence, that Ezekiel, Daniel, Zechariah, and Revelation can be shuttled back and forth over the centuries and placed wheresoever the whim of the critic demands? Biblical apocalypses, including Daniel, are in striking contrast to the non-canonical ones in that they are securely tied down to definite places in history. They use persons and places whose existence can be demonstrated by external evidence. The kings of Daniel are definite persons of history; but, if Daniel had been written like the Jewish apocalypses, he would hardly have mentioned a king or a place by name. Thus Daniel cannot truthfully be classified as an apocalypse of pre-Christian Judaism.

(5) It is claimed by critics that the apocalyptic literature

that flourished among the Jews in the two centuries before Christ borrows heavily from the canonical books of the Old Testament. This is undoubtedly true, but it does not follow that this is a proof for the lateness of the Book of Daniel. The Jewish apocalypses borrow in a slavish manner without any creativeness on their part. It could hardly be asserted that Daniel borrows from any predecessor or contemporary. His visions are unique in the Old Testament; there is no canonical book that is like it. This does not mean, of course, that Daniel has no relationship with other Biblical books. It has long been felt that Daniel cannot be interpreted alone or apart from other books of the Old and New Testaments. Such books as Ezekiel, Zechariah and Revelation must surely be taken into account as we interpret Daniel. The Jewish apocalypses depend heavily upon the Old Testament for their material, but they add nothing to our knowledge of God's revelation; but the apocalypses of Scripture, related as they are to one another but not to outside sources, interpret in turn, each adding a significant segment to the totality of God's revelation, the course and outcome of the kingdom of God.

We must add here a proof for the early date of Daniel that has not, so far as we know, been given the emphasis that it should properly have. We have just been speaking of the attempt that critics make to place Daniel in Maccabean times because of the supposed similarity between Daniel as an apocalypse and the Jewish apocalypses of the late intertestamental period. The point we refer to now is just this: It is a well-known fact that, in the second and third centuries after Christ, there arose in the Church a vast body of apocryphal gospels, acts, epistles, and apocalypses, written after the style of the genuine New Testament books and under the assumed name of one of the apostles or some other notable person. We could just as well argue, on the basis of the critical claim about Daniel, that the New Testament books did not originate until the second or third centuries because the genuine books of the New Testament bear similarities with the pseudepigraphical literature of the later date. But every critic worth his scholarship knows that the genuine books of the New Testament came first and that the later literature is, at best, but a poor and adulterated imitation of the genuine. By analogy, we believe this same argument will hold when applied to Daniel in the Old Testament. The book of the historical Daniel represents the genuine and unadulterated in God's revelation; it was written, like the New Testament literature, by a man of God inspired by the Holy Spirit. But the apocalypses of pre-Christian Judaism, like the fraudulent literature of sub-apostolic Christianity, represent the ungenuine and adulterated. It is first the spiritual, then the natural; first God's unadulterated Word, then man's vain attempt to imitate.

Having thus now covered the main arguments offered by the critics for their claim that the Book of Daniel was not written by the historic Daniel of the Exile but rather by some pseudo-Daniel of the time of Antiochus Epiphanes, and having seen that these arguments are invalid when weighed against objective facts, we are now ready to pass on to the other claims made by the critics about the Book of Daniel.

B. *The Book of Daniel Is Historical*

One of the gulfs that separates the liberal from the conservative concerns the historical credibility and trustworthiness of the Sacred Scripture. Critics as a class have little hesitation in attributing mistakes in matters of history to the writers of Scripture. There is hardly a more outstanding example of this characteristic of negative criticism than is found in their attitude toward the Book of Daniel. We must, therefore, deal with this subject adequately but at the same time briefly.

1. The critical claim. We have previously alluded to the critical position here. In order to make their side as clear and concise as possible we mention here the points most often emphasized by the critics.

a) The critical concessions. Even the most radical among the liberal school will concede that there are some statements in the Book of Daniel that will stand the test of

S

history. We have previously mentioned these and need not here repeat them. But these are mere crumbs which will not, we are told, satisfy the true historian in his search for historical data.

b) The critical claim. But it is confidently claimed that there are some real mistakes in Daniel which no amount of explanation can explain away. Some of these mistakes are in the historical statements (to be dealt with below) and some in the prophetic statements (such as the forecast of the speedy arrival of God's kingdom to put to an end the persecutions inflicted by Antiochus Epiphanes). We shall deal with the critical claims regarding the unhistorical character of statements found in Daniel in our presentation below of the conservative side.

2. The conservative claim. No fear should dominate the conservative in dealing with the historical accuracy of Holy Writ. It is no *a priori* theory of Biblical inspiration that compels us to look upon Scripture as true history. In one sense we admit that we cannot believe that a God of truth would inspire His servants to record inaccurate accounts of history. But it is largely on the basis of objective investigation of the available evidence, to which any man has access, that we are led to put our faith in the absolute historicity of the Book of Daniel. Why, then, may the conservative be so confident as he deals with the critic on the score of Daniel's credibility in the historical realm?

a) Statements in Daniel now absolutely confirmed. Here the critic joins hands with the conservative. There are some statements in this book that no longer need to be debated. We would, however, remind the critics that they are the ones who have had to change their view regarding these historical statements. No conservative has ever denied that Nebuchadnezzar built Babylon or that Belshazzar was a real person. But the critics, due to the compelling archaeological evidence, have had to revise their estimates and make concessions to the conservative side.

b) Statements that do have a solution but the solution is not acceptable to the critical side. Let us note some of these: (1) The statement in Daniel 1:1 regarding the date of Daniel's deportation can be reconciled with other statements (Jer. 25:1; 46:2) on the basis that Daniel is employing the Babylonian (rather than the Jewish) mode of reckoning dates. If this be so, as it most likely is, then there is no contradiction here in Daniel. (2) Nebuchadnezzar's madness is naturally not found on the monuments, although there is the legend of Megasthenes (discussed by Boutflower, *In and Around the Book of Daniel*, ch. 10) that may point to the Biblical description in Daniel. Josephus and Eusebius have recorded statements from earlier writers that reflect upon Nebuchadnezzar's sanity. (3) The use of the term "Chaldean" in Daniel does not necessarily reflect an age later than the historical Daniel. Herodotus (about 440 B.C.) uses this term in a similar way. Too little is known of this term and its usage to make dogmatic statements derogatory of Daniel's accuracy. (4) The description of Belshazzar as king in Daniel (5:1) has been criticized as inaccurate. But the Aramaic word *malka* (king) may not necessarily mean an absolute monarch. It is almost certain, in view of the cuneiform evidence, that there was a co-regency between Nabonidus (who was often away from Babylon) and his son Belshazzar. That there was such a co-regency is implied in the statement that Daniel would become the third ruler in the kingdom. The Jews of the Exile would naturally look upon Belshazzar as the real king and call him such. There is nothing in the fifth chapter of Daniel that contradicts known history; in fact R. D. Doughtery in his *Nabonidus and Belshazzar* (1929) considers this chapter as having high historical value. Even J. A. Montgomery in his *Commentary on Daniel* (ICC series) looks upon Doughtery's work as antiquating much of the earlier skepticism about Daniel's historicity.

c) Statements in Daniel which have a possible solution. Here we cite the classic case concerning "Darius the Mede" (5:31; 11:1). Many identifications have been made of this person (such as equating him with Cambyses, Astyages, Gobryas or some other person). It can be said that, at the present time, our archaeological evidence is too scanty to make an absolute identification possible. But this does not mean that Daniel is at fault. He undoubtedly had access to knowledge as a contemporary that is no longer available to us. It is possible that our solution to the problem awaits the next great discovery in archaeology. We recall how Sargon's debated existence was confirmed by a great archaeological excavation at Nineveh.

d) Statements in Daniel which are "mistakes" because of the critical viewpoint. We cite two such "mistakes." (1) The critics affirm that the author of Daniel conceived of a separate Median kingdom between the Babylonian and the Persian. History knows nothing of such a kingdom, for it is an established fact that the Persians conquered the Medes before Babylon fell. In the Book of Daniel it is an indisputable fact that the Medes and Persians are considered one nation (cf. 6:8). But because the critics demand that the visions of Daniel terminate in the time of the Greek Empire, they must find three empires that precede. So they have, after their own fashion (but not after Daniel's), the Babylonian, the Median, the Persian, and the Greek. But this is to make Daniel contradict himself to support a critical theory. (2) The other case is where the "muddled mind" of the author of Daniel made him, as the critics assert, bring Darius the Great from his later place in history and make him the one who conquered Babylon in 538 B.C. as "Darius the Mede." Thus we are told that the author confused the conquest of Babylon under Cyrus (538 B.C.) with the later one under Darius the Great (521 B.C.). But this confusion is altogether of the critical fancy and should not honestly be attributed to Daniel. Daniel by no means identifies "Darius the Mede" with Darius the Great. It is highly possible that "Darius" is a title like "Caesar" or "President" and could be applied to several in a line who held a similar office. Too little is known on this subject at the present to impute historical inaccuracy to Daniel.

Thus we have briefly surveyed the main historical problems connected with the Book of Daniel and have seen that there is not a single case where it can be categorically affirmed that the author of this book fell into error in his account. To be sure, we are not able to explain sufficiently at the present time all the historical problems, but this admission should by no means be interpreted that such problems are insoluble. We could almost venture the prediction that the time will come when Daniel will be as firmly established as a historical record as Luke's writings are in the New Testament. Archaeology is a recent science and the future will undoubtedly bring additional confirmations of the Bible from this fertile source.

C. *The Book of Daniel Is Prophetic*

Having shown that the Book of Daniel is a genuine production of the historical Daniel of the Babylonian Exile, and also having shown that this book is historical in all its descriptions, we turn our attention to the prophetic character of this book and thus deal with another subject of controversy between the liberal school of criticism and the conservative.

1. The critical claim. The liberal school maintains with a great deal of assurance that the Book of Daniel is not prophetic in the sense of being predictive of events beyond the author's time. The following reasons are advanced for this viewpoint.

a) It is quite dogmatically asserted that the visions of Daniel are simply history masquerading as prophecy. The author was so clever in his deception that he made the Jews (and Christ and the Christian Church) believe that he was really predicting future events. If we understand this device as a "pious fraud," we shall not be shocked at the fact that the "prophecies" did not actually come to pass.

b) The visions all terminate in the time of Antiochus Epiphanes — so we are confidently informed. This means that the author related as visions what has already taken place. He was clever enough, however, to use symbols to veil somewhat in mystery-form the history already covered.

c) As confirmation of the positions already mentioned, the critical school advances such proofs as the following. (1) The fourth kingdom of the prophet's visions is said to be the Greek kingdom. This kingdom had already arisen and had already become divided into its four parts by the time of the writer of Daniel. (2) Not only that, but we are told just as assuredly that the prophecy of the seventy weeks (Dan. 9) terminates in the time of Antiochus Epiphanes. That the period from the beginning of the Exile (606 B.C.) to Antiochus (165 B.C.) is not seventy weeks or (as is generally understood) 490 years makes little difference to the critics, who find here an additional reason for historical inaccuracy of the book. (3) Further confirmation of the critical view is found, so it is claimed, in the supposed fact that, when the author really did try to make a prediction, he failed miserably. Here the critic is accustomed to cite the supposed fact that the author blundered in his reference to the end of Antiochus and also in his prediction that the kingdom of God would soon appear on the scene.

2. The conservative claim. Conservatives may be divided on some points of interpreting Daniel's prophecies, but they are united in their conviction that in this book we have real, supernatural prophecy that is beyond the ability of non-inspired men. Is this a matter of mere dogmatism with them, holding persistently to an idea because it is traditional, or is it a truth that can be defended by reasons that should appeal to every thinking man? This second alternative is undoubtedly the true one, and that for the following reasons.

a) Our first proof, which might be considered as the strongest, is that our Lord Jesus Christ calls Daniel a prophet and cites a prophecy as yet to be fulfilled (Matt. 24:15). We do not believe that any theory of kenosis (Phil. 2:7) can be legitimately used to teach that our Lord is not to be accepted as a final authority in the interpretation and application of the Old Testament. Any sane exegesis of our Lord's words would justify the view that he considered Daniel a real prophet and also believed that one of his prophecies at least had not yet been fulfilled. If our Lord was mistaken here, we do not see how He can be accepted as an authority in any matter dealing with the Old Testament Scriptures. It can, therefore, be believed that Daniel is prophetic on the basis of our Lord's use of his prophecies. Other statements used from Daniel by our

Lord will be cited when we come to deal with the Messianic character of this book.

b) Our second proof of the prophetic nature of the Book of Daniel will be drawn from the use made of Daniel's prophecies in the New Testament generally. Here we note the following facts.

(1) Daniel's visions in chapters 2 and 7 are undoubtedly the basis of the eschatological teaching given by Christ (Matt. 24; Mark 13), Paul (II Thess. 2:1-12) and John (Rev. 13). Paul's "man of sin" and John's Antichrist find their adumbration in Daniel's "little horn" (ch. 7).

(2) Furthermore, the destruction of Jerusalem, spoken of as the abomination that makes desolate (Dan. 9:26f), surely reached its fulfillment when Titus destroyed that city A.D. 70 (cf. Luke 19:43f). Thus Daniel, like Micah (3:12) and Christ (Matt. 24:2), predicted the complete destruction of Jerusalem.

c) Our third proof for the prophetic character of Daniel is found in the fact that this is the only view that makes sense in the book itself. We cite these facts.

(1) The "little horn" of chapter 7 is certainly not the same as the "little horn" of chapter 8. The one mentioned in chapter 8 is identified as the king arising out of Greece (8:23). This person is undoubtedly Antiochus Epiphanes, whose career is further described in chapter 11. But the "little horn" of chapter 7 is a different person as can be easily seen if the descriptions in the two chapters are compared. Thus, unless the author is guilty of serious fumbling of his material, the "little horn" of chapter 7 must be a different and later person than Antiochus Epiphanes.

(2) In the critical view the author of Daniel made a serious error when he predicted the soon-coming of the kingdom of God to defeat the powers of Antiochus (cf. 2:44; 7:22, 27; 9:24-27). How such a "prediction" could have helped the Jews during their persecutions or how such a prophet could ever have been considered as worthy of reception into the same canon with Jeremiah (whose prediction came true literally, cf. Dan. 9:2; Jer. 25:11f; 29:10) is a mystery beyond comprehension.

(3) The critical view makes Daniel confused. He knows enough to tell us that Nebuchadnezzar (or the Babylonians) represents the first great empire, but he does not know enough to distinguish between the Median and the Persian kingdoms. Of course, history knows nothing of a separate Median and Persian kingdom existing after the Babylonian, but such separate kingdoms are demanded by the critics in order to make the Greek kingdom the fourth. But if Daniel is really prophetic, as conservatives believe, then Daniel's predictions are literally fulfilled in the four great kingdoms, the Roman being the fourth.

d) Our fourth reason for the prophetic character of the Book of Daniel is derived from our view of revelation as a whole. We believe that God is back of His Word and that God can foresee the future (cf. Isa. 41:22; 42:9; 43:9; 44:7f; 45:21; 46:10). If God cannot foresee beyond the present, then God is just like man — finite and limited in knowledge. The God of Christian theism, however, is One who is infinite in all His attributes. If Daniel is a part of Scripture, then Daniel is "God-breathed" (II Tim. 3:16). If, therefore, Daniel wrote under the inspiration of God's Spirit, he wrote down what God revealed to him concerning the future. We cannot allow for one moment that God was mistaken in His view of the unfolding of history; and for the reason that Daniel was a messenger of God, we cannot allow that Daniel was mistaken in his predictions concerning the course of world history.

D. *The Book of Daniel Is Messianic*

Here we reach the very heart of the difference between the higher critical approach to Daniel and the conservative. Critical scholarship differs widely and radically from conservative scholarship on the issue of the Messianic character of this book. Again we present the two sides of the controversy.

1. The critical claim. That the critical view is radically different from the conservative will be evidenced as we put down here the main propositions that represent the critical position.

a) The purpose of the Book of Daniel does not concern the Messiah but rather concerns the terrible persecution visited upon the Jews during the time of Antiochus Epiphanes. The pseudo-Daniel, living during the time of this awful tyrant, was not predicting the advent of Jesus Christ, but was telling the Jews how to bear up under their present persecutions. Thus the critics confidently inform us that the Messiah is not in Daniel's forevision.

b) Likewise the critics tell us that none of the features of the book demands a Messianic interpretation. It is argued that chapters 8 and 11 undoubtedly depict the history of Antiochus. Here the critics cite the fact that even conservatives take this view of the two chapters just mentioned. With this much granted, they affirm that the other visions (chapters 2, 7 and 9) terminate at the same point in history as chapters 8 and 11. Since there is no Messiah in chapters 8 and 11, and since these chapters depict the same events as in chapters 2, 7 and 9, they argue that there is no Messiah in the latter chapters. Thus, by a process of logical deduction, we are informed that the Messiah is not in Daniel.

c) Furthermore, the "predictions" of Daniel fit far better, we are told, into the time of Antiochus Epiphanes than they do into the time of Jesus Christ. Since conservatives make much of the minute fulfillment of prophecy, it is maintained that such a fulfillment is more easily and naturally seen in the events of Antiochus than in the mission of Jesus Christ to earth. Using chapter 9 as an example of the critical identifications with the times of Antiochus, we note the following "fulfillments": (1) The anointed one (9:25f) is Onias III, an honored high priest. (2) The prince (9:26) is Antiochus Epiphanes himself. (3) The seventy weeks (that is 490 years) designate the period from the final deportation (586 B.C.) to the decree of liberation granted to the Jews by Cyrus (538 B.C.). (4) The last week, in the midst of which the sacrifices were abolished (9:27), represent the pollution of the Temple at Jerusalem by Antiochus (165 B.C.), the height of which was reached when he sacrificed a sow on the sacred altar.

Thus, according to the critical reconstruction of Daniel, there is no place left for the Messiah.

d) However, since our Lord Jesus obviously cited Daniel (as we shall see below) as applicable to Himself in a Messianic sense, it is fitting that the critics find some way of justifying their non-Messianic interpretation in the light of our Lord's teaching. The device resorted to, to accomplish this task, is known as the kenotic theory. Using a wrong interpretation of Philippians 2:7 ("he emptied himself"), the liberal school claims that Christ divested Himself of absolute knowledge regarding questions of date and authorship of Old Testament books and that His references to such subjects are to be accepted or rejected on the basis of scientific investigation conducted by modern scholars. It is sometimes said by such scholars that they know more about such subjects than our Lord knew. Thus, it is claimed, the references that our Lord made to Daniel cannot be taken today as representing absolute facts. Christ, in His limited way, did not know what the modern critic presents as the true meaning of the Book of Daniel.

2. The conservative claim. Conservatives will be naturally inclined, in view of their general attitude toward God's revelation as a whole, to think of Daniel in terms of its Messianic significance. This is not due to a preconceived supposition as to what Daniel or any other portion of Scripture must contain. It is rather due to good and cogent reasons, the most important of which will be included in the brief summary that follows.

a) The most compelling reason for believing that Daniel is Messianic (that is, that it contains promises and predictions that found their fulfillment in the Lord Jesus Christ) is found in the fact that the Lord Jesus supports this view indirectly and directly.

(1) Indirectly our Lord substantiates this view by His appeal to the Old Testament, as a whole, as bearing witness to Him. This is the burden of His post-resurrection ministry to His disciples (cf. Luke 24:27, 44f). Christ showed His disciples in "all the scriptures the things concerning Himself." If Christ could find Messianic promises in the Law

of Moses and in the Psalms and in the Prophets, He could surely find such references to Himself in the Book of Daniel. The burden of proof is on those who would exclude the Messiah from Daniel.

(2) Directly our Lord appears, in several ways, to apply Daniel's prophecies to Himself. The self-designation of Jesus as "the Son of Man" surely goes back to Daniel's prophecy (Dan. 7:13f). Moreover, it would appear that this same prophecy in Daniel forms the basis of our Lord's teaching about His second advent (Matt. 10:23; 16:27f; 19:28; 24:30; 25:31). Our Lord undoubtedly applied Daniel 7:13 to Himself as He stood under oath before the Jewish Sanhedrin (Matt. 26:64). Furthermore, we should not forget that the last book in the New Testament is "The Revelation of Jesus Christ" (Rev. 1:1), and in that book we find a number of statements applied to Christ that have their origin in Daniel. Compare, for example, the description given in Daniel 7:13f with what is found in Revelation 1:7, 13-15; 14:14; or the description in Daniel 10:5f with Revelation 2:18.

b) Our second reason for believing that Daniel is Messianic is found in the fact, which we hope to prove briefly in the remarks that follow, that there are a number of indirect proofs for this viewpoint in the New Testament.

(1) Christ's announcement of "the kingdom of heaven" as "at hand" (Matt. 4:17, etc.) surely is based upon Daniel's prophecy that the God of heaven would set up a kingdom during the time of the fourth (or Roman) world-empire (Dan. 2:44). Christ came during the time of the Roman Empire and this is one proof at least that He was the true fulfillment of Daniel's prediction.

(2) Moreover, although Daniel 9:24-27 is not quoted as such (except in Matt. 24:15) in the New Testament, there are a number of indirect allusions to this great prophecy of the seventy weeks. Practically all conservatives believe that this prophecy pre-dates the time of the Messiah's advent. This is the view that has been held down through the Christian centuries among orthodox interpreters. This interpretation means, as put very briefly, that Christ began

His ministry (A.D. 26) at the beginning of Daniel's seventieth week. To signalize this momentous event He was baptized or anointed as the Messiah (that is, the Anointed One; Dan. 9:25f). Thus the Messianic time was fulfilled and the kingdom of God was at hand (Mark 1:15). The Jews, not knowing their own prophets (Acts 13:27), did not know the time of their visitation (Luke 19:44).

It is a significant fact, independent of our interpretation of Daniel's prophecy of the seventy weeks, that scholars of all shades of theological belief are inclined to limit our Lord's ministry to a period of approximately three and one-half years. This length of time is surely confirmed by the Gospel of John. Christ's death is, therefore, placed at about A.D. 30. Thus He, in the middle of Daniel's seventieth week (or three and one-half years after He began His ministry to Israel), caused "the sacrifice and oblation to cease" (Dan. 9:27) by His own complete and once-for-all sacrifice of Himself on the cross. The veil in the Temple was rent in two to symbolize dramatically the end of the Old Testament sacrificial system (Matt. 27:51). Thus also did Christ fulfill the promises in Daniel 9:24. By His death He brought in "everlasting righteousness."

There is another significant detail that, we believe, confirms the interpretation given above. We refer to the fact that Christ was constantly aware that His whole life on earth had been carefully planned and that He had a predetermined "hour" ahead of Him which no force or circumstance could change (Matt. 26:18; John 2:4; 7:6, 8, 30; 8:20; 17:1). That significant and epoch-making "hour" was the fulfillment of Daniel's prophecy (Dan. 9:24-27). He could not die on the cross until that pre-determined "hour" had arrived. In the middle of Daniel's last and seventieth week (that is, three and one-half years to the date after His baptism or anointing), He abolished the Old Testament sacrifices and introduced the new covenant in His blood as He died as the Lamb of God (John 1:29).

c) Our third reason for believing in the Messianic interpretation of Daniel is gathered from the fact that this is the only interpretation that gives meaning to this book for the child of God. The learned critic may deal with this book as a medical student deals with a corpse, but the believer must always recognize in Scripture a divine meaning and import. The believer will admit that Daniel's prophecies do concern the terrible Antiochus Epiphanes (chapters 8 and 11); but he will not admit that all of Daniel's prophecies terminate at that same time. In chapters 2, 7 and 9 he will see parallel prophecies concerning the coming of the Messiah. In chapters 2 and 7 he sees the course of human history from Daniel's time to the Messiah's advent symbolized by the image of a man and by wild animals. In the fourth, or Roman kingdom, the Messiah comes to earth to establish God's kingdom. But the Roman Empire, as we well know, covered an extended period. Something more definite was needed to pinpoint the exact time in the fourth kingdom when the Messiah would come. So we have the wonderful and unique prophecy of the seventy weeks (Dan. 9:24-27) to tell exactly when the Messiah would come, so that the Jews would have no reason to reject Him, since He came at the time appointed (Gal. 4:4).

Here is the great contrast between the conservative view of Daniel and that held by liberals. The former group believes that the prophecies of Daniel pointed to the Messiah and can now be used, as Calvin used them, to prove the supernatural origin of the Bible. The liberals deny that these prophecies point to Christ and even deny that the "prophecies" of the pseudo-Daniel, regarding the expected arrival of God's kingdom, had any fulfillment at all. One view makes sense and confirms our faith; the other view makes nonsense out of Daniel and leads to unbelief.

IV. CONCLUDING REMARKS

Although we have left out other matters that could have been used in our defense of the conservative and historic view concerning Daniel, we must conclude this subject with the following remarks.

A. *Dead Sea Scrolls and Daniel*

At the present stage of the study of these scrolls, it is impossible to say what exact bearing they have on the dating of Daniel. One thing can, however, be said: there is nothing in the discovery of these scrolls that jeopardizes the conservative view at all, but there are implications that would seem to call in question the dating (165 B.C.) found among liberals. We cannot say at the present that this discovery has invalidated the critical dating. We can almost make the prediction that either through these scrolls, or through some other significant discovery, the critical dating and view of Daniel will be completely overthrown on archaeological grounds and that the historic and true view of Daniel will be eventually vindicated.

B. *Daniel Among Conservatives*

In our presentation of the conservative view regarding Daniel, particularly his prophecy regarding the seventy weeks (9:24-27), we assumed as the true interpretation that one, which finds in the seventieth week its true fulfillment in the ministry and death of our Lord. We are well aware of the fact that among those who call themselves dispensationalists there is an interpretation that makes the seventieth week the same as what they call "the great tribulation" at the end of this age. We cannot accept this interpretation as the true one. However, these same dispensationalists join with other conservatives in holding to the prophetic and Messianic character of Daniel. We could wish that they could see in the prophecy of the seventy weeks the life and death of our Lord and could thereby use this great prophecy, as the older, historic view does, in confirmation of an event that has already been fulfilled in our Lord Jesus Christ.

CHAPTER NINE

CRITICISM AND INTERPRETATION

It can be truthfully said that almost every book written about the Bible is an attempt to interpret its meaning. And it can just as truthfully be affirmed that the Bible has been interpreted in many different ways down through the centuries. F. W. Farrar's *History of Interpretation* (London, 1886) illustrates what we are speaking of, although its presuppositions are different from our own. On some debated portions or sections of Scriptures the various interpretations have run into the dozens — to speak conservatively. So much is this true that some have despaired of any success in arriving at the real meaning of Scripture. In fact, one of the stock objections of unbelievers is that no one knows exactly what the Bible means in any given place.

The picture, however, is not as bad as it is often painted by unbelief. In spite of many differences, there is, nevertheless, a deep unity of agreement among sincere interpreters of the Bible regarding its basic meaning. Though we may never hope in the present world to have absolute uniformity, even among those who hold the Bible to be the Word of God, yet, as we humbly submit our minds to the Divine Author of the Word, we can believe that our interpretation of Scripture will more and more harmonize with that which was originally intended by the Holy Spirit.

In the present chapter, therefore, we shall attempt to survey the vast field of Biblical interpretation in the light of criticism. There are many points of importance that must be passed by in our effort to present the problems of interpretation in a constructive manner. What we offer will, we believe, lead the student in the right direction in his own interpretation of God's Holy Word.

I. NEED OF INTERPRETATION

No one will debate the fact that there are parts of the Bible so simple that no one could possibly misunderstand their meaning. If this were true of all parts of the Bible, there would be no need for further interpretation. But it is perfectly evident that such a situation does not actually exist. There are portions of the Bible — even verses and words — about whose meaning commentators and theologians have differed widely and sometimes violently. The need of interpretation is due more or less to one of the following factors.

A. *The Bible an Oriental Book*

Though the Bible, in a very definite sense, is the universal Book of mankind, yet at the same time it bears the marks and characteristics of the age and people of its origin. This simply means that in order to properly understand its message we need to know something of the modes of thought and linguistic peculiarities of the people to whom the Sacred Oracles were first of all committed. We are not to interpret literally what was meant to be understood figuratively. Many a queer interpretation of Scripture has arisen because the western mind was unable to put itself in the place of the original readers. The ancient message of God's infallible Book still has a message for the modern world, but the modern man must understand the Bible from the standpoint of it historical origin and environment.

B. *The Bible a Spiritual Book*

The Bible is not merely a book of history or a record of an ancient people. It is God's message of redemption to the human race. As such, though written in human language and in words that are simple, its real message cannot be comprehended except by those who have "eyes of faith" to grasp its meaning. The natural man simply cannot understand the deeper meaning of the Word of God (cf. I Cor. 2:14). It is required that our hearts be illuminated by the Spirit of God. Thus a great scholar, erudite in the technical knowledge of the Bible, may be blind to the real meaning of the Bible. He knows its letters but is ignorant of its meaning. This does not mean, of course, that the believing child of God should minimize the technical side of Biblical knowledge. It is for this reason that the conservative scholar will prize most highly a knowledge of the original languages of Scripture and will reckon such knowledge a part of his God-given equipment for the better understanding of the Word of God. But he will never overlook the fact that the deeper knowledge of the message of the Sacred Word will come only as he submits his will humbly to the Divine Spirit who wrote it.

II. THE INTERPRETER

Having seen briefly why the Bible is in need of interpretation, we turn our thoughts now to the interpreter himself. Every reader of the Bible makes some interpretation or application of its message to his heart and life. Our more immediate concern is to deal with that person whose office or function makes it necessary for him to interpret the Bible in a private or public way to others. Concerning such a person the following remarks will be more or less applicable.

A. *The Interpreter's Background*

No one can approach the Bible with an absolutely neutral attitude toward it. Other books may be dealt with from an objective standpoint, but not the Bible. By its very nature and claims, it challenges us. We must either believe it as coming from God or reject it. There is no mid-point between these positions. Men must either subjectively believe the Bible as God's message or subjectively reject it. It is not a matter of the intellect alone — our whole spiritual nature assumes an attitude of acceptance or rejection.

Therefore, it is perfectly obvious that those who approach the Bible with the presupposition of naturalism as their philosophy must reject, twist and pervert all of the Bible that assumes the supernatural. This explains why men who are academically equipped, though biased against the supernatural, are usually found in the camp of destructive critics. It is from this source that some of the most extravagant theories (most of which are now exploded) have been advanced in the name of higher criticism. As we instinctively

T

reject a physician of questionable practice and unsavory reputation when a person is in a critical condition, so, for similar reasons, we reject as our interpreter of Scripture a scholar whose attitude toward the supernatural claims of the Bible is negative and destructive. The Christian Church must not accept as her recognized interpreters men whose writings are saturated with the poison of unbelief. It is for this reason that the true Church has rejected Celsus, Porphyry, Voltaire, Paine and their imitators in the modern world. On the other hand, the Church has accepted such men as Augustine, Calvin, Luther, Bunyan, John Owen, Waterland and their spiritual kinsmen in the world today.

B. *The Interpreter's Knowledge of the Bible*

The interpreter's office is tremendously important, for he is dealing with men's souls and with eternal realities. If he errs he will undoubtedly receive judgment from the hand of God. He, therefore, simply cannot enter upon his task lightly or irresponsibly. There is nothing in all the universe that demands more serious and concentrated study than the Bible. Whatever, therefore, will enable the interpreter to know the meaning of Scripture better must enter into his equipment for his task. The following list could be expanded.

1. Academic knowledge. When God had great revelations to make, He chose such men as Moses and Paul who were trained in all the knowledge of their day. And the same can be said in regard to the men most signally used in the history of the Church to interpret the Bible. In fact, it can be truthfully said that few men have attained eminence as interpreters of the Bible who did not also possess a knowledge of the languages and literature of the Bible. God does not bless ignorance, as such, among those who pose as expositors of the Word.

2. Spiritual appreciation. As we have already indicated, no man can qualify as an expounder of Holy Writ unless he is in spiritual sympathy with its message. The Bible simply will not unfold its deeper meaning to the man whose approach is negative and hostile. Academic equipment,

though it be the best that the world can offer, can never be a substitute for spiritual understanding and appreciation. The believer must ever be the better interpreter than the unbeliever — such is God's law!

3. Comprehensive knowledge. The wider the expositor's knowledge of the Bible the more able he should be for his task. The specialist has his place, but he is not thereby always the best interpreter. One of the weaknesses of the modern study of the Bible is that men have concentrated on minute sections of the Book but have been largely ignorant of its larger scope. Or, to look at the same situation from a different angle, scholars have been very erudite on questions regarding the text of Scripture and can tell us all about J, E, D and P, but these same scholars are less than babes when it comes to the message and theology of the Bible. In order to interpret the Bible correctly, the Biblical scholar must be just as much at home with Moses as with Paul. Such a task may seem very difficult, but it is not impossible. One of the glories of the giants of Biblical interpretation among the Reformers, and those who followed them in the sixteenth and seventeenth centuries, is that they were men who knew the whole Bible.

4. Knowledge of other views. As far as possible, the Biblical interpreter must have a comprehensive knowledge of the various views that have been held down through the centuries in the realm of criticism and theology. On the surface this might appear quite impossible. It is, however, well within the range of the sincere student of the Word of God. A competent interpreter must, we believe, know such things as, for example, the different views of the Lord's Supper (Roman Catholic, Lutheran, Zwinglian, and Reformed) or the different views of eschatology (premillennial, dispensational, postmillennial and amillennial) or some of the major views in the realm of criticism. Such knowledge will enable him to weigh the reasons which have been advanced for, or against, some of the major interpretations of Scripture.

III. Sources of Misinterpretation

The sources of the misinterpretation of the Bible are many and varied. It would be impossible in our limited space to list all these sources. Let it be sufficient for our present purpose to enumuerate briefly some of the major ones.

A. *Wrong Presuppositions*

A man's interpretation of the Bible is colored considerably by his presuppositions. If he approaches the Sacred Book from the standpoint of naturalism, he will, of course, rule out, or explain away, practically everything that assumes the supernatural. For this reason it is to be expected that all who accept Deism or some similar view will interpret the Bible in line with the philosophy of their system. Miracles, predictive prophecy and supernatural truths will simply be rejected as inconsistent with the philosophy of naturalism. It is for this reason that so much of what is called "higher criticism" is destructive of the supernatural claims of the Bible. Higher criticism is a legitimate science in itself, but when it is wedded to the philosophy of naturalism, as has been the case in many instances, it cannot but produce a de-supernaturalized Bible.

But a man may be a sincere believer in the supernatural and may even be conservative in theology, and yet, because of the acceptance of a system that will not fit into the Bible's teaching, he may give to the Scriptures an interpretation that it will not sustain. Many such instances could be cited. One must suffice for the present. We refer to the theory, widely accepted in certain evangelical circles, that the purpose of the first advent of Christ was to set up the earthly kingdom presumably promised to David. Such a theory carries with it the idea that the Church Age is not foreseen in the prophets and that this present age of grace is a "great parenthesis" made necessary by the Jewish rejection of the earthly kingdom proffered to them. This theory, which we can but briefly delineate here, must run contrary to some of the plainest statements found in the Bible and must twist certain phrases (e.g., "the kingdom of heaven") to mean just the opposite of what they were intended to mean (that is, "the heavenly kingdom").

No person or group, it will be seen, is entirely free from the possibility of error in the interpretation of Scripture. We must all recognize the fact that the infallible Word of God has been often misinterpreted by fallible men.

B. *Wrong Translations*

Not all of us can be translators of the Bible. We must, therefore, accept the translations already made. But the true interpreter will not be a slave of any man-made translation. He must ever test the translation by the original languages and must never adopt the attitude that the translation is inspired or above criticism. Right here is where some make a serious mistake. Because of prestige or for other reasons, some look upon certain translations as above reproach or criticism. Some, of course, lack the ability to examine a translation as to its agreement with the original languages of Scripture. But the true interpreter must ever be on the alert for errors that appear in translation. If the error is serious, he is bound to make known that fact — no matter how much some would like to cover it up.

The writer has had occasion, in the course of a study on Greek words, to examine a number of translations of the Bible. Three of these were made by groups of scholars (AV, ASV, RSV); others were made by individuals (Goodspeed, Weymouth, Verkuyl, Moffatt, Montgomery, Williams). It is not his purpose here to evaluate these translations as to their merits or their weaknesses. It is perfectly obvious, if one will examine these translations, that no two translations generally agree. Where one translator will choose one English word for the Greek original, another will not be satisfied unless he has exhausted the English synonyms for the word under consideration.

But our more immediate concern is to point out some ways by which translations give or convey a wrong meaning. The following list is by no means exhaustive; it is given merely to indicate some of the faulty translations that appear in various versions of Scripture.

1. Sometimes the article is left out. The prophecy in Isaiah 7:14 definitely concerns "*the* virgin." The same article appears in the quotation in Matthew 1:23. Paul was speaking about "*the* apostasy" in II Thessalonians 2:3. One may consult the introductory section in Young's *Concordance* for many more illustrations.

2. Sometimes the translation uses the wrong English word. A noted professor in one of the outstanding universities of our country wrote a book in which he criticized the Bible for its pre-scientific view of the world. This writer cited the reference in Genesis to the word "firmament" as a proof for his contention. But the first marginal reading in ASV informs us that the Hebrew word translated "firmament" means expanse — which would surely agree with the learned professor's science.

3. Sometimes the translator becomes an interpreter. In I Thessalonians 4:4 Paul uses a word which means "vessel." Interpreters are divided as to whether he meant by that word the believer's "body" or his "wife." Paul simply said "vessel"; but RSV translates that word by "wife" — which is not translation. There is another word in the Greek that means "wife." In Luke 1:34 RSV makes Mary say that she has no husband, which is exactly what the woman at the well said to Christ (John 4:17); but Mary said that she did not "know" (sexually) a man. Mary's affirmation emphasized her virginity, but the translation referred to puts her in the same category (as far as her virginity is concerned) as the woman (prostitute) at the well. Even a novice in Greek would understand that "know" and "have" are different words.

4. Sometimes our English translation fails to bring out the syntax of the original. In Matthew 28:19 the word translated "them" is masculine although it refers to "nations" — which is neuter in Greek. This fact shows that Christ is not speaking of the conversion of nations but of individuals in the nations. Other examples may be seen in Matthew 25:32 and Revelation 20:8, where one should consult the Greek.

5. Sometimes a change in the punctuation can consider-

ably alter the meaning. There is hardly a better example of this than that found in Romans 9:5. One should note the difference between ASV (which applies the statement to Christ) and RSV (which makes it a doxology to God). This vast difference is effected by punctuation alone.

6. Sometimes translations use conjectural emendations of the original text. A notorious example of such is found in RSV at Psalm 45:6. On the basis of a conjecture as to what the original text might have been — for which conjecture there is not an iota of real evidence — the ascription of deity is changed to a flat statement about a throne. This translation goes against the reading in the Septuagint, the Latin Vulgate and the quotation in Hebrews 1:8.

7. Sometimes translations fail to give the best manuscript evidence. No textual critic will debate the fact that "only begotten God" is supported by better textual evidence than "only begotten Son" in John 1:18. The vague way in which some translations refer to "some ancient authorities" or "many ancient authorities" as supporting different readings can but confuse the simple reader.

8. Sometimes devices of an obnoxious character are used to give a wrong implication. RSV, for example, invented the idea of using the old English "Thee," "Thou," and "Thine" when deity is referred to; whereas when human beings are addressed "you" is used. In some places (e.g., Matt. 16:16) Christ is addressed as "you" — which is surely an implication that He is human like other people. In a marginal note on John 9:38 ASV states (or at least implies) that Christ is a creature.

C. *Other Causes of Misinterpretation*

There are many other causes of the misinterpretation of Scripture which we cannot deal with here. We simply mention a few of them. There are those, for example, who are unfamiliar with the historical background of a book and thereby give to it a fanciful meaning. There are those who are so wedded to literalism that they make the Bible appear absurd when they make figurative statements literal. There are those who are so obstinate in their rejection of the simple meaning of Scripture that they will not accept the truth. All isms find their origin and continuation right here. A cultist will make white black and black white in his twisting the simple meaning of Scripture. The writer once heard a lecturer give twenty-four reasons why Saturday should be observed instead of Sunday, but all the reasons were "manufactured." There is no limit to the arguments that can be adduced to support an error.

IV. FOUR MAJOR APPROACHES TO BIBLICAL INTERPRETATION

There are, generally speaking, four main methods by which the Bible is interpreted in the modern world. Most expositors of Scripture will be found to line up fairly definitely with one or another of these methods. The party-lines are well established. Those who adhere to one group will hardly ever be found in the company of those of another group. Practically all books written today about the Bible will be found, on careful examination, to follow the principles of Biblical interpretation generally adopted by the party or school to which the author has given his intellectual assent. It will be our purpose, then, to enumerate the chief characteristics of each school of interpretation in order that the reader may easily detect them in his reading or hearing. Two of the schools are definitely supernatural-istic; the other two are just as definitely anti-supernaturalistic in their tendency.

A. *The Anti-Supernatural Approach*

This division contains two of the four main approaches to Biblical interpretation. They have differences which divide externally; but they have agreements that unite them internally. They are both on the left side of center in the realm of Biblical criticism. One, however, is more extreme than the other, although the less extreme position is the more subtle and dangerous. Let us look at each briefly.

1. The radical school of Biblical interpretation. This school represents a synthesis of such systems of thought as is represented by Deism, Rationalism, Skepticism and the like. The yardstick by which everything is measured by this school is the philosophy of naturalism. The Bible is a human book

written by men who were just as fallible as other men. The Bible does not contain a special revelation from God, but is rather the product of man's continuing search for God. There are no miracles, no predictive prophecies, no supernatural truths, no divine salvation in the Bible. Israel's religious development is after the same pattern as such development among other peoples and is determined, at every stage, by the evolutionary progress of the race. Scholars of high repute in the modern world have adopted these principles in their interpretation of the Bible.

2. The modern, liberal school of interpreters. This approach, as indicated above, has much sympathy with the view just sketched. Its basic philosophy is practically the same, although those who hold this view, due to their failure to see their logical inconsistency, have not yet gone as far in their rejection of the supernatural. All the members of this group cry loudly against the doctrine of an infallible Book. They will also minimize to the lowest denominator the miraculous in the Bible. And most predictive prophecy they will reject as an attempt on the part of the author to project back to a previous time and thus make his readers believe that the prophecy is genuine. Most members of this school will also accept the theory of evolution and apply it more or less to the development of Israel's religion. There are some in this group who still hold on to such truths as the virgin birth, deity, sinlessness and resurrection of Christ; but their testimony to these truths is vitiated by their negativistic attitude toward the Bible as a whole. It is obvious that those who adopt the principles of this school will be defenders of the higher critical approach to the Bible and most of them will still be in the Graf-Wellhausen-Driver-Pfeiffer camp.

B. *The Supernaturalistic Approach*

Here we also find two divisions. Each is definitely supernaturalistic in dealing with the Bible. There are real differences but there is, nevertheless, an underlying unity that binds them together in the major concerns of the kingdom of God. Let us look at each group briefly.

1. The historical, orthodox approach. This view, held by the majority of those who have been considered orthodox down through the Christian centuries, holds unreservedly to the full inspiration and authority of the Holy Scriptures. It accepts unhesitatingly the miraculous and predictive elements of the Bible and holds to the great doctrines of theology — the virgin birth, sinlessness, deity, vicarious atonement, resurrection and second coming of our Lord Jesus Christ. It believes that the Old and New Testaments are organically related to one another and that the old covenant prepares the way for, and is fulfilled, in the new covenant introduced by the advent of Jesus Christ. This is the view that is summarized in the ancient creed of the Church and re-emphasized and expanded in the classic creed of the Reformation era. It is, without doubt, the view of the Bible that must still be classified as historic and orthodox.

2. The dispensational approach. This view shares with the orthodox the same high view of the inspiration and authority of the Bible. It has the same abhorrence of anti-supernaturalism as the orthodox, historical school of interpreters. It differs primarily in its presuppositions and its methods of interpretation, especially in its adherence to a literalistic interpretation of prophecy. The differences of the dispensational approach to Scripture will be seen in the following details:

a) The Old Testament is primarily about Israel. Israel's greatness as a nation and her glory under King Messiah constituted the message of the prophets.

b) The prophets did not speak about the coming Church Age. We are not to find, according to dispensationalism, prophecies in the Old Testament about the Christian Church.

c) When Christ appeared on earth, He came to fulfill the promises made to Israel as a nation. These promises centered in the Davidic covenant (II Sam. 7) with its announcement that King Messiah, at His advent to earth, would sit and rule on David's throne. John the Baptist and Christ announced the contemplated and intended advent of this kingdom when they proclaimed the kingdom of heaven as at hand.

d) When Christ was rejected as Israel's King, two things necessarily followed in the dispensational interpretation. On the one hand, it became necessary for Christ to announce His intention to go to the cross and die for man's sin. Thus He actually changed His message and mission from the (material) kingdom, which was rejected by the Jews, to the (unexplained and unpredicted) cross. On the other hand, and yet connected with the foregoing, it became necessary for the present gospel age to be introduced, although it had not been announced in the Old Testament plan and prediction. Dispensationalists characteristically call the present age of grace a "great parenthesis" which was unknown as such to the Old Testament prophets. It was Paul who was chosen to explain and unravel the mystery of God's departure from His announced plan.

These ideas and others connected with the second advent have been incorporated in a vast literature and have been given wide publicity in the notes of a famous Bible.

In order that the reader may have a better conception of the four views delineated above, we mention the fact here that the great divide between the two great schools — anti-supernaturalistic and supernaturalistic — concerns the unique inspiration and infallibility of the Bible as the Word of God. To the former, such an idea is highly repugnant; to the latter, it is the very essence of their conception of Scripture. Most of those who claim to be liberal or modern or who hold to the theory of evolution will be found taking the interpretation of the anti-supernaturalistic school. Those who call themselves conservatives will be found in the supernaturalistic group.

V. THE MESSIANIC INTERPRETATION OF THE OLD TESTAMENT

The Christian Church since the first advent of Christ has believed that the great burden of predictive prophecy in the Old Testament revolved about the coming of the promised Messiah. From Genesis 3:15 to the end of the Old Testament, the Church, following the example of her Lord and supported by the testimony of the ancient Jews, has found in the Old Testament repeated references to the

Messiah, the Lord Jesus Christ. But the Messianic inter-pretation of the Old Testament is questioned by some and debated by others in our modern world. And even among conservatives there are important problems regarding the Messianic predictions found in the Old Testament. It will be our purpose, then, to survey briefly some of the major problems and questions regarding the Messianic interpreta-tion of the Old Testament.

A. Does the Old Testament Predict an Incarnation?

Upon this question conservatives are united against the anti-supernatural school. The orthodox view, held from early times, maintains that the Old Testament predicts a real incarnation of the Messiah, that is, that the Son of God will come down and dwell on earth. Conservatives have held that "the angel of the Lord" mentioned in the Pentateuch and in some of the other books of the Old Testament was none other than the Lord Jesus Christ. It is also believed that in such passages as Isaiah 9:6 and Micah 5:2 we have explicit references to the incarnation of Christ. And in spite of liberals who object, the Bible-believing child of God still believes that there are references to the virgin birth of Christ in the Old Testament Scriptures (Prov. 30:19; Isa. 7:14; Jer. 31:22—on which, see ASV or AV rather than RSV).

B. Is the Messiah a King or the Saviour?

This is a question that agitates the conservative camp. The old, historic view of the Church has always been that the Old Testament predicted the coming of Jesus Christ in order that He might die for the sins of the world. Isaiah 53 was interpreted, according to this view, as depicting Messiah's vicarious suffering for the sins of mankind. And the New Testament (cf. Luke 24:26f, 44f) gives abundant support to this ancient view. In the last century there has arisen, however, in evangelical circles the dispensational teaching that the Old Testament uniformly taught that the Messiah was to come to be King of Israel and reign on a temporal throne in Jerusalem. Certain Old Testament pas-sages were interpreted literally to make out a case for this supposition. Another aspect of this problem will be seen under the following heading.

C. *Was the Messiah to Come for National or Spiritual Israel?*

The same dispensational view just referred to maintains that the Messiah's advent was primarily, if not exclusively, for the posterity of Abraham. Thus those who could claim kinship with Abraham had a prior claim on the Messiah. His coming would elevate them nationally and individually to places of honor in the earthly kingdom about to be set up. On the other hand, the older church view has always been that the Messiah's coming had primarily in mind the union of Jews and Gentiles in one mystical body, the Church, which is His Body. Thus a Gentile who believes in Christ as his Saviour is more of a real Jew than that physical Jew who rejects Christ as his Saviour (Rom. 2:28f; 9:6-8; Col. 2:11). If the Old Testament is truly interpreted — with the New Testament as our key — we must believe that the Old Testament had spiritual Israel primarily in mind in the Messiah's advent to earth.

D. *Are the Old Testament Prophets to Be Understood Literally?*

There are, as all will admit (cf. Isa. 2:1ff), glowing descriptions in the prophets of the blessings that would accompany Messiah's advent. These are real predictions and must have a meaning and fulfillment. The issue concerns whether such prophecies are to be taken literally or figuratively. None, except the radical and the liberal, will deny that there are real prophecies in the Old Testament concerning the nations, Israel and the Messiah which have been literally fulfilled. The Gospel of Matthew frequently calls attention to the fulfillment of Old Testament predictions about Christ. The question, however, among conservatives concerns whether the glowing descriptions in the Old Testament depicting Israel's glory and blessings still await a fulfillment in an age after the second advent called the "millennium." This is a debate between the premillennialists and dispensationalists on the one side and the postmillennialists and amillennialists on the other side. We shall not attempt here to solve the problem. However, we will suggest the thought that the New Testament never presents to the Jews such a hope for their future.

E. *Does the Old Testament Present a Unified Messianic Hope?*

It has been contended that there is no uniformity in the picture of the Messiah presented in the Old Testament. This concerns the problem, already partly dealt with above, regarding a suffering and reigning Messiah. Some passages, it is maintained, present the Messiah as King (Ps. 2); others present Him as the Suffering Servant (Isa. 53). These are said to be conflicting views. There have been four answers to this apparent conflict. We briefly give them here.

1. The radicals and liberals, rejecting Messianic prophecy as such, solve the problem from a purely naturalistic standpoint. The "prophecies" concerning the coming king find their "fulfillment" in some local king of Judah or Israel. The "suffering servant" of Isaiah 53 is perhaps some pious individual or the godly remnant of Israel or even the Jewish nation itself. This is also the view of reformed Judaism today.

2. The orthodox Jews insist that the Messiah has not yet come. The Jews of Christ's time had so understood their Old Testament Scriptures of a reigning Messiah that they could not accept the claims of Jesus Christ, who came rather as a servant. The Jews have no place in their expectation for the fulfillment of Isaiah 53. Their Messiah is king.

3. The dispensational view sides with the Jews to a large extent. It maintains that, apart from subsequent revelation that was made necessary by the Jewish rejection of Christ, the Jews of Christ's time were perfectly right in expecting their Messiah to appear in the role of a sovereign king. The "suffering servant" aspect of the Messianic advent could not have been realized, according to dispensationalists, until after the Messiah had appeared as king and been rejected in that capacity.

4. The older, orthodox view gives undoubtedly the true

answer regarding this problem. It affirms that Christ fulfilled both the suffering and reigning aspects of Old Testament prediction in His first advent. He came, as the Old Testament announced plainly (Isa. 53 and Ps. 22), to suffer and die for man's sin; He also came to introduce a kingdom and reign as King on the promised "throne of David" (Acts 2:29-35; I Pet. 1:9ff). He suffered and died that He might enter into His glory (Luke 24:26f, 44; Heb. 2:9). Christ's post-resurrection ministry, it would seem, was spent in expounding to His disciples the true meaning of His mission and reconciling the apparent differences between the Old Testament predictions concerning a suffering and a reigning Messiah (cf. Luke 24:45ff; Acts 1:3).

F. *Did Christ Really Fulfill the Messianic Predictions?*

This problem is closely related to the one just discussed. It is asserted by some that Christ did not actually fulfill the promises made in the Old Testament concerning the Messiah. Those promises concerned a literal restoration of the Jewish nation at Messiah's advent and the consequent blessings that would be poured out upon the Jewish people as a result of His advent. These things did not actually happen when Christ came. The conclusion must be, therefore, that Christ did not really fulfill the Messianic predictions. There are three possible solutions to this problem.

1. Some affirm that the Jews, on the basis of the literal and obvious interpretation of the Old Testament predictions, were right in rejecting Christ as their Messiah. This is the view, of course, held by most Jews and is still their argument for rejecting Christ. Some dispensationalists, by the nature of their view, implicitly hold to this also.

2. Some affirm that Christ really misunderstood the Old Testament predictions concerning the Messianic advent and wrongly applied them to Himself and His mission. This would imply that Christ was ignorant regarding the real meaning of the Old Testament. This view, if correct, would justify the Jews in their rejection of Christ.

3. The true view, of course, is that which holds that Christ truthfully interpreted the real meaning of the Old

Testament predictions and rightly applied such predictions to Himself (cf. Luke 24:27). This would carry as a corollary that the Jews completely misunderstood the real meaning of their Scriptures. Paul uses three chapters in one of his major works (Rom. 9-11) to justify God's dealings with the Jewish people with references to the promises made to them.

G. *Is the Messianic Hope Actually in the Old Testament?*

This question is a distinctively modern one. It has arisen out of the critical debate regarding the Old Testament and the application of naturalistic principles to Israel's religious development. It is obvious that there are two answers to this question.

1. The old, orthodox view has always been that the Old Testament contains the Messianic hope. This view maintains that the New Testament, by its frequent appeal to prophecies that were fulfilled by Christ, completely substantiates the Messianic interpretation of the Old Testament. The fulfillments in every case were real and honest and the intended ones. There was an exact equivalence, in God's plan, between the prediction in the prophets and the fulfillment in the Gospels.

2. The liberal, radical view, on the other hand, maintains that there is no real or intended connection between the Old Testament "prediction" and the New Testament "fulfillment." The "fulfillments" are due to the desire of the Early Church to find some support for its view of Christ. In their effort to elevate the Man Jesus into the Godhead these early disciples of the Prophet of Nazareth searched around in the Old Testament for some "proof-texts" to vindicate their claims. Thus, as an example, Isaiah 7:14 really never predicted the virgin birth of Christ. It concerned some unmarried woman in Isaiah's time. But due to the unfortunate (?) rendering of the Hebrew word in the Septuagint by the Greek word meaning "virgin," Matthew naively took the quotation from Isaiah and applied it to the birth of Christ. This view, it will be seen, does not find in the Old Testament any *bona fide* prophecies of the Mes-

siah. The applications found in the New Testament have been "manufactured" by the early disciples of the Man of Galilee in order to elevate Him further in the process of final deification.

H. *Is the Messianic Hope Original to the Old Testament?*

This is another problem that has arisen out of the modern study of the Old Testament — influenced considerably by the study of comparative religion. There are actually only two answers to this question.

1. On the one side the orthodox Church has always maintained that the Messianic hope is original to the Old Testament revelation. God revealed to our first parents the original promise of the coming of the Messiah (Gen. 3:15). This promise was repeated in greater clarity to each succeeding generation until the end of the Old Testament canon. Since this revelation was originally made at the very dawn of the human race, it is quite natural for us to find among other nations and peoples contemporary with Israel echoes and reverberations, considerably corrupted by man's depravity, of the Messianic promise. Christ is the original and only true Messiah.

2. Liberals and radicals are not satisfied with such a simple solution. With their de-emphasis of almost everything that is unique in Israel's religion, it is to be expected that they will not allow Israel the privilege of originating the Messianic hope. In line also with their desire to minimize Israel and magnify the Egyptians, Babylonians, Greeks and other pagan nations, it is natural for them to affirm that Israel borrowed her Messianic hope from one of the contemporary, pagan nations — the exact one largely determined by the proclivity of the scholar who follows this line.

VI. THE MESSIANIC INTERPRETATION CONFIRMED BY THE NEW TESTAMENT

If Christ and the New Testament are to be taken as infallible guides in determining the meaning of the Old Testament, then it is perfectly obvious that the older revelation is to be understood as containing many explicit predictions concerning the coming of the Messiah. In order to make

U

our study more specific, we shall confine our attention to the quotations from the Book of Psalms found in the New Testament writings. We have examined practically all these quotations and come up with the following results.

A. *Prophecies Cited As Literally Fulfilled*

Many of the Psalms are cited as literally fulfilled in some event during the life of Christ or the Early Church. The facts concerning the defection and apostasy of Judas are described as being predicted in the Psalms (Ps. 41:9; 69:25; 109:8; Acts 1:16, 20f). The rage of the Jewish and Gentile world against Christ fulfilled the prophecy of Psalm 2:1 (Acts 4:26f). The resurrection of Christ from the dead was preannounced in Psalm 16 (Acts 2:25ff).

B. *Old Testament Prophecies Are Christo-centric*

If anything stands out in the use which the New Testament makes of the Old Testament, it is that Christ is the very center of Old Testament prediction. From the New Testament standpoint the whole life of Christ is vividly portrayed in the prophecies of the older revelation. Christ spent a great part of His post-resurrection ministry in "opening" the minds of His disciples regarding the Messianic significance of the Old Testament (Luke 24:25f, 44f). The rejection (Ps. 118:22; Acts 4:11), resurrection (see above), ascension and rule (Ps. 110:1; Acts 2:34), and priesthood (Ps. 110:4; Heb. 5:6; 7:21) of Christ are found in the Old Testament. Likewise the New Testament goes to the Old Testament for such truths about Christ as His eternal generation (Ps. 2:7; Heb. 5:5), His humiliation as Son of Man (Ps. 8:4ff; Heb. 2:6ff), His deity (Ps. 45:6; Heb. 1:8), His absolute purity (Ps. 45:7; Heb. 1:9), His eternity (Ps. 102:25ff; Heb. 1:10ff), His absolute obedience to the Father in death (Ps. 40:6ff; Heb. 10:5ff), and other great truths. It is not an exaggeration to say that the New Testament looks upon the Old Testament as saturated in the Messianic hope.

C. *Old Testament Predictions and Gospel Truths*

If Christ and His redemption are major themes of Old Testament revelation, it is self-evident that gospel truths connected with the Messiah's death will also be abundantly found in the Old Testament. And this is exactly what the New Testament says. The doctrine of justification by faith is the center of the Christian's faith and that doctrine was taught and illustrated in the Old Testament (Ps. 32:1f; Rom. 4:1-8). Paul draws mainly from the Book of Psalms for his description of the depravity and corruption of the human race (Rom. 3:10-18; Ps. 14:1ff; 5:9; 140:3; 10:7; 36:1). The rejection and spiritual blindness of Israel is confirmed by the Old Testament (Rom. 11:9f; Ps. 69:22f; I Pet. 2:7f; Ps. 118:22). The graces of the Christian life are illustrated from the Psalms (I Pet. 3:10ff; Ps. 34:12ff).

D. *The Old Testament Is Inspired and Authoritative*

In a previous chapter we have dealt with the inspiration of the Old Testament. We need not, therefore, repeat what we have already said. Suffice it here to call attention to the fact that, in quotations from the Old Testament, the New Testament always considers the older revelation as the absolute utterance of God. The Holy Spirit is the One who authored the warning against rebellion against God's voice (Heb. 3:7ff; Ps. 95:7ff). The Holy Spirit spoke the word concerning the defection of Judas (Acts 1:16; Ps. 69:25; 109:8). David in the Holy Spirit calls Jesus Lord (Matt. 22:43ff; Ps. 110:1). David by the Holy Spirit foresaw the opposition to the Messiah (Acts 4:25ff; Ps. 2:1f).

The references cited above could have been greatly multiplied if we had taken into account all the quotations from the Old Testament found in the New Testament. But we have limited our attention purposely to the Book of Psalms and even there have not used all the quotations cited in the New Testament. The quotations cited, however, are illustrative of the incontestable fact that the New Testament considers the older revelation to be the source of the Messianic promises fulfilled in Jesus Christ and the Christian Church. No other explanation will satisfy the data as presented above.

VII. CRITICAL ATTEMPTS TO EVADE THE MESSIANIC INTERPRETATION

Since Christ is at the very center of Christianity and since He also, as we have already shown, is the very heart of the Messianic predictions in the Old Testament, it is quite natural that scholars who approach the Old Testament with an anti-supernaturalistic bias will make every effort possible to evade the Messianic interpretation of the Old Testament. Supernaturalism rests its case right here. It is willing to defend its case at this point, believing that, if it can be successfully defended here, the same will hold true at all other essential points. There is no secret of the fact that the rationalistic approach to the Old Testament has vigorously attempted to "explain away" the references to Christ in the Old Testament. That this is so will be evidenced by the article "Psalms" in J. Hastings' *Dictionary of Christ and the Gospels* (1908), vol. 2, pp. 450-54, from which the illustrations that follow are mainly gathered. Here, then, are some of the ways in which the liberal school attempts to rob the Old Testament of its Messianic hope as fulfilled in Jesus Christ.

A. *Anti-Messianic Features in Messianic Psalms*

It is contended that there are features in some Psalms considered as Messianic which nullify the Messianic interpretation. Thus Psalm 2, which is definitely Messianic according to the New Testament (Acts 4:25f; 13:33; Heb. 1:5), is said to contain a statement (verse 9) which is inconsistent with its Messianic interpretation. But liberals characteristically ignore the justice and wrath of God and do not like to see such ideas imputed to Him. But the New Testament, which firmly upholds such attributes, sees no inconsistency in applying the disputed verse (Ps. 2:9; cf. Ps. 110:5f) to Christ (Rev. 2:27; 12:5; 19:15). We must, therefore, conclude that the debated verse does not rob the second psalm of its Messianic import and message.

B. *Historical Background Ignored in Messianic Interpretation*

It is affirmed by the liberals that the Messianic interpretation of the Psalms ignores the historical background. Psalm

69, for example, is said to be too vindictive (verses 22-28) to be applied to Christ; it must, it is claimed, be applied to some contemporary king of Israel or Judah. But two facts support conclusively the Messianic interpretation of this Psalm. There is, for example, a striking similarity in thought and spirit between this Psalm and the twenty-second Psalm, which is definitely Messianic. On the other hand, this Psalm is quoted both by Christ (John 2:17; Ps. 69:9) and by Paul (Rom. 15:3; Ps. 69:9) and applied to Christ. In the light of what we have said under the previous heading, the debated verses (Ps. 69:22-28) can well be understood in the light of such New Testament references as Matthew 23:13-36; Luke 21:20-24; Acts 28:25-28; I Thessalonians 2: 14-16, etc.

C. *Psalms Better Applied to Others than the Messiah*

It is claimed by the critics that the Psalms can be better applied to other persons than the Messiah. In fact, it is definitely implied that the Messianic interpretation is forced and far-fetched. The natural and obvious interpretation, it is affirmed, is to find some historical character. For example, Psalm 8 is said to apply to the human race as such and Psalm 22 is applied to the same "suffering servant" as Isaiah 53, although in neither case is the application made to the Messiah. There are two major objections to the critical view here given. On the one side, such an interpretation ignores the New Testament application of both of these Psalms to Christ (Ps. 22:1; Matt. 27:46; Ps. 8:4ff; Heb. 2:6ff). The New Testament never even mentions the possibility of any other application. And it is not unreasonable to suppose that any other application would be highly obnoxious. On the other side of the picture, the critics are not able to agree as to who the "suffering servant" actually is. When the Messianic interpretation is rejected, men are left on a wide sea of uncertainty and speculation. Here, as in so many other places, we must choose to stand with Christ and His apostles rather than with the most brilliant modern critic.

D. *Christ Did Not Understand the Psalms Messianically*

It is maintained that Christ did not teach, nor did He instruct His disciples to teach, that the Psalms and other portions of the Old Testament applied to Himself. This position can be upheld oniy by ignoring the clearest kind of evidence in the New Testament itself. For, first, Christ surely endorsed the Messianic application of Psalm 110:1 to Himself (Matt. 22:44f). Then, secondly, Christ surely taught His disciples to find in the Psalms references concerning Himself (Luke 24:27, 44f). And, thirdly, it is clearly evident that as soon as the apostles began their ministry they followed their Lord in finding many references to Him in the Old Testament (Acts 2:25ff; Ps. 16:8ff; Acts 2:34f; Ps. 110:1; etc.). The Psalms did not have meaning apart from their reference to Christ. He alone is the sacred Key that unlocks their treasures.

E. *Uncertain Textual Evidence for Messianic Interpretation*

It is claimed by the critical school that uncertainties regarding the original text wipe out the Messianic interpretation. The example most often cited is the quotation in Hebrews 10:5ff of Psalm 40:6f. A similar case is found in the quotation of Amos 9:11f in Acts 15:16ff. In both cases the New Testament follows the Septuagint rather than the original Hebrew and in both cases there are some striking differences between the original Hebrew and the Septuagint. We cannot enter at this point further into the textual questions here involved. Suffice it to say that if inspired men adopted an uninspired translation we must believe that there were some good reasons why this was done, even when the uninspired translation (the Septuagint) differed from the original Hebrew. We see nothing here that lowers the inspiration of the original Hebrew. Paul's inspiration was not lowered when he cited heathen poets to confirm certain truths (Acts 17:28; Tit. 1:12). As we see it, God providentially turned the translation into a vehicle to bring out the deeper meaning already latent in the original.

F. *The Messianic Interpretation Not in the Original*

The most desperate and daring effort made to rid the

Old Testament of its Messianic meaning is to resort to some textual emendation of the original text itself. The most notorious example of such tampering with the original is found in the translation of Psalm 45:6 in RSV. The translation of this verse as found in AV and ASV is supported by three lines of textual evidence — the Septuagint, the New Testament (Heb. 1:8), and the Latin Vulgate — not to speak of other evidence. In spite of the overwhelming evidence for the rendering in AV and ASV, RSV has the effrontery to put into its text here a reading that has nothing back of it except the speculation of certain "brilliant" scholars who concocted this reading out of their fertile imagination. All sensible scholarship, no matter what name it applies to itself, ought to blush with shame at the arrogant liberty taken with the Word of God. Not even a classical writer would be treated with such reckless defiance of the facts.

We have now covered some of the attempts made by the rationalistic school of critics to get rid of the Messianic interpretation of the Old Testament. Illustrations of all these attempts could be found in many books, commentaries, and dictionaries written about the Bible from the liberal viewpoint. We have not put up a man of straw just to knock him down. Many of the books in which these negative views are presented are written by men of high standing in ecclesiastical and theological circles in present-day Christendom.

VIII. THE TRUE INTERPRETATION OF THE OLD TESTAMENT

It is now in order to ascertain which view of the Old Testament is our best guide for its real interpretation. In order to make our conclusion more realistic, we shall pass in review each of the four major views already presented and point out wherein they fail or succeed.

A. Views that Fail to Interpret the Old Testament Rightly

Here we place all those approaches to the Old Testament that fail in one way or another to interpret the Old Testament correctly.

1. The radical-liberal approach fails. We put the radical and the liberal approaches together because there is an es-

sential kinship between them. The radical is by far the most consistent logically. The liberal-modern *is* an unstable synthesis of radical and conservative elements with a leaning toward the radical. The radical-liberal interpretation of the Old Testament fails for the following reasons.

a) It puts the Old Testament on a level with other literature and destroys the uniqueness of Israel's religion. Because of its rejection of an infallible revelation committed to Israel and because of its acceptance of the theory of evolution, it is not qualified to interpret the Old Testament aright. We may as well expect a blind man to describe the beauties of the sunset as to find among those who adopt the radical-liberal view a true understanding of the Old Testament faith.

b) It wipes out the true, Messianic meaning of the Old Testament. Men who spend their intellectual efforts with the fixed purpose of denuding the Old Testament of its Messianic hope can never enter into the real meaning of Scripture.

c) It undermines the moral authority of the Old Testament. One cannot hold the Old Testament in high esteem as an authoritative guide in moral matters when one considers it as erroneous in historical matters and as untrue in its predictions. The radical-liberal reconstruction of the Old Testament in modern times has been the most influential movement in the discarding of the Old Testament as a supernatural revelation.

2. The dispensational interpretation fails. This view, although held by some conservatives and evangelicals, seriously fails to interpret the Old Testament correctly. This statement will be justified when we properly evaluate the following facts.

a) It interprets the Old Testament too literalistically. No one who believes the Bible as the Word of God will debate the fact that there are many prophecies in the Old Testament that have been fulfilled literally. Prophecies concerning Israel, Egypt, Assyria, Babylon, and the Messiah could easily be cited in substantiation of our assertion. Admitting this, we are not thereby driven to the position that all prophecies in the Old Testament are to be interpreted literally. The true import of this statement will be seen in the discussion below.

b) It has no place for the New Testament age of grace in its interpretation of the Old Testament. Dispensationalists affirm quite dogmatically that the prophets did not see the present Church Age. What they foresaw concerned the literal kingdom promised to Israel but not the Church and the blessings of the Gospel Age. Thus there is a serious blind-spot among the proponents of this school. They can see only Israel and the Davidic kingdom; they cannot see the Church and the grace of God as made known to us in the death of Christ.

c) It ignores the New Testament interpretation of the Old Testament. Much of dispensational literature by-passes the New Testament. If they would but follow the New Testament they would see that Christ is now on the promised throne of David (Luke 1:32f; Acts 2:25-36, esp., 31f; Heb. 2:9; 8:1). They would also understand that the "last days" follow the first advent rather than the second advent (Acts 2:16ff; Heb. 1:1). We are now living in the days foretold by the prophets (Acts 3:24). The present age is not a "great parenthesis" in God's plan, unrevealed in the Old Testament, but is rather the climax of God's redemptive program for the world. When Christ returns it will be the end of world history and the introduction of eternity (I Cor. 15:23f; Matt. 24:14). We, therefore, simply cannot recognize the dispensational interpretation as the right one.

B. *The True Understanding of the Old Testament*

The older revelation of Scripture was surely meant to be understood. The views we have just presented (the radical-liberal and the dispensational) fail considerably and seriously in getting at the real message of the Old Testament. The error of the radical-liberal is in his heart — his opposition to the supernatural; the error of the dispensationalist is in his mind — his adoption of a theory that appears quite plausible but simply will not fit the facts and will not square with the New Testament. The radical-liberal wilfully opposes the truth in the face of clear evidence against his position; the dispensationalist, professing great reverence for the Word of God, misinterprets the Word because of his failure to consider his theory in the light of the New Testament revelation.

There is, however, a true interpretation of the Old Testament that is given to us in the New Testament and has been held by orthodox expositors down through the Christian centuries. It is well represented, for example, in the sainted Matthew Henry. The elements in this interpretation will be succinctly presented below.

1. Basic presuppositions. There are two basic presuppositions that undergird this orthodox-historical view of the Old Testament. We shall deal with each briefly.

a) Against the radical-liberal school this interpretation maintains that the Old Testament is a true, historical revelation firmly grounded in facts. God has revealed Himself to man in a supernatural way from the very beginning of history. In the center of this history stands the promise concerning the Messiah, the Redeemer of the world. All of the Old Testament is pregnant with hope and blessing of His coming into the world.

b) Against the dispensationalist the orthodox-historical view maintains that the main promise of the Old Testament did not concern the restoration of national Israel at Messiah's advent but rather the gathering of all who believe into one body, the Church, as a consequence of the Messiah's death for our sins. God did choose Israel for a purpose (Rom. 9:1-5) but that purpose was fulfilled when Christ came of her seed (Rom. 15:8, 9; Acts 13:27, 32, 33).

2. The orthodox-historical view more fully presented. This viewpoint can be more adequately presented in a series of propositions regarding the Old and New Testaments in their mutual bearing one on the other.

a) The Old Testament is the necessary introduction to the New Testament and neither can be properly understood apart from the other. The relationship here is organic and fundamental. One may as well try to read Hebrew without an introductory course in the language as to try to understand the New Testament without the Old Testament.

b) The Old Testament anticipates the New Testament and harmonizes with it. Practically all the truths ·in the later revelation find their source back in the earlier revelation. We go to the Old Testament for basic truths in Paul's theology rather than to the pagan mystery-religions. The great words of the Christian faith — righteousness, faith, holiness, redemption, etc. — are found in the Old Testament in their pristine glory. When the two revelations are put together they harmonize with and supplement (but do not contradict) one another (Heb. 1:1; 11:39f).

c) The Old Testament revelation illustrates and typifies the basic truths of the New Testament revelation. The things of old were written for our instruction and our admonition (I Cor. 10:6, 11). Many of the bare historical events of the Old Testament were incorporated in the Sacred Record because of their typical significance (e.g., John 3:14; 6:31ff). With the New Testament in our hands we can now interpret many things in the Old Testament which appear to be simply the recital of trivial facts (e.g., Gal. 4:21-31; Hebrew 12:16-29; 13:10-16). The Books of Exodus, Leviticus and Numbers, with their portrayal of the ceremonial legislation, receive new meaning as they are now interpreted in the light of their typical significance (as in the Epistle to the Hebrews).

d) The New Testament is the climax and fulfillment of all that was predicted in the Old Testament. The orthodox-historical view maintains that the New Testament is the final revelation to mankind and is the final stage of human history until the consummation of all things in the eternal world introduced by the second and final coming of Jesus Christ. Therefore, this view looks upon the Old Testament Scriptures as containing many things about the present Church Age. One will need, however, the New Testament as his guide as he goes back into the older revelation. There, if he uses his key aright, he will find many truths hidden away in the prophets and other writings of the Old Testament about Jesus Christ and His spiritual kingdom. He will find Christ in the types, in the mystical sections (Song of Solomon), in the prophecies, in the histories, and in the figurative language often employed to signify Messiah's advent ('e.g., Isa. 55). If he uses his key aright, the Old Testament will become a well, springing up with new life and vitality.

A SELECTED BIBLIOGRAPHY

BOOKS DEFENDING OR EXPLAINING THE MODERN (LIBERAL) VIEWPOINT:

Bewer, Julius A., *The Literature of the Old Testament* (New York: Columbia University Press, rev. ed., 1933).

Briggs, Charles Augustus, *A General Introduction to the Study of the Holy Scriptures* (New York: Charles Scribner's Sons, 1899).

Clarke, W. K. Lowther, *Concise Bible Commentary* (New York: The Macmillan Co., 1953).

Davies, G. Henton; Richardson, Alan; and Wallis, Charles L., eds., *Twentieth Century Bible Commentary* (New York: Harper & Brothers, rev. ed., 1955).

Driver, S. R., *An Introduction to the Literature of the Old Testament* (New York: Charles Scribner's Sons, rev. ed., 1913).

Farrar, F. W., *The Bible: Its Meaning and Supremacy* (New York: Longmans, Green & Co., 1897).

Fosdick, Harry Emerson, *A Guide to Understanding the Bible* (New York: Harper & Brothers, 1938).

Hahn, Herbert F., *The Old Testament in Modern Research* (Philadelphia: The Muhlenberg Press, 1954).

Kraeling, Emil G., *The Old Testament Since the Reformation* (New York: Harper & Brothers, 1956).

Manson, T. W., ed., *A Companion of the Bible* (New York: Charles Scribner's Sons, 1947).

McFadyen, John Edgar, *Old Testament Criticism and the Christian Church* (New York: Charles Scribner's Sons, 1908).

————, *The Approach to the Old Testament* (New York: George H. Doran Co., n.d.).

Meek, Theophile James, *Hebrew Origins* (New York: Harper & Brothers, rev. ed., 1950).

Pfeiffer, Robert H., *Introduction to the Old Testament* (New York: Harper & Brothers, rev. ed., 1948).

Richardson, Alan, *Christian Apologetics* (New York: Harper & Brothers, 1947).

————, ed., *A Theological Word Book of the Bible* (New York: The Macmillan Co., 1950).

Rowley, H. H., *The Rediscovery of the Old Testament* (Philadelphia: The Westminster Press, 1946).

————, ed., *The Old Testament and Modern Study* (Oxford: Oxford University Press, 1951).

The Interpreter's Bible (New York: Abingdon-Cokesbury Press, 1952-57).

317

BOOKS DEFENDING OR EXPLAINING THE HISTORIC (CONSERVATIVE) VIEWPOINT:

ON INSPIRATION:

Bettex, F. *The Bible the Word of God* (New York: Eaton & Mains, 1904).

Boettner, Loraine, *The Inspiration of the Scriptures* (Grand Rapids: Wm. B. Eerdmans Publishing Co., 1940).

Burrell, David James, *The Teaching of Jesus Concerning the Scriptures* (New York: American Tract Society, 1904).

Ellicott, Charles, *Inspiration of the Holy Scriptures* (Edinburgh: T. & T. Clark, 1877).

Engelder, Th., *Scripture Cannot Be Broken* (St. Louis: Concordia Publishing House, 1944).

Gaussen, L., *Theopneustia: The Plenary Inspiration of the Holy Scriptures* (Chicago: The Bible Institute Colportage Ass'n., n.d.).

Lee, William, *The Inspiration of Holy Scripture* (Dublin: Hodges, Smith & Co., 1864).

Manly, Basil, *The Doctrine of Inspiration Explained and Vindicated* (New York: A. C. Armstrong & Son, 1888).

Stonehouse, N. B., and Woolley, Paul, eds., *The Infallible Word* (Grand Rapids: Wm. B. Eerdmans Publishing Co., 1953).

Warfield, Benjamin Breckinridge, *Revelation and Inspiration* (New York: Oxford University Press, 1927).

Watts, Robert, *Faith and Inspiration* (London: Hodder & Stoughton, 1885).

ON REVELATION:

Auberlen, Carl August, *The Divine Revelation: An Essay in Defense of the Faith* (Edinburgh: T. & T. Clark, 1867).

Bavinck, Herman, *The Philosophy of Revelation* (Grand Rapids: Wm. B. Eerdmans Publishing Co., 1953).

Berkouwer, G. C., *General Revelation* (Grand Rapids: Wm. B. Eerdmans Publishing Co., 1955).

Candlish, Robert S., *Reason and Revelation* (London: T. Nelson & Sons, 1864).

Given, John James, *Revelation, Inspiration and the Canon* (Edinburgh: T. & T. Clark, 1881).

Mead, C. M., *Supernatural Revelation* (New York: Anson D. F. Randolph & Co., 1889).

Orr, James, *Revelation and Inspiration* (Grand Rapids: Wm. B. Eerdmans Publishing Co., reprint, 1952).

Zwemer, Samuel M., *The Origin of Religion* (New York: Loizeaux Brothers, 3rd. ed., rev., 1945).

IN DEFENSE OF THE CONSERVATIVE VIEW OF THE BIBLE:

Allis, Oswald T., *The Five Books of Moses* (Philadelphia: The Presbyterian and Reformed Publishing Co., 1943).

————, *The Unity of Isaiah* (Philadelphia: The Presbyterian and Reformed Publishing Co., 1951).

Atkinson, Basil F. C., *Is the Bible True?* (New York: Fleming H. Revell Co., 3rd. ed., 1934).

Boutflower, Charles, *In and Around the Book of Daniel* (London: Society for Promoting Christian Knowledge, 1923).

————, *The Book of Isaiah: 1-39* (London: Society for Promoting Christian Knowledge, 1930).

Davidson, Francis, ed., *The New Bible Commentary* (Grand Rapids: Wm. B. Eerdmans Publishing Co., 1953).

Davies, L. Merson, *The Bible and Modern Science* (London: Pickering & Inglis, n.d.).

Davis, John D., *A Dictionary of the Bible* (Grand Rapids: Baker Book House, 4th ed., reprint, 1956).

Dawson, W. Bell, *The Bible Confirmed by Science* (London: Marshall, Morgan & Scott, n.d.).

Finn, A. H., *The Unity of the Pentateuch* (London: Marshall Brothers, Ltd., 2nd ed., n.d.).

Free, Joseph P., *Archaeology and Bible History* (Wheaton, Illinois: Van Kampen Press, 1950).

Green, William Henry, *Moses and the Prophets* (New York: Robert Carter & Brothers, 1883).

————, *The Higher Criticism of the Pentateuch* (New York: Charles Scribner's Sons, 1896).

————, *General Introduction to the Old Testament: The Canon* (New York: Charles Scribner's Sons, 1898).

————, *General Introduction to the Old Testament: The Text* (New York: Charles Scribner's Sons, 1899).

————, *The Unity of the Book of Genesis* (New York: Charles Scribner's Sons, 1910).

Hamilton, Floyd E., *The Basis of Christian Faith* (New York: Harper & Brothers, rev. ed., 1933).

Harris, R. Laird, *Inspiration and Canonicity of the Bible* (Grand Rapids: Zondervan Publishing House, 1957).

Kyle, Melvin Grove, *Moses and the Monuments* (Oberlin: Bibliotheca Sacra Co., 1920).

————, *The Problem of the Pentateuch: A New Solution by Archaeological Methods* (Oberlin: Bibliotheca Sacra Co., 1920).

————, *The Deciding Voice of the Monuments in Biblical Criticism* (Oberlin: Bibliotheca Sacra Co., 1924).

————, ed., *The International Standard Bible Encyclopaedia* (Chicago: The Howard-Severance Co., rev. ed., 1930).

Leupold, H. C., *Exposition of Genesis* (Grand Rapids: Baker Book House, 1950).

Manley, G. T., ed., *The New Bible Handbook* (Chicago: The Inter-Varsity Fellowship, 1948).

Möller, William, *Are the Critics Right?* (London: The Religious Tract Society, 2nd ed., 1903).

Orr, James, *The Problem of the Old Testament* (London: James Nisbet & Co., 1906).

Pilter, William Turnbull, *The Pentateuch: A Historical Record* (London: Marshall Brothers, Ltd., 1928).

Unger, Merrill F., *An Introductory Guide to the Old Testament* (Grand Rapids: Zondervan Publishing House, 1951).

————, *Archaeology and the Old Testament* (Grand Rapids: Zondervan Publishing House, 1954).

Vos, Geehardus, *The Mosaic Origin of the Pentateuchal Codes* (New York: A. C. Armstrong & Son, 1886).

Wilson, Robert Dick, *A Scientific Investigation of the Old Testament* (Philadelphia: The Sunday School Times Co., 1926).

————, *Is the Higher Criticism Scholarly?* (Philadelphia: The Sunday School Times Co., 1922; 9th ed., 1948).

————, *Studies in the Book of Daniel* (New York: Fleming H. Revell Co., first series, 1919; second series, 1938).

Young, Edward J., *An Introduction to the Old Testament* (Grand Rapids: Wm. B. Eerdmans Publishing Co., 1949).

————, *The Prophecy of Daniel* (Grand Rapids: Wm. B. Eerdmans Publishing Co., 1949).

————, *Thy Word Is Truth* (Grand Rapids: Wm B. Eerdmans Publishing Co., 1957).